DATE			

FREDERICK L. COVAN, PH.D.
with Carol Kahn

SIMON & SCHUSTER

New York   London

Toronto   Sydney

Tokyo   Singapore

CRAZY all the TIME

Life,
Lessons,
and
Insanity
on the
Psych Ward of
Bellevue Hospital

SIMON & SCHUSTER
Rockefeller Center
1230 Avenue of the Americas
New York, New York 10020

SIMON & SCHUSTER and colophon are registered trademarks
of Simon & Schuster Inc.

Designed by Hyun Joo Kim
Manufactured in the United States of America

1   3   5   7   9   10   8   6   4   2

Library of Congress Cataloging-in-Publication Data
Covan, Frederick L., date.
Crazy all the time : life, lessons, and insanity on the Psych Ward of Bellevue Hospital / Frederick L. Covan, with Carol Kahn.
p.   cm.
1. Psychotherapists—Supervision of—Case studies. 2. Interns (Psychiatry)
3. Psychotherapy—Case studies. 4. Bellevue Hospital—Miscellanea.
I. Kahn, Carol. II. Title.
RC459.C68 1994
616.89'14—dc20
93–35900
CIP

ISBN: 0-671-79159-1

To Diane

Acknowledgments

My sincere gratitude to my students and colleagues at Bellevue Hospital, especially those in the Department of Psychiatry, for all we have shared while growing and learning together; to the Bellevue patients who teach us so much; to my mother, Mary, for her continuously inspirational love of life; to my wife, Diane, for her encouragement, wisdom, and love; to my son, Alex, for his warmth; to my son, Dan, for his spirit; to my son, Zac, for his openness; to my son, Ben, for his joy; to my friends, Tony and Becky Robbins, for motivating me and this project; to my editor, Gary Luke, for believing in this book; to my writer, Carol Kahn, for generously giving the ideas form and life; and to my agent, Susan Lee Cohen, for her vision, support, and constant calm.

Contents

Drinking the Blood of Virgins

Chapter 1

Yesterday it was mountains, streams, blue sky, crickets chirping. Today it's traffic on Fifth Avenue, horns honking, drivers yelling, buses belching, sirens screaming, pedestrians strolling across the street like they owned it. Every time I come back from vacation, it's the same jarring reentry as I negotiate my motor scooter through New York traffic. Most people think I'm crazy to commute on something not much bigger than my three-year-old's tricycle—maybe I am, and that's why I love it at Bellevue.

Something was happening up ahead. I couldn't see a thing from where I sat, but I sure could hear it.

"Yo, Lieutenant Columbo, get outta there."

"You trying to get killed?"

"Get the creep."

A wolf whistle was followed by a catcall. "Hey, babe. Over here." A loud raucous voice with a thick Brooklyn accent bellowed from the line of yellow cabs in front. "Hey, Mistah. Ya know where you belong? Bellevue!"

Pathologically nosy, I risked amputation at the knees, maneuvering between a mail truck and a pickup filled with lumber. I pulled abreast of the taxis at the next light. And then I saw it. The brown baggy pants rolled up over a pair of jeans. Over that, a pink, polka-dot dress, cinched at the waist with a purple velvet bathrobe belt. On the head was a wool cap and on top of that a trooper's hat. The cabbie was right. The guy did belong at Bellevue. It was Mr. Greenblatt, one of our recently discharged psych patients, directing traffic on Fifth Avenue.

Better have his doctor check out his medication, I thought, nodding to Greenblatt. He gave me a high five. Patients invariably direct traffic in the direction it's already flowing, which is a good strategy. The cars stream forward as they wave them onward and then halt when they put up their hand. It makes them feel powerful, as though they, not the traffic lights, command this immense river of people and machinery. There is even a lesson to be learned from their madness—you get what you want by accepting the inevitable.

These musings were interrupted by an ambulance attempting to blast by megaphone and siren through the thicket of traffic. Skirting my way along the jagged edge of cars pulled to the right, I swung in behind the ambulance and followed it east on 30th Street as it headed for the emergency entrance to Bellevue Hospital. An unusually large trauma team awaited it, their faces alert with battlefield readiness. I stopped to watch as the cab door of the ambulance opened and a trembling female paramedic stepped down. The team of doctors and nurses crowded around her, ignoring the stretcher that emerged from the rear. What's going on? I wondered, as I overheard the doctor in front ask tensely, "Have you got it?" She held up what appeared to be a plastic bag. Suddenly there was an outburst—gasps, giggles, everyone talking at once. A redheaded nurse clapped her hand to her mouth and shrieked. "What's the matter, Rosie?" yelled the doctor who was now holding the bag. "Haven't you ever seen a penis before?"

WELCOME TO BELLEVUE—THE HOSPITAL OF CHOICE, proclaimed the red letters flowing across the message board in the elevator corridor. After three weeks of not smoking, I congratulated myself on successfully passing through the glassed-in entryway without joining the nicotine addicts taking a final puff before entering the smoke-free hospital. The plastic couches in the towering lobby were already filled with people eating, waiting, sleeping. Along the wall in the back, armed correction officers were lead-

drinking the blood of virgins

ing a line of chain-linked prisoners in handcuffs and leg-irons to the service elevator that would take them to the psychiatric prison ward. A hospital policeman checked the stream of people passing into the elevator corridor for IDs or visitor passes. I waited at the elevator with attending physicians in their expensive suits, white-coated interns, grubby street people, staff members protecting their cardboard trays with coffee and danishes, visiting dignitaries, patient visitors, and uniformed correction officers. It felt good to be back.

It was my thirteenth consecutive year at Bellevue. I began as an intern here in 1969, returning in 1980 as chief psychologist in the Department of Psychiatry. My first office, spacious with high ceilings, overlooking the East River, was in the Bellevue Psychiatric Pavilion. But that red-brick 1937-vintage building, surrounded by a ten-foot-high, spear-topped, wrought-iron fence, oozed history—along with vermin and water from broken pipes. In 1985, psychiatry joined the other departments in the modern, twenty-three-story Bellevue Hospital. The old building became a shelter for the homeless, and instead of a room with a view, I had a cramped, windowless office.

Now I was there with David Anderson, starting his first day as an intern. I was going to be one of his supervisors. The phone was ringing off the hook. "Sorry for the interruptions. This is a really crazy day, as if there's any other kind around here," I said to David. I picked up the phone, and my secretary, Lucy Rosselli, appeared at the door. "Fred, the psych emergency room wants to talk to you right away but your phone's continually busy."

I excused myself from the first call and picked up the second. "Dr. Covan."

"Fred, it's Amy Hensen in triage. The cops brought in a kid who's been carrying on for half an hour wanting to see you. He says you're his doctor and you'll vouch for the fact that he's crazy. Hold on a minute, Fred, okay?"

I turned to David. "Someone in the ER says he's crazy and I'll know it."

David looked bewildered. "Huh?"

"Not so unusual," I said. "We often get homeless people looking for three hots and a cot, but they don't usually ask for me by name."

"Anyway, Fred," said Amy back on the phone, "can you come down and talk to him since he refuses to see anyone else?"

"What's his name?" I asked.

"Chris Mueller."

"Tell him to hang on. I'll be down as soon as I can."

I hung up. "Look, David, I have to go to the psych ER. Want to come? We'll talk on the way."

As we headed down the narrow corridor connecting the row of offices in the psychology department, I filled him in. "The kid we're going to see is a seventeen-year-old student at Bellevue's school, and he's also in my adolescent therapy group."

"Bellevue has a school?"

"P.S. 106 on the twenty-first floor," I said. "It's for emotionally disturbed kids from six to twenty-one. The school provides the education and we provide the therapy."

David was one of eight students who had just arrived to start the internship required for a Ph.D. in clinical psychology. I'd been interviewing him to see where in the hospital he should be assigned. Besides the more than 350 psychiatric beds, there are fourteen outpatient clinics for everyone from two-year-old children to the elderly; eight hundred people a month in the psych ER alone; and a prison for mentally disturbed prisoners. Matching the students with the right settings and patients is a real challenge.

"Chris has failed careers as a student and as a mini-criminal," I continued. "He's not too bright. Somehow he's always the one left holding the bag while the other guys get away."

"Has he ever been psychotic?"

"No. It's more likely he's scamming. Anyway, telling what's real from what's not is half the job around here."

Kitty Webster, one of the new interns, greeted us. At the same moment, Rhoda Schlossberg, a staff psychologist, poked her head out of her office, smiling broadly.

"Hi, I'm Dr. Schlossberg," she said to the students. "If you need anything, my door is always open."

I watched, amused. Rhoda, at age sixty-two with thirty-five years at Bellevue, is brilliant and feisty, a true cynic who manages to see the cloud in every silver lining. But every September, when the interns arrive, she gets a new lease on life. While everyone on the staff loves to train, I suspect that some of Rhoda's enthusiasm comes from the possibility of making converts to her religion of classic psychoanalysis. She never lets us forget that when she was a kid, "giants" like Freud and Adler walked the earth.

"Great crop of students," said Rhoda, beaming at David and Kitty, who were already deep in conversation. "They make me feel energized."

"I know what you mean," I said. "It's like drinking the blood of virgins."

She looked at me quizzically. "God, Fred, what a thing to say."

"You know what I'm talking about, the ancient rituals where the elders sacrifice virgins and drink their blood to be rejuvenated. Not that we sacrifice our students, we just feed on their energy and youth, their naïveté and idealism. We nurture them and they keep us alive."

Pulling me aside, she rose to the top of her five feet two inches and whispered, "With the exception of Wayne Roderick, of course."

"Well, you know how I felt about him," I whispered back.

"Damn that Carl. Wayne has the social skills of a hermit."

"He was Carl's first choice," I said. "So what do you expect? We all go for candidates like ourselves."

We were talking about what happened last February when Carl Zelecky, a strong-willed, opinionated psychologist fought like a pit bull to get the one intern he especially wanted. This was the final phase of a selection process that had begun six months earlier when three hundred applicants from around the world competed for a slot at Bellevue. It is one of the most sought-after internships and usually only the top students apply, willing to accept $15,000 for their year's work because the job gives them an invaluable opportunity to learn. They have spent at least four years in a psychology graduate program learning theory, psychological testing, and psychotherapy techniques, and have already had clinical experience as part-time externs. After each candidate was interviewed by two members of the staff, the list was winnowed to about seventy. The final selection was made in an intensive two-hour free-for-all in which the staff members cajoled, argued, and politicked in the psych department's equivalent of a slave auction. As each candidate came on the block, so to speak, we loudly championed our favorites—"Look at that GPA," "Did you ever see such recommendations?" "Look what she's done with her life"—until four men and four women made the final cut.

"Wayne has good credentials as a researcher, and Carl has to win a few just like the rest of us," I reminded Rhoda.

"You're right," she sighed. "Let's hope it works out."

I rejoined David and Kitty, who were now chatting with two more students, whose arms were crammed with printed matter.

"Hi, Dr. Covan," they chorused.

"Hi, gang. How's it going?"

"Great," said one of the students. "I'm just going down to get my shots." The others groaned.

"I'll see you all in the conference room at two o'clock and I'll tell you about those forms," I said.

I turned to David. "You ready for the ER?"

"You bet," he said. "Catch you guys later."

We opened the locked door of the psychology department and walked into the secretarial area, where there is only one secretary for the twenty-three psychologists on the staff. One of the psychologists, Mike Warner, was scanning the anouncements of conferences, colloquiums, and workshops that filled the walls.

"Fred," he said, turning around, "you're just the person I want to see."

"Can it wait, Mike? I'm busy."

"It's kind of important. We're out of test forms and I got a patient waiting to be tested."

"Hasn't that order come in yet? Weenie said he'd find the money for forms three weeks ago," I said, using our less than flattering nickname for Malcolm Weiner, one of the more annoying administrators.

"For God's sake, Fred, if we can't get psych test forms at Bellevue, this city's really in trouble."

drinking the blood of virgins

"Tell me about it," I said. "Listen, why don't you try the guys in rehab? Maybe they have forms."

"And they've probably borrowed from some other department. Sounds like bulb snatching."

I shrugged. "Better than sitting in the dark."

As David and I hurried past an adult psychiatric inpatient unit, he pointed to the sign on its double doors: BE CAREFUL WHEN OPENING DOORS, RISK OF ELOPEMENT.

He jerked his thumb at the sign. "I know they're talking about escapees, but that's how I think of my girlfriend—elopement risk."

"Are you thinking of getting married?"

"Officially, we're engaged, but I'm not ready yet. By the way, what happened to the floors?" he asked as we stepped single file onto the walkway—a couple of two-by-sixes nailed together—that led to the elevators.

"It's kind of a million-dollar screw-up," I said over my shoulder. "They put in beautiful wood floors but the grain was facing the wrong way. So when they mopped, the tiles sponged up the water and expanded."

"And then they started to buckle," said Maria Santiago. "Excuse me, Fred, I don't mean to be so intimate."

I laughed as Maria and I did a little face-to-face dance in order to pass each other on the gangplank.

"David, this is Dr. Santiago," I said, as she and David came abreast. "She's one of our psychologists and you'll be seeing a lot of her."

Maria turned around and walked backward to talk to David. Even walking backward, she was elegant. "You should have been here when the tiles started popping. One of our staff members was in Vietnam and he jumped two feet into the air every time he heard the sound."

"So what are they doing now?" asked David.

"They're putting in linoleum," I said. "But first they had to put in a layer of concrete because the tiles were almost two inches thicker than the linoleum. It's a mess. The hospital is suing the contractor and the contractor is suing the manufacturer."

"Can you imagine the cost?" Maria grumbled. "Which reminds

me, Fred, I still haven't received tuition reimbursement from the hospital for those workshops I took."

"I know."

"But, Fred, it's been two years. I'm starting a second workshop series and I still haven't been paid for the first."

"Maria, they owe me too. But I'll get on their case."

She walked with us to the elevators, two of which had been boarded up for repairs. A small crowd was waiting.

"Uh oh," Maria said. "Don't look now, but here comes Weenie."

"Fr-ed," he said, his nasal voice managing to make two syllables out of my name. "I need you to do something for me."

"What is it, Malcolm?"

"I got this request from downtown. They want an ethnic breakdown on your department. So send me a list of how many you have of whatever you've got."

"Right, Malcolm. What categories are we using today?"

"Yeah," said Maria. "Like am I lumped under white or Hispanic? Or is it Latino or, to be precise, Latina?"

"Can I include sexual orientation also?" I asked.

Weenie pulled sharply at the ends of his red polka-dotted bow tie and looked at me. "Just show that we're diversified and have it on my desk by this afternoon," he said.

David and I managed to squeeze onto the elevator. All the floors between twenty-one and twelve, where the elevator went express to the ground floor, were lit up. It was going to be a long ride.

"How'd you get into this business, anyway, Dr. Covan?" David asked me as we rode down.

"I always wanted to be a shrink," I said.

"Why? Was anyone in your family in the field?"

"Only on the receiving end. I had an aunt who jumped from the sixth floor during a postpartum psychosis. Another aunt was a chronic schizophrenic. And one of my grandfathers hung himself."

"No wonder you're interested in bizarre behavior."

"Or maybe it was my unconventional upbringing in Greenwich Village. My mother owned an avant-garde clothing boutique and I'd sit on the floor pretending to play with my toys while I listened to the women shoppers talk about their lives. In the evenings, our home was like a salon, where artists, musicians, neighborhood bohemians liked to hang out. I guess I got hooked on people's stories and why they do the things they do."

"Yeah," David smiled.

On the ground floor, we turned away from the lobby and walked toward the psych ER. David looked at the crowd milling in front of the elevators. "It's like Times Square. This place is famous even in my hometown in Michigan."

"We get them all," I said. "The people who make the six-o'clock news and the people who watch it. The ones who hold up traffic on the Brooklyn Bridge while they threaten to jump, the killers and their victims. El Sayyid Nosair and Rabbi Kahane, the man he was accused of killing, were both brought here. So was Mark Chapman, who shot John Lennon."

"I'd like to get some famous patient like that."

"I'll see what I can do," I said dryly.

I opened the door marked PSYCHIATRIC EMERGENCY ADMITTING SERVICE. "Hi, Roberto," I said to one of the hospital police officers sitting on a bench along the wall.

"Hi, Chief. I hear you got a personal invitation to come down here. He was making quite a racket until I convinced him you were on the way. He's in there," he said, pointing to one of the interview rooms.

David and I passed the metal detector, used to screen patients, and stepped across the thick red line painted on the floor. Once that line is crossed, the patient is under the jurisdiction of Bellevue and cannot leave on his own; he is evaluated and either "treated and released" or admitted to a ward upstairs. David tried not to gawk at the scene around us. Several patients were stretched out on brown Barcaloungers, snoozing or watching the TV bolted to the wall with its Plexiglas screen cover to protect it from acting-out critics. A woman with parts of her scalp showing where her hair had been removed—from the looks of it forcibly—was strapped to a chair with a fabric waist restraint while she ranted in short incomprehensible bursts. A man in a neck brace, his arms handcuffed to a wheelchair, yelled to no one in particular. "I want meds. I want meds."

We walked to the interview room where Chris was waiting for us. "Can you tell me what happened, officer?" I asked the city cop who was standing just outside the door.

"He tried to snatch a gold necklace from a female undercover cop," he told me. "After we arrested him, he started going crazy, yelling, 'Take me to Bellevue. I'm a patient there. I hear voices. Ask Dr. Covan.' So I brought him here to check it out."

"Dr. Covan, it's me, Chris," yelled Chris from inside.

David and I walked in and found him shackled to a chair.

"Hi, Chris."

"See," Chris yelled to the undercover cop who continued to wait outside. "I told you I knew him. I hear voices. Tell them, Doc."

"So what's this about trying to steal a necklace?"

"The voices told me to do it."

"Chris, you never told me you heard voices."

"You know how messed up I am, Dr. Covan? How many problems I have? Now I've started hearing voices."

"Really?" I said, nodding. "What do they say?"

"Bad things, like 'steal something.' They keep repeating it, you know?"

"Is it a man's or a woman's voice?"

"It's a man's voice. Yeah. A man's voice."

"Uh huh. Do you recognize the voice? Is it anyone you know?"

He thought about it for a moment. "Uh no. No, I don't recognize it."

"Okay. So which ear do you hear them in, Chris? This ear or this one?" I asked pointing to each ear.

He cocked his head as though listening and then moved his eyes from one side to the other. Then he said brightly, "Right ear, Dr. Covan. Yeah, right ear."

"I'm sorry, Chris, but you know you're not hearing voices." He looked down sheepishly. "Why did you tell the cops that?"

"I dunno. I was scared and I saw this program on TV where this guy was hearing voices and they didn't take him to jail. They took him to the hospital."

"Look," I said, "you're going to have to go with the police to the precinct. I want to help you, but not by pretending you're crazy. I'll call the school and tell them what happened. Anyone else I should call?"

"Yeah. Call my grandma."

"So how'd you know the kid was faking?" asked David, as we made our way back to my office.

"Well, he just failed the standard Bellevue test. Someone who's really hearing voices hears them in his head, just like you hear my voice now, not in one ear or the other."

"Neat," said David.

"Leave it to Chris," I sighed. "He blew his con as badly as he did the robbery."

We got off the elevator on the twentieth floor and I stopped by the secretary's desk to pick up my messages. "Weenie called twice," Lucy said. "The first time he said it was important and the second time urgent. The unit chief of one of the adult psych wards wants to discuss a change in policy. Your wife says to leave a message on her machine what time you'll be home for dinner. Kitty, a new intern, called to change her appointment."

The phone rang while I was standing there.

"It's Dr. Mahoney from microsurgery. Says it's important."

I told Lucy I'd take it in my office. Mahoney and I had worked together on several cases. He'd stitch up their bodies and then turn them over to me for what he called "psychosurgery"—meaning shrinking, not lobotomizing as the term is used in psychiatry. Surgeons, pardon the pun, are known for their cutting humor, which, I suppose, allows them to continue in their daily labor of violating human flesh.

"Fred, hold on to your crotch," he warned. And then he told me about his latest patient. "Oh my God," I said, simultaneously reacting to what he said and recalling the scene with the ambulance I had witnessed this morning in front of the emergency entrance. I looked at David, sitting there, unsuspecting, thumbing through a thick manual on Bellevue policy and procedures. "Guy," I said, "I have just the intern for you."

The Unkindest Cuts

Chapter 2

At the first meeting of our seminar on psychological testing today, one of the interns asked me, "What is normal?" I told her, "Stay with that question for the rest of your life." The older I get, the more I think that "normal" describes an arbitrary segment of the continuum of human behavior from the Charles Mansons to the Mother Teresas. We see that continuum every day at Bellevue. But when I look around, Bellevue appears like a microcosm of New York City and New York City a microcosm of the world.

Sometimes what appears abnormal is a normal reaction to a crazy-making situation. This week it's the latest round in budget cuts. During the best of times, we are understaffed, overworked, and woefully lacking in the barest essentials like pencils and paper. The present fiscal crisis in New York has brought new indignities, unkind cuts that range from slashing lines of support staff to withholding mouse traps because the mouse population has not yet reached the designated density. Today, I am faced with an even unkinder cut. In addition to our secretary, the one typist allotted to my department will now be filled by a severely disturbed outpatient from a psychiatric rehabilitation program.

Bellevue's cuts are one thing, but the kind that we or others inflict upon ourselves are the unkindest cuts of all. Of these, the ones that seem to push the envelope of normality are acts of self-mutilation. One of the most bizarre was committed by the young man referred by Dr. Guy Mahoney, the microsurgeon, and whom I had just assigned as David Anderson's first case.

David was the epitome of clean-cut with his short brown hair brushed high over his forehead and dressed in a button-down oxford shirt, chino slacks, spit-polished penny loafers. Unlike most of the new trainees, he had a kind of cocky self-confidence that came from five years of research and practice in an ivory-tower university clinic after graduating from the University of Michigan. He had even published some articles on behavior modification. But along with his midwestern casual manner, there was a prissiness and self-righteousness that he needed to give up if he was to develop the kind of empathy, that fellow feeling with the patient, which for me is far more important than a particular "school" or approach to psychotherapy.

So it was to David, with his gym-trained and vitamin-fed perfect body, that I handed the chart on Matthew Nichols. The patient, who had been operated on, was recovering nicely, at least from the surgery. Nobody could be further from David than Matthew was. At age twenty-three, only a few years younger than David, Matthew was a study in failure. After a series of incompletes in his second year of college, he had dropped out and drifted from one low-paying menial job to another. A social misfit, he had no friends, either male or female, and had not had a girlfriend since his freshman year in high school. To introduce some order into his chaotic life, he had joined a strict Pentecostal religious group. In the end his inability to make it on his own either financially or socially had forced him to move back in with his parents. We have a term for it in the mental-health field—"failed at independent living."

I watched David thumb the pages and then freeze as he started to read it. He bit his lip and, unaware of what he was doing, crossed his thighs and read on. Finally, he looked up, his face drained of blood as well as of all the eagerness he had displayed just moments before.

"Welcome to Bellevue," I said.

"How could he do it?" David squealed, his throat constricted with tension and anxiety. "How could he cut off his penis?"

Just then the phone rang. Today it was even worse than the usual average of ten times an hour since our secretary had a dental appointment and Yolanda Barrantes, the rehab patient slash typist, had yet to make an appearance. "Hold that thought," I said to David and picked up the phone. It was Weenie.

"Fr-ed, one of your externs didn't fill out a chart completely. She's been in your department since June so you'd think you would have taught her how to do it by now." The externs are second- or third-year unpaid graduate students who work half time.

"What exactly is missing?"

"She failed to countersign the third paragraph on page five."

God, I hate this stuff, I thought. But then, Malcolm was only doing his job. "No kidding? She must've been busy doing something else, like treating somebody. But, hey, that's no excuse."

"Fred, this isn't the first time this has happened. I don't have to tell you that proper documentation is the top priority around here."

"No, you certainly don't, unfortunately."

"I mean, if somebody somewhere down the line were to question something, and it wasn't countersigned, where would you be?"

"You know, Malcolm, you're absolutely right. In fact, Mal, I've been thinking a lot about documentation recently. Do you realize that it gives us the power of life and death? We can bring someone back from the dead."

There was an exasperated pause at the other end of the line. "Covan, just what are you talking about?"

"Well, the way it is around here, if you don't write something down, it didn't happen. So if somebody died and no one wrote it down, then he didn't die."

Another pause. "I don't get it. Of course he's dead."

"Forget it. While I've got you on the phone, do you think you could get us some number-two pencils? We're down to using burnt match sticks."

"Fred, we have a pencil shortage."

"I know. That's what I just said."

"It's not my fault. Everyone blames everything on me." His pitch level was rising rapidly. "You'd think that I was personally responsible for slashing ten percent of the operating budget, not counting inflation."

"Speaking about that, Mal, do you have any idea what happened to the rehab typist? She hasn't shown up today. And we have reports to get out, not to mention charts to be filled out. Or is that in?"

"You know, I'm never sure which one it is," Malcolm said. "Out or in."

I let him chew on that awhile. "I'll have the student sign the form if you give me the pencil to do it with."

"What are you talking about? All forms have to be signed in ink."

"We're out of pens, too."

"I'll see what I can do. But I'm not promising anything."

Administrators, they make me crazy. I hung up the phone and turned back to David, who was laughing and looking considerably more relaxed. "Now where were we?"

He looked at me a little sheepishly. "Um, I was just wondering how he managed to cut off his penis."

"David, you read the report. He did it with scissors."

"C'mon, Dr. Covan. You know what I mean. How could he do such a thing? I mean, do guys really do this?" He had crossed his thighs again and in the tight corner of my office our knees almost touched.

"Call me Fred. You'd be surprised. It doesn't happen every day, but we do get a fair number of self-inflicted penisectomies. Just last month, we had a transsexual in the unit, a really attractive young woman in every sense of the word but one, who had gone to a sex-change clinic to have his penis removed. But they didn't think he was psychologically ready and the operation is incredibly expensive. So he did the job himself with a razor blade."

"Ouch," he yelped, reflexively putting his hand over his crotch.

"At least with the transsexual it was a clean cut. In Matthew's case, it must have been a much harder job. I mean, imagine using your mother's pinking shears. *Pink-ing* shears," I said, drawing out the syllables. I wanted him to experience the full horror and not back off so that he could be there with the patient, be able to lis-

the unkindest cuts

ten with the feeling of, *Oh yes, that's what it's like.*

"You know what they are, David? Those big scissors with the little Vs along the edges so the material won't unravel after you've cut it?" I added, just in case he was having trouble visualizing the implement.

David whined. "Fred, I know what pinking shears are . . . and, uh, what they do."

I raised my eyebrows inquisitively as if I was interested in hearing about his experiences with them. The blood rushed to his face and he added quickly, "My mother had a pair."

"And did you ever . . . ?"

"Fred, stop that."

"Actually, as it happened, it made the surgeons' job a lot easier. In order to reattach it, all they had to do was line up the edges. And, voilà, they're locked together. It won't even twist off."

David winced. A big wince with his eyes squinched shut and his mouth pulled up into a tight line. "How can you joke about this?"

"Because joking about it helps distance us from the horror. Because it is self-protective. Because gallows humor is a survival mechanism. Have you ever heard cops at a homicide or surgeons during an operation? And you think I'm bad!"

David nodded solemnly. This kid is even serious about joking, I thought.

"Actually, all kidding aside, you have a lot of work ahead of you and not much time in which to do it. Thirty-five days, to be exact. We are a diagnostic and disposition center. If he's not out of here in thirty-five days, he'll come up for a special review as to exactly why he isn't. And the last thing I want is more lectures from administrators about length of stay and documentation. Capish?"

"Thirty-five days," David repeated.

"That's all the time you have to make sure that the surgeons' handiwork doesn't come undone. You're going to find that sticking his penis back on is a lot easier to do surgically than it is psychically. So your first job is to find out what made him do it in the first place." I looked at my watch. "C'mon, I've got an appointment on the second floor. We'll talk about it on the way out."

CRAZY ALL THE TIME

We walked into the corridor and through the locked door that separates the staff offices from the secretarial area. Although the room contains several desks and typewriters, no one was there. The new typist had yet to show up, and the reports to be typed were piling up in her IN box. And while we had no typist, hospital administrators were proliferating like a disease. One statistic tells the whole story: The Health and Hospitals Corporation—which runs Bellevue and the fifteen other municipal hospitals—has increased the number of administrators over the last decade by 155 percent while the total employment in all other job categories—from housekeeper to physician—has gone up only 25 percent. So far it seems that productivity has gone up in only one area: paperwork.

As usual the elevator was as packed as a rush-hour subway car. Elevators at Bellevue are more than a vertical conveyance with blinking numbers. They are a way of life, a rite of passage between floors that can take longer to complete than the daily four-mile scooter run from my Upper West Side apartment to the hospital. The random, unpredictable nature of the elevator ride, in which a lit-up floor number is no guarantee that the car will actually stop there, generates a kind of grudging fellowship among the passengers who are involuntarily boxed together for an indefinite period of time.

We all love to eavesdrop, and overheard conversations are prized. The best snatches are repeated and circulated throughout the hospital like the latest sick joke or staff rumor. Mindful of this, staff members play a kind of elevator one-upmanship in which they let fall a juicy tidbit of gossip just before exiting or loudly regale their neighbors with an outrageous anecdote, meanwhile monitoring the conversations around them. The competition, made all the more fun by the oblique references necessary to obey the strictures against discussing patients while on the elevator, can be fierce.

Today was no different. Four or five animated conversations in varying degrees of intensity were going on around us. "Hold the door." It was Rhoda Schlossberg, her short, bustling figure rushing toward the door, instinctively raising her padded shoulders as she wedged her way into the car.

the unkindest cuts

"I hear someone's been playing fast and loose with the scissors," she said jocularly as we started our lurching descent. The conversations around us became a little quieter. David blanched and tried to press his tall body farther into the immovable wall of people behind him. Rhoda craned her head up at him and rolled her eyes. "Self-multilation's a classic. Look at Oedipus."

Bill Morris, an anesthesiologist, balancing his lunch tray precariously with one hand while recounting a story he had just heard in surgery about a naked couple rolling in the snow, turned his head in our direction.

"Yes," I said hesitantly. "But it's not really applicable. It's not eyes we're talking about cutting off. It's penises."

Bingo! We won the competition hands down. All conversation came to a halt.

"Getting off," Rhoda yelled as the elevator rattled to a stop. "You got a point, Fred. Anyway, men are too attached to their penises, don't you think?" And with that verbal thrust, she was gone. The whole car turned in my direction. Half the people seemed waiting to hear more, while the other half had the same look on their faces David had during our session. I imagined that, collectively, all the men were squeezing their thighs together. A heavily muscled man with a VISITOR badge glued to his tank top glared at me.

"Get ready to escape," I whispered to David. On the ground floor, we stepped gingerly around a patient standing at the very front, hugging his portable IV unit close to his body so that he and it would not become separated when he got off. David disappeared into the crowd; I waited for a local elevator that would take me back up to the second floor for my meeting.

When I returned from lunch, a tense and angry-looking David was waiting for me along with a very agitated Lucy and the new typist, Yolanda, who was staring at the wall. "She's been doing that for the past hour," said Lucy. You can always tell how Lucy is feeling by the way she wears her copper-colored hair. Today it was pulled into a bun, signaling that she would be brisk and in no mood for nonsense.

I wondered which of the three to treat first and decided on

Yolanda. Extending my hand, I said, "Hi. Good to see you. I'm Dr. Covan."

She grabbed her pocketbook from her desk. "Hullo, Dr. Covan," she said in a toneless voice.

"When did you get here?" I asked as pleasantly as possible.

"Sorry I'm late. I had trouble getting here. The sidewalk opened up in front of me."

I imagined that she was talking about some construction in front of her house. It struck me as a clumsy excuse, but I let it slide. It was her first day. I pressed on. "Why are you staring at the wall, Yolanda?"

"What else is there to do? And it's not Yolanda. It's Josephine."

"Josephine," I repeated.

"All her forms say Yolanda, but she calls herself Josephine." Lucy shook her bun indignantly.

I turned back to the woman, who was now hugging her bag to her chest.

"Josephine," she repeated in an intense monotone. "Yolanda's not here today."

"Okay, Josephine. Now you can start by typing this report on the top of the IN box. Lucy, would you please show Josephine how the report is set up?"

I nodded to David, who was clenching and unclenching his fists, to come with me. Lucy followed me to the door. "This isn't going to work, Fred," she said ominously.

I patted her shoulder. "With your help, Lucy, it will."

She glanced back at the woman and whispered to me, "She's a fruitcake."

"Yeah, but she can type."

Lucy reared up, her ears ever ready to detect the slightest hint of criticism. It isn't that Lucy can't type. It's just that typos are sprinkled through her copy as liberally as salt on a pretzel.

"Just what is that supposed to mean?" she fumed.

"Nothing. Except that we have a lot of typing to get done." Pushing David ahead of me, I hurried through the door but not before she handed me a stack of phone messages.

"Fred," he accosted me as soon as I closed the door to my office.

the unkindest cuts

"Did you know he was tied down? Trussed up like a Thanksgiving turkey? His wrists are tied to the bars on the side of the bed. He can't turn over. It's barbaric."

For a moment, I didn't know who he was talking about. Then I remembered Matthew. "It's cruel," I agreed. "But it's a necessary precaution. It's newly attached and he might pull it off."

"You mean he might try it again?"

"We've had penisectomies do it two, three times over. You have no idea how determined some people are. And we still don't know what made him do it in the first place."

"You'd think . . . I mean, just the pain. How could he continue after the first cut?"

"When the mind says 'do it' the body responds," I told him. "Several years ago we had a forty-five-year-old man who was brought in after he cut his arm off with a radial-arm buzz saw. You know, the kind they use in lumberyards. He was plagued by homicidal impulses against people—his neighbors, his boss, a brother-in-law. But he was devoutly religious and guilt-ridden about his thoughts. So he did what he had been taught to do when he was troubled. He went to the Bible and opened it at random with the idea that the first passage his eyes lit upon would be a clear instruction from God. As luck would have it, the passage was 'If your right hand offends you, cut it off.' "

David groaned. "Oh no."

" 'Okay, sure, Boss. Whatever you say.' He went at it like a trooper. First he got a tourniquet ready, which he planned to secure with his remaining hand and teeth. It took him four passes with the saw until he was clear through. Imagine that. You have to go through skin, nerves, muscle, and then bone. That takes work. Perseverance."

David nodded. "So you're saying any guy who could do that once could do it again."

"I'm saying that you're right to be upset. Anyone would be. You don't get as upset at someone who loses their arm because of an accident. But it challenges our basic survival instincts when someone deliberately chops off his arm with a saw or his penis with scissors. Because who in their right mind would do such a thing? And the answer is no one. These people are not in their right mind."

David smiled, looking a lot better than he did when he entered the office. "So," I said, "did you get any ideas about why he did it?"

He shook his head. "I tried. I really did. But it just sort of went from bad to worse. I started off by asking him what brought him to the hospital and he said, 'The ambulance brought me.' And I thought, How am I going to deal with this kind of concrete thinking? But I played along. I said, 'So why did the ambulance bring you?' And then he gets very defensive and says, 'You know why. It's on my chart. Don't play games with me.' Fred, I've got to tell you, I couldn't get to first base with this guy. When he wasn't being literal, he was being evasive. Then he just told me he was tired and ended the interview just like that. Ten minutes after it began. And all the while I couldn't take my eyes off his bound wrists."

David ran his hands through his hair and grimaced. "To be honest, it wasn't just the cruelty of tying him that got me. It was that it constantly reminded me of what he had done."

I was behind schedule. I had two students waiting outside my door and a meeting in fifteen minutes. "I want you to bear in mind there's no yawning gap between Matthew and you. As Harry Stack Sullivan, the great psychoanalyst, said, 'We are all more alike than we are different.' So, I'll see you at ten tomorrow, David, and then we'll talk about the subtle art of getting a patient to talk."

David's face brightened. "I sure could use the help. Because I gotta tell you, Fred, I don't think behavior modification will help this patient."

I was pleased. Like the newly converted, many trainees take to a particular school of therapy with a religious fervor. Part of my job, as I see it, is to get them to give up the search for a magic "method" and see that the secret of effective psychotherapy lies within the psychotherapist as much as in the method used. David had already started to make a name for himself in the field of behavior modification, yet on his first case here he was ready to see that it might not be applicable to every situation. Behavioral therapy works best as a treatment for getting rid of unwanted repetitive actions such as smoking. But I was ready to bet that cutting off one's penis was not an ingrained behavior that required deconditioning.

I let David out and ushered in two other interns, Kitty Webster and Wayne Roderick. Kitty was always so perfectly dressed in suits with matching accessories, so accommodating and apt to preface her remarks with "I'm sorry," that she reminded me of a stewardess. I had assigned her a paranoid schizophrenic woman whom the trainees had managed to keep out of the hospital for the past twelve years. After a few of her customary apologies, Kitty gave a sympathetic, perceptive portrayal of her patient's delusions that strengthened my conviction that she had the makings of a superb therapist once she stopped serving refreshments and took command of the aircraft.

Wayne was another story. I was still chafing from Carl's insistence that we take him on as an intern. He was certainly intelligent and no doubt an excellent researcher, but he seemed rather cold and emotionless and often buried himself in a book rather than taking part in conversations with the other trainees. He seemed careless about his dress, his clothes never quite fitting or matching. Nor was his appearance helped by his thick lenses, which made his eyes and upper cheeks look as if they were being viewed through the wrong end of a telescope. Since he had had experience working in a college counseling center, I decided to start him off slowly with a young woman in her senior year of college who was confused and anxious about what to do after graduation. I hoped that he would be able to relate to someone just a few years younger than he was—at twenty-four, he was the youngest intern—and that his logical, problem-solving mind would be helpful to a patient who was having trouble thinking clearly.

It had been a long day and I was looking forward to my own form of therapy, riding my motor scooter through rush-hour traffic. I've been riding a scooter to work ever since I came to Bellevue in 1980 in the midst of a transit strike. After the first one was stolen, I decided to apply a little urban camouflage, spraying it bubble-gum pink and taping it to make it look damaged so that no self-respecting thief would want to be seen on it. I also painted two eyes on the front to attract the attention of jaywalkers who ignored my horn. As I said, my friends think I ought to get my head examined. But I'd rather deal with the perils of traffic than the cattle-car conditions, unpredictable delays, and other calamities of New York's subways.

Tonight, however, I was denied a clean getaway. As I was unlocking my bike, Carl Zelecky appeared. Short and compact, Carl at fifty-odd years still possessed the wrestler's body of his college days. A psychologist of great erudition, Carl would rather write than teach, spin theories than practice. He can be arrogant, pompous, and abrasive, and from the expression on his face, I knew I was headed for trouble.

"Covan," he began threateningly, "where the hell is the special report I handed in to be typed three days ago? Weenie and his gang are breathing down my neck."

"Carl," I began sympathetically, "I know you're upset—"

"Damn straight, I am. Not only do I spend my days and nights researching the literature on compulsive gambling but then I'm persecuted for getting the report in late. All I'm trying to do is keep this guy from gambling himself into bankruptcy and attempting to kill himself a second time."

"Carl, you know the rules. The patient stays more than thirty-five days, you have to answer to the evaluation team."

"Dammit, Covan, whose side are you on?"

"Look, we all have to live with the regulations. But—"

"Anyway, that's all beside the point. The point is I did my duty and wrote that report before his thirty-five days were up and it's been sitting on your desk for three days."

"Not my desk, the typist's. But you have a legitimate complaint. It's just Lucy's been out having her mouth renovated and Josephine, the rehab typist, didn't get in until one o'clock because she said the sidewalk opened up in front of her, whatever that means."

"Josephine? I thought her name was Yolanda."

"Today, it's Josephine."

"What is she, a multiple personality?"

"Paranoid schiz, more likely."

He gave me a withering look. "Wouldn't it make more sense to hire professional typists, instead of paranoid patients?"

"Oh no, this is Support Mental Health Week and the administration is demonstrating their good intentions by letting patients work for free rather than hiring staff."

"Great. Maybe they ought to let the patients work as therapists as well."

I couldn't resist. "Don't they already?"

"Very funny," Carl snarled. "But what I'd like to know is where is the logic in all of this? Wouldn't it serve administrative ends better if the evaluation team got their report on time?"

I had to agree.

"And won't getting the report in late make us look bad?"

Again, there was no argument. Part of being chief psychologist is having to agree. Another part of being chief psychologist is having to reconcile two or more agreed-upon situations that are, in effect, unreconcilable. I got on my scooter and gunned the little motor. "I'll make sure that your report is the first thing on Yolanda's, er, Josephine's desk tomorrow," I promised before speeding away.

The next day went no better for David. In our morning supervisory session we talked about Matthew's resistance to talking. David had gotten off the track from the very start just by asking the question "Why?" I expressed my belief that nobody really knows *why* they do anything. They might have an idea, but it might be only part of the story or just what sounds plausible to them. Then there's the issue of unconscious motivation, particularly with someone like Matthew who is resisting any kind of discussion.

"David," I said, "what's your favorite ice cream flavor?"

"Vanilla."

"Why?"

He paused. "I don't know."

"See what I mean? Next time," I said, "ask Matthew something like, 'What was it like to cut off your penis?' That's a question that's less likely to elicit an 'I don't know.' " There is an art to structuring questions, I pointed out. "Never start off a request with 'Do you want to . . .?' because most likely the patient doesn't want to. It's like asking your child, 'Do you want to clean up your room now?' 'No way,' says the kid. 'If I wanted to clean my room up now, I'd be doing it.' "

David was clearly dubious. "But what if the guy just won't talk?"

he insisted. "What if it's something that made him feel really guilty and that guilt is keeping him from talking about it now?"

"You're probably right about that. But at the same time you've got something going for you. Matthew is in conflict. Part of him wants to tell. Everyone is in conflict about wanting to share their pain rather than carry it around alone. The art is in being seductive enough so that you become the person to whom they want to unload all their stuff."

At that moment David himself was in conflict. He was nodding at what I was saying, but he had a profoundly skeptical look on his face. "So how do you become this person?" he asked half defiantly and half wanting to know.

"You do it by being *curiageous*."

"*Curi* who?"

"It's my word for a combination of curiosity and courage. Really wanting to know what makes the guy tick and having the courage to ask the hard questions. This is the one place where you can be really nosy. And you can do it if you are coming from a place where you really care about people. Then you listen and communicate your caring and compassion in a nonjudgmental way. Really, all that is, is being a good human being. A *mensch*."

The phone rang. It was staff psychologist Maria Santiago, wanting to know what happened to all the Rorschach tests. I told her I was with a student at the moment, but I'd see if I could find one as soon as I was free.

"Sometimes the most effective prod to a patient is to confront him with his behavior in a paradoxical way. Like you might say to a patient who is his own worst enemy, 'It's really great you hate yourself. Since you act in pretty despicable ways toward people, your self-hatred is proof of your integrity.' And chances are, if it's really coming from the caring we've been talking about, after a double take, he'll say, 'You're right, Doc.' "

We role-played, with me feeding David some lines to try out on Matthew. "Don't try to be me, just do what we're talking about in your way in your words. Try it and let me know what happens. If it doesn't work, we'll try something else."

As David left my office I couldn't help feeling that Matthew wasn't the only one being resistant. Normally, I might have taken a few more minutes to find out what was going on in my student's mind, but at that point the usual disorder at Bellevue was reaching chaotic proportions. Yolanda/Josephine had yet to arrive, reports marked "stat" were overflowing her basket, and staff members forced to do their own photocopying were having to wait almost a half hour just to get to the machine. Carl was irate about his special report not being ready. Even Maria, legendary for her ability to sail with dignity, grace, and humor over life's severest bumps, was rushing around in a frenzy looking for a Rorschach test kit to complete a psychological testing on one of her patients.

At times like these, I practice what I teach at stress-training seminars. I take a deep breath and mentally summon up my favorite spot. For some people it is a beach with sparkling diamonds of sand and the whitecaps unfurling in a perfect wave. For others, it is a mountaintop with the smaller hills and valleys falling away into the distance and fluffy white clouds almost at eye level. For me, it is the carpentry shop at my country house where I focus on a specific aspect of a current woodworking project. What it does in reality is lower my blood pressure a few points, give my crowded head a little breathing room, and let me tackle these other issues without being overwhelmed. It is a little like the detachment of Zen, letting things flow over you rather than eat away at you. But sometimes I think Buddha himself would have lost it at Bellevue.

Five minutes later, Lucy came bouncing through the door. "Hi, Fred," she sang out, waving her long, red fingernails at me. "Don't you look cute in that bow tie?" Maria looked up from the file cabinet and gave me a conspiratorial wink. "Hi, Maria, what're you looking for?" Lucy bent her tall frame so that she was next to her at the cabinet. "Maybe I can help." Today, her hair was loose and flowing, coppery ringlets falling about her face and shoulders like a Pre-Raphaelite maiden, a sure sign that she was feeling bubbly and flirtatious. She told me she had met microsurgeon Guy Mahoney on the elevator and he had asked me to call and tell him how his "zipper repair case" was holding up.

I declined asking her if she had spent the morning having her teeth cast in platinum. At least she was here, which was more than

CRAZY ALL THE TIME

I could say for Josephine. Eventually, around two P.M., Josephine put in an appearance, although today she was back to being Yolanda. And I also learned what she meant by the sidewalk opening up in front of her. She meant that the sidewalk opened up in front of her, like your own personal San Andreas fault appearing in front of you wherever you walk. And if she didn't watch out, she would fall in and vanish from the face of the earth. Lucy was right. Carl was right. This wasn't going to work.

My day ended as it began, with David in my office. It wasn't his scheduled supervision session, but he had asked for a few minutes to talk about his problems with Matthew.

"How'd it go?" I asked.

"Terrible." He blew his cheeks out with little puffs of air. "He's not cooperating. He's fighting me."

I motioned him to a chair. "Why shouldn't he? He doesn't think you're on his side. It's not his job to cooperate. Did you think it was going to be easy? The guy cuts his penis off and you expect to have a nice conversation? Wake up."

David slumped into his seat. "Ah, you're right."

"What else is bugging you?"

"It's just that this is such a big case. Everybody at the hospital seems to have heard of the guy who cut off his penis with his pinking shears."

"Well, you got your celebrity case."

David and I talked about his anxieties for a few minutes—a celebrated patient, the pressure to do well, and the difficulties involved in meeting a solid wall of resistance. He seemed to perk up a bit, but as he reached the door he stopped.

"I still can't understand it, Fred. How could he do such a thing? It's so . . ." He searched for the word. "Sick. I think about it when I get dressed in the morning, and every time I go to the bathroom. I even thought about it last night in the middle of making love to my fiancée. I mean, how could he . . . ?" He shook his fists, unable to continue.

"I know," I said, patting his shoulder. "It's really frightening. It's like when you have a suicidal patient and you think just for a moment, 'I wonder what it's like to blow your brains out.' And then before you know it, you're actually visualizing that moment. We'll talk some more about it in the morning." And then because I thought he could use some lightening up I invited him to our Wednesday get-together lunch the next day.

At least one thing got cleared up that day. As we were walking through the reception area, I passed by Yolanda, typing away. Out of the corner of my eye, I glimpsed a familiar black and white image at the level of her calf. "See you tomorrow," I yelled to David. Then I turned back, reached into Yolanda's wastepaper basket and pulled out a stack of Rorschach inkblots.

"Yolanda," I inquired as sweetly as I could, "what are these doing here?"

She bolted out of her chair. "Dr. Covan," she said accusingly. "What are you doing with those?"

"I'm putting them back where they belong. Did you throw them out?"

"Don't you know those pictures are against the law? They're obscene. They're pornographic."

I looked at the black blotches in my hand. True, each person puts together the meaningless spots and splotches in his own way and many people see sexual imagery in them. That's how they work, as a key to one's unconscious thoughts and feelings. But obscene pictures?

"All of them," she continued. She flipped through the cards. "See, a vagina and a penis and a man who is doing . . ." She handed them back to me. "Oh, it's so disgusting. What could you possibly want with these?"

It was the usual hectic lunch scene at Penne's Italian Restaurant when we arrived. White-shirted waiters careened around the room, trays aloft, oblivious of the constant flow of diners coming and going and waiting for seats. The babble of voices bouncing off the exposed brick walls and columns sounded like a roaring football stadium. The rich aroma of garlic and olive oil emanated from the kitchen each time the door swung open.

CRAZY ALL THE TIME

Carl tucked a napkin under his chin. "I've been dreaming of spaghetti and clam sauce all week."

"There's nothing here under a thousand calories," announced Maria.

"As if you have to worry," snorted Rhoda. She was right about Maria, a willowy woman in her late forties.

"You can always have pasta without the sauce," said Pam Wyatt, a young psychiatric social worker with owlish glasses and hair pulled back over the top of her ears.

"Pasta without sauce is like whiskey without alcohol," declaimed our resident Irish poet and raconteur Parnell Walsh, who was an attending psychiatrist in the psych emergency room.

With Kitty Webster, David, and myself also in attendance, it was an interdenominational table—students, psychologists, a psychiatrist, and a social worker. It was our once-a-week attempt to re-create the late, lamented table at the student-faculty cafeteria at New York University across the street from the old Bellevue building. There we gathered every lunch hour, an outrageous, raucous group who delighted in put-downs, ranking each other, competing with jokes. We have a cafeteria in the new high-rise concrete structure, but most of us don't use it and it's just not the same.

Rhoda started the ball rolling by asking David, "How's your patient with the autopenisectomy?"

"Self-multilation is a rather fertile ground for research, don't you think?" asked Carl. "People do the craziest things to themselves just to hurt other people. I remember there was this guy back when I was in college, a battle-scarred veteran, very angry. He was having a psychotic episode and they brought him into the local hospital."

"Oh, Carl," said Rhoda, "not that story. Not when I'm eating squid."

"And he put out his eyes while he was in the observation room."

"Aaarghhh." Kitty and David made the same strangled sound.

"They didn't do a very good job of observation," observed Pam.

"When they asked him why he did it, he said people kept coming in and were harassing him, teasing him, making fun of him. And the only thing he could think of to get back at them was to put out his own eyes. Psychologically, it is equivalent to the high school student who refuses to study because he doesn't like his teacher. 'I'll show her. I'll fail.' Or the adolescent who hangs himself because he's angry at his parents."

"Do I really want to do this for a living?" asked David. We all laughed, having asked ourselves that question more than once.

"There is something about the juxtaposition of sexual parts and mutilation," observed Parnell in his dry, sophisticated voice, "that has a kind of repellent attraction for us. When I was doing my residency at the hospital, a naked couple was brought in, still in flagrante delicto. They were coupled together like two boxcars."

"I thought that only happened with dogs," said Carl. "The bitch's vagina clamps down on the swollen member so the male can't remove it."

"Well", here it wasn't a case of *vagina dentata,* but rather the tail end of an IUD that had managed to grab onto the man's foreskin like a hook in the mouth of a fish."

Even I had to cross my legs at that one.

"So there they were fully conscious, still involuntarily engaged in the most intimate act known to man and exposed to every doctor, nurse, and orderly who found some excuse to go into that room."

"Did you ever notice when there's a real catastrophe, like the World Trade Center bombing, how much real caring goes on in this hospital? But just let something like that IUD thing happen, where there's no real danger to the participants, and suddenly everyone's a voyeur," I said.

"But how did they get them apart?" asked Kitty, looking worried.

"Oh they just did a circumcision."

"While he was inside her?"

"Um," nodded Parnell, taking a swallow of Perrier. "Very delicate surgery."

"Talk about indecent exposure, the worst story I ever heard," I said, "was at a seminar on sex crimes. One of the cops told about a flasher whose MO was to go into a Seven Eleven when there was a female cashier on duty and hang out in the back until the store was empty. Then he'd pick up several items—a can, some milk, a bunch of bananas—and put them on the checkout counter along with his penis.

"The clerk would be busy moving things along, ringing them up on the cash register, and suddenly she'd grab it and scream. So one day," I continued, "he got a can of pork and beans and some other things and put them all on the counter with his penis, and this particular clerk, who was real streetwise, picked up the can of pork and beans and brought it down. Smash."

"Oh no."

"Yikes."

"The pain knocked him out, of course. And when he came to there was the cop who told the story to us standing over him. And the cop said, 'Next time buy something softer, like a loaf of bread.'"

Kitty said, "I've got one—" Everyone turned toward her. She began to blush. I smiled encouragingly. Kitty began hesitantly, her voice going up at the end of each sentence Valley-girl style so that every statement ended up sounding like a question. "I was a nursing aide at Mount Sinai? I thought I wanted to be a nurse? They brought in this guy one day? He was bent over like a pretzel and he couldn't straighten himself out? Isn't that funny?" We all looked at her uncomprehendingly. "I'm sorry. I mean, no one had ever seen anything like that before."

"No one had ever seen anyone whose back was in spasm?"

"No, I mean, I'm sorry."

Spit it out, Webster, I thought.

"I mean it was the *reason* his back was bent over? He was trying to, um, do it to himself?"

"Good Lord," said Parnell. "And I thought 'go fuck yourself' was only an expression."

"Not that. I mean in his mouth?"

"Autofellatio," mused Carl. "Seems to me I saw a paper about that in *Experimental Psychology*."

Maria almost choked on her salad. "Some experiment!"

"You mean this guy was trying to give himself a blowjob?"

"At least he solved the problem of finding a willing sex partner," chuckled Rhoda.

the unkindest cuts

"I don't know," I said. "It sounds like a cock and bull story to me." And then I ducked as all the napkins flew at me.

David saw Matthew for the next few weeks, reporting to me at each session that he was getting nowhere. In fact it seemed that the patient had taken an active dislike toward my student. It began just at the point David thought he was finally making a breakthrough. They were discussing religion, specifically religious laws and injunctions. For the first time, Matthew was really talkative. Then he asked if David attended church.

When David admitted he had stopped going a few years ago, the young man turned his head to the wall. "Then none of this means anything to you," he had said bitterly. David tried to protest, he told me, but it was useless. He had gleaned enough from Matthew to know their values and way of life were miles apart. Although they had both been brought up in middle-class homes, Matthew was an only child who had been raised strictly, punished severely for disobedience, taught to believe that sex was forbidden outside of marriage and a necessary evil inside. Women were temptresses who could bring a man to ruin. To Matthew, David might have been from Mars, a man who moved and spoke with a kind of ease that was beyond him. He saw David as someone who was trying to batter down his wall of silence and secrecy and invade his world, which, however tormented and distorted, was still safer than the world outside.

But for David, what Matthew had done was doubly terrifying. He had destroyed not only his bodily integrity but the symbol of his sexuality and manhood. Matthew's act of self-mutilation was so horrendous to him, so repugnant, that he could see nothing of Matthew in himself or of himself in Matthew. But it is exactly that ability to see ourselves in others that enables us to forge the therapeutic alliance between us and our patients, which allows healing to take place.

David acknowledged he was having trouble telling the messenger from the message, the patient from the pathology. He knew the self-inflicted penisectomy was not all there was to Matthew, but still he could not get beyond it. This is a common phenomenon in city hospitals, where it is often difficult to distinguish the criminals who are brought in from the crimes they have committed. One emergency room surgeon makes it a practice never to inquire about patients who have just been arrested for fear that it will interfere with his ability to operate. He made this decision after he removed a bullet from the lung of a man who had just murdered, raped, and cut up the body of a twelve-year-old girl, throwing the pieces into a dumpster. Throughout the procedure, the doctor had to fight an urge to just let the man die.

"Somehow," I said to David, "you have to search that continuum of behavior between Mother Teresa and Charles Manson to find some attribute that you can identity as being part of a fellow human being."

"Matthew is both criminal and victim," said David. "So which part am I supposed to identify with?"

"Neither," I said.

He looked at me, perplexed.

"Not the role, but the person behind the role."

David got up from his chair and began pacing in my cramped office between my chair and desk and the few small chairs I have for visitors. "You know what I feel like?" he asked, his tone a mixture of defiance, bravado, and hurt. "I feel like your surgeon friend. To me, Matthew is a *monster*."

"You mean, he has no right to live?"

"I mean, I've seen him . . . what's it . . . ten times now? And he has yet to utter one single word, make one gesture that would identify him as that human being we're always talking about. Even when we were talking about religion, it was like he was lecturing me." David waved his hands about agitatedly. "He was didactic and patronizing, talking to me like I was some kind of child."

The phone rang. It was Weenie asking me if I had included Jenny Noh, the new psychologist I had hired, in the diversity survey.

"No, Malcolm," I said. "I gave that to you two weeks ago."

"But she's Asian."

"So?"

"So it's more diversity."

"But you said downtown wanted it right away. Isn't it too late to add it now?"

"It's never too late," Weenie said. "Type on an addendum and have it on my desk—"

"This afternoon," I said, finishing the sentence for him.

Hanging up, I said to David, "As I was saying, Matthew's not there to charm you or be your friend. Stop thinking about *you* and just try to get to know this other human being. Just go in there with sensitive curiosity and find out what makes him tick and why he was so desperate to do such a desperate act."

But David just stared at me.

"C'mon," I said. "What's really on your mind?"

"What's on my mind is, I spend an hour every day, whether I feel like it or not, in the gym, lifting weights, pedaling away on that damn Lifecycle, because I care about health. I care about my body. And then this idiot goes and cuts his dick off. I mean, it really makes me sick, if you want to know the truth. And I don't care what you say, I'll never be able to empathize."

I just sat there, unable to say anything. No matter what I tried to do to get David to connect with Matthew, it hadn't worked. I seemed to be having as much trouble breaking through to David as he was with his patient.

David took a deep breath. "I got to tell you, Fred. I don't think I'm really the right person for this case. What I'm saying is, I don't think I can work with him."

I looked at his tightly drawn face. It was his first case at Belle-vue and I didn't want him to fail. *I* didn't want to fail. But I knew that the only way he was going to succeed was to reach more deeply inside himself to find a way to connect with Matthew.

From the time I first interviewed each of them, the interns knew that a morgue visit was to be part of their Bellevue experience. My rationale is simple—I want them to face death. Although the AIDS epidemic has made death a reality for many younger people, most of our students have never seen a dead body.

I believe that death has a special place in psychotherapy. If our students are ever to be good therapists they must be able to acknowledge their own feelings about death. In one of his books, Carlos Castaneda says that death is our ally. I know what he means.

CRAZY ALL THE TIME

Death is a silent partner who often helps me treat my patients. Most people and, I am sad to say, even most therapists avoid the subject of death, particularly their own. But when I have a patient who refuses to examine his or her life, I often ask, "Are you prepared to die as miserable as you are now? Because unless you make some crucial changes, that is how you will live out the rest of your life, whether it is a few more weeks or decades." When I say that, I see in my mind a corpse I once saw in the morgue. I believe that image, which is still so vivid, helps make that confrontation more powerful.

When we started out for the morgue, two days after my session with David, everyone was understandably nervous. I told them the "field trip" was to be a quiet, meditative process. They should observe themselves as much as the corpses. "Don't ask me any questions or talk while we are there," I said. "This is to be an inner journey. We'll talk about it afterward."

There was some giggling and small talk as the seven interns and I took the elevator from my office down to the first floor. The eighth intern, Elizabeth Driver, who often couched her remarks in ideological and feminist terms, called the morgue visit "an exercise in paternalism" on my part and refused to go. We crossed the lobby and changed elevators to get one that went to the basement. "Orpheus descending," nervously joked Nick Torres, a bit of a rebel with his black ponytail and gold hoop earring.

The only sounds were our shoes clattering on the tile floor as we entered the morgue. In the air was an amalgam of body odors, formaldehyde, and ammonia. Overhead, the fluorescent ceiling panels cast a cold shadowless light on the three aisles of double-tiered stainless-steel refrigerator doors. There were sixty doors on a side, each about the size of a man's torso.

I put on a pair of rubber gloves and looked down the row of doors. On the first door was a sign that said BABIES. Everybody looked at me as if to say, "No, not those!" They had nothing to fear because in all honesty I don't want to deal with that one. Earlier that day, I had come down and selected five bodies, male and female, young and old, to give them a sense of the life cycle. I opened

the unkindest cuts

the first door and slid out the tray on its metal gliders. Until a few years ago, the bodies were naked on the tray. But now they are wrapped in white plastic like a piece of frozen meat. The group gathered around as I cut away the wrapping. There was an audible collective gasp at the body of a young muscular black man, whose chest bore gaping bloodless holes.

Kitty and David stood apart from the group and I eased them in closer. Putting his finger to his lips, David stared at the corpse intently, seeming almost not to breathe. Sometimes people look a little green, but in all the years I've been doing this I've never lost anybody. The next corpse was a twenty-five-year-old white woman, an IV tube still attached to her thin arm. It is not unusual for medical equipment, feeding tubes, or paraphernalia used for resuscitation to be left fixed to their bodies as if death were an inconvenient interruption of modern survival technology.

We looked at three more bodies that afternoon. One was a large middle-aged man, postautopsy, with a Y incision across his upper chest and down to his abdomen. Sewed back up with black wire, he was a grotesque rag doll. But it was the last body, that of an old man, which transfixed the group. He was the image of a Bowery bum. The network of red veins splayed across his bulbous nose bespoke years of alcoholism. A stubble of beard covered his cheeks. He was in rigor mortis. His back and neck arched like a bow, his eyes like those of a dead fish, his mouth open in its final gasp. It was as though he had seen Medusa and turned instantly to stone.

In the eerie quiet, the sound of the tray sliding back into place was unnaturally loud. I pushed against the door to close it and when it failed to close all the way, gave it an extra shove with my shoe until it slid into place with a heavy, muffled thud. As always happens, the people on the elevator ride going up in the midst of their animated conversations stared at our silent group. We, on the other hand, felt as though we had rejoined the living.

Nick began the debriefing session, seemingly more comfortable than the others because of his years as an AIDS volunteer. "I've sat with so many AIDS patients, held their hands, talked about their feelings about dying. I've even been on death watches. But this was so different. These people were . . . so . . . so . . ."

"Dead," said Wayne. The laughter that followed sounded more like a sigh of relief.

"Yeah," Nick agreed. "To tell you the truth I found nothing spiritual about it. If there is a spirit, it had long ago left these bodies. They reminded me of discarded clothes. Fred, do you know why that young guy was shot?"

Usually I didn't know, but this victim had made the papers. "For his lambskin jacket," I said.

"Jesus," Nick groaned. The others exchanged stricken glances as if hearing about a friend.

"What got to me," said Garrison Bernstein, who had been in medical school before deciding to become a psychologist rather than a medically trained psychiatrist, "was how different this was from cutting up cadavers in anatomy class. These were people, individuals. They had life stories, like that young woman with her wasted body or that black kid killed for a jacket."

Sitting in the back of the room, Ginger Baron was nodding. "I wondered about all those people. That young woman. What killed her? Did she have children? A lover? And that old man," she shuddered. "I'll never forget that last gasp of death."

"It's funny," said Wayne hesitantly. "I never think of death as real, as something that could happen to me."

"I know what you mean," said Garrison.

"But when I looked at those dead bodies," Wayne continued, "I could have sworn that I saw their chests move."

"That's a common hallucination," I said. "A momentary denial of death. But I think that what you'll all find over the next few weeks is that life will become more real."

Kiesha Wright, an African-American intern, shifted restlessly in her seat. "I guess you people didn't grow up in the ghetto," she said with a somewhat bitter laugh. "My uncle was stabbed to death in a fight when I was fourteen. I saw it. That same year my best friend was pushed off the roof of her six-story house when her boyfriend found out she was pregnant. Just last week, my neighbor's seven-year-old boy, a really good kid, was killed in a drive-by shooting."

the unkindest cuts

"My father died when I was eight," said Kitty softly. "I just came home from school one day and found my mother sitting with a neighbor. My mother took me in her arms and said, 'God has taken Daddy from us. You must be very strong.' That's all she said. The next day they buried him and they didn't even take me to the funeral. I never saw him in his casket. It was as though he hadn't died at all. He had simply *disappeared*."

There was silence as Kitty wiped her eyes. Then she smiled. "I'm sorry," she said. "I didn't mean to be so morbid."

"It's sad," I said quietly, "that when parents try to protect their children from the reality and pain of death, they do more harm than good."

The meeting was over. Only David had not said a word.

The next day, much to my surprise, David arrived for our supervisory session brimming with excitement and pleasure. In fact, he looked a lot like he had the first day before I had assigned him Matthew.

"David," I exclaimed. "What's going on? Fill me in."

He shook his fists like an athlete who had just won a big game. "Fred, I had a breakthrough. I know why Matthew cut off his penis."

I walked over to our chairs. "Great. Sit down and tell me all about it."

He remained standing. "I will in a minute. But first I want to tell you what happened with me. When I got home last night, I saw this plastic bag of old clothes that I've been meaning to give to a homeless shelter. Then I thought about that black guy in the morgue who had been *killed* for his jacket. And I remembered what Nick said about the bodies in the morgue seeming like discarded clothes. Suddenly it all seemed so useless, my clothes that at one time meant a lot to me, and that man, young and muscular like me. His life was over. Useless and discarded.

"And then something struck me. You know how we talked about how Matthew was not his penis? I mean he isn't any more than I am my muscles, or that man was his muscles. Yet our bodies are part of us. So it's like we both are and are not our bodies. Then I thought, and I know this sounds funny, how much of me is old clothes? Like what can I discard and still be me? My old girlfriend once said that every man's self-concept was in his dick. 'Without a dick,' she said, 'a man would have no identity.' I'm sure that's true for many guys and maybe it was true for me at the time. But then Matthew did the very thing that she was joking about and he is still Matthew. So I know the whole thing is very confusing, but somehow I came to the realization that at the root of Matthew's problem is the fact that he detaches himself from his body. Otherwise he could not have done what he did. And at the root of *my* problem was the need to detach myself from Matthew, to repress my own fears of death, and deny the fact that at some point in life we all have to separate from our bodies. In the final analysis, we are not our bodies, and what Matthew did is a reminder of that. Our bodies are not us. At least not all of us."

I waited for him to sit down, but he still wasn't finished.

"Clearly our penises are important parts of our bodies."

I had to agree.

"The thought of living without one, cutting it off from the rest of me, is unthinkable. Every time I met with Matthew I could hear my own voice inside me saying over and over, 'How could you do this?' And in the process I wasn't listening to what Matthew was trying to tell me. All I can say is that last night something clicked, and the proof of it is what happened this morning."

Then he sat down and told me.

He went into Matthew's room and found him sitting up in bed, although his hands were still tied to the bed railing with padded canvas straps. David began to chitchat a little and for the first time Matthew was beginning to respond to him. Perhaps it was because David was sitting with him, making eye contact, and listening to Matthew rather than the little voice in his head. Finally David said to him, "Matthew, I would really like to understand what made you cut off your penis."

Matthew turned away as usual. But this time he mumbled, "I can't tell you. It's too embarrassing."

David remembered what I had said about confronting a patient in a paradoxical way. "I know that what you did, cutting off your penis, was very difficult," he said. "It must have taken a lot of guts, determination. You must have had a very good reason for doing it. Because I know you would not have done it otherwise."

Matthew nodded his head slowly. "Yeah. You're right. I had a reason."

"Would you share it with me?"

For a moment, their eyes locked, and Matthew looked, as David put it, "like he was about to spill the beans." Then he pulled back. "I can't tell you. You wouldn't understand."

Ordinarily David would have pulled back, too, resentful that the guy was so ungiving. Now he leaned forward. "Try me," he said.

"Well," Matthew began tentatively. "I kept having these thoughts." And then he stopped.

David pressed on. "What kind of thoughts?"

"Nasty thoughts, really bad thoughts. I just really can't even talk about these things."

Then David had a brainstorm. "You know, Matthew. I have a really terrible imagination. And when people say they've been thinking about something and they won't tell me what it is because they're embarrassed, my mind is so weird and outrageous that the things I come up with are even worse than anything they could possibly conceive of."

Matthew looked at David suspiciously. "Really?"

"Yeah. And I'll tell you something else. To do what you did because of those bad and embarrassing thoughts, you have very high principles."

Matthew bit his lip and said nothing, but he didn't look away.

"When did you first start having these thoughts, Matthew?" David held his breath in anticipation. He felt his heart beating fast, hoping that the part of Matthew that wanted to talk would win out against the part that wanted to hold back.

"The first time was about a month ago," Matthew said finally. "I was sitting watching "Jeopardy." It's my mother's favorite program. She never misses it. She walked into the living room and sat down next to me on the couch. She had just taken a bath and was wearing a bathrobe and her hair was wrapped up in a towel like a turban. And then she did something she never does. She leaned her head against my shoulder. And like I said, she had just gotten out of the bath, and she smelled, you know, good. And then out of the blue this thought comes into my head."

He stopped. David waited. But after a few minutes of silence, David said, "C'mon, Matthew, you're not going to stop there."

Matthew actually smiled. For the first time since they had been meeting, David began to relax. They were making contact.

"It was just a fleeting thought," Matthew continued. "It was . . ." He closed his eyes. Then he opened them and looked at David, who wanted to hear what he had to say with all his heart. *What would it be like to have sex with my mother?* It was like someone else was saying it. Like the devil was speaking through me. And I just jumped up. And my mother said, 'Hon, what is it? Can I get you something? Do you want something to drink?' And I just yelled at her, 'No, I'm going to my room.' And I shut the door and turned on the radio real loud. It was a rock station and she hates rock music. But she came after me anyway. She knocked on the door and said, 'Are you all right?' And I yelled, 'Go away.' And then after she left, I tried to put the thought out of my mind, but I couldn't. Like it wouldn't go away. It just kept happening at home, at church, everywhere. Sometimes I would even get pictures in my mind, like my mother's bathrobe opening. I was so sick and disgusted. I tried to think about other things, talk to people, listen to the radio, read. I tried to read the Bible, but it made me feel even more dirty, like I shouldn't even be touching it. It was like the devil speaking, really. *Why else would I think such thoughts?* I tried banging my head against the wall, trying to drive the devil out. But I couldn't stop it. I even tried drinking to block out the thought. I wanted to drink until I couldn't think anymore. Drink myself into a stupor. But all that happened was I got sick and nauseated. Sometimes I even felt twinges in my penis when I thought about it. And then I thought, what would my mother do if she knew I had such thoughts? She would be so disgusted with me. When I was little, if I said a bad word, she'd wash my dirty mouth out with soap. I thought, that was it. *God was finally telling me what I had to do to stop the thoughts.* I went downstairs to the basement, where my mother has her sewing room. I went through her sewing basket and I found the pinking shears. And I didn't want to do it but I knew I had to. And the first cut hurt so much. I never felt such pain. It was like my whole body was on fire. But I just kept on. *Because this was my salvation.*"

"You did good, David," I said when he had finished talking. "You really connected with him."

David smiled broadly. "Thanks. I feel good. But I got to tell you, Fred. I don't know what to do next."

"Oh that's easy. Next time you tell him he cut off the wrong organ."

"What?"

"The most important sex organ in the human body is the brain. The penis is only following orders. He should have cut off his head."

"So I have to change his thoughts not just his behavior."

"Right," I said. "And it's the way he thinks about thinking that has to change. Matthew has to see that there is a fundamental difference between thoughts and action. Thinking about having sex with his mother is not the same as having sex with his mother any more than wishing someone was dead is the same as killing him. Someone else might be upset by thoughts of sex with his mother but probably wouldn't decide that chopping off his penis is the proper remedy. Thoughts are separate and somewhat uncontrollable. Our actions are under our control. He has to become more accepting of his thoughts, even, or especially, sexual ones. It may be that he doesn't like to think about sex, that it's against his religion and his value system, but the thoughts are normal. That doesn't mean he has to act on them."

"It's normal to think about having sex with your mother?"

"It's within the realm of normality. Psychoanalysts believe that those thoughts are often a bridge from childhood dependence upon the mother to psychological separation from her during puberty and the eventual development of a fully adult male identity. Matthew has yet to make this transition. But we have to help him recognize that it is normal. He has to learn to tolerate an occasional, passing thought about any kind of sex, even if it is with his mother."

"If he accepts his thoughts, then he can accept his penis."

"Right."

"So we are completing the surgeon's job," said David happily. "We're the psychic reattachment team."

"So next time tell Matthew that sexual arousal comes from erotic thoughts and that he should have cut off his head. See what he does with that. The paradox might just prove to be the pinking shears he needs to cut through his denial of his feelings."

"Maybe we need a regular scissors here," David said mischievously. "We want his denial to unravel, don't we?"

That evening, I saw Carl Zelecky approaching me again in front of the building. "Fred," he called. "Wait up." When he came abreast he said, "I just wanted to say you were right. Yolanda, whatever her name is, did a great job typing up the report."

"No, Carl, you were right. Your report was the only thing she got done in a week."

He gave me a friendly clap on the back. "Well, maybe the next one will be better."

"The next one?"

"Haven't you heard? Yolanda quit. Seems like there were some dirty pictures lying around that she found offensive."

"God knows what they were," I said, getting on my scooter.

Sex, Drugs, and Other Addictions

Chapter 3

During a recent group-therapy session, one of my patients talked about putting her feelings in a box. The problem, I told her, is feelings have a life of their own. Hidden from the light of day, they fester, growing teeth, and horns, and tails. Then, when you least expect it, these demon feelings burst out of the box and overwhelm you.

Suppressed feelings and desires are often the source of our obsessions, addictions, and violent actions, either against ourselves or others. A serial killer, who would rather murder than face his sexual desires and fears of rejection, is just an extreme example of what happens to boxed-up feelings. The same inability to acknowledge our deepest urges takes place on a societal level when we demonize sex, drugs, or rock and roll.

But of all the subterranean impulses that drive us, none has more power to create mischief than our sexuality. And as I was soon to learn, it was the spark that lit the fire in the dark, unexplored reaches of the heart of our trainee Wayne Roderick.

My day began with intern Kitty Webster uncharacteristically bursting into my room without knocking. "Fred, I'm sorry to interrupt you like this, but . . . but . . ."

Noticing that her hands were shaking, I put down the report I was working on and moved the stack of papers from the chair to the floor. "Kitty, what's the matter? Sit down."

CRAZY ALL THE TIME

Perching herself on the edge of the chair, she said nervously, "It's Brenda Coleman? My patient? She said she was going to come after me." She was talking about a paranoid-schizophrenic woman with delusions she was working with.

"Kitty, sit back, take a deep breath, and then tell me what happened."

She did and continued in a steadier voice. "Everything went just fine with Brenda during the session. We talked mostly about how she couldn't sleep because she was staying up late watching all those movies on TV about her life. But just as she was about to leave, she noticed the coffee container that I had thrown into the wastepaper basket. I always have coffee and a bran muffin before I start work. Suddenly she goes like this."

Kitty stood up, her arms outstretched, acting it out for me, emphasizing each word like a conductor calling out train stations. " *'God's wrath be on this generation. I, His emissary on Earth, promise retribution against drug addicts, cigarette smokers, and coffee drinkers.'* Fred," she said, returning to her normal voice, "I don't even smoke."

Back in her seat, she clasped her hands together tightly. "Do you think I have to worry? Do you think I should be scared of her?"

"Not if you don't drink coffee and smoke."

She smiled, but I could still see the fear in her eyes. Although Brenda had never been known to actually hurt anyone, the fact that she was delusional and had pushed and shoved people in the past meant that there was always the possibility that she could do real harm.

"Keep the door open when you meet with her," I cautioned. "And sit closer to it than she does. Watch her and listen very carefully to her words, especially those concerning losing control."

Kitty came back an hour later with Wayne for their joint supervision appointment. I prefer to do supervision in groups of two or three, since the students learn not only from me but from one another. Although it was more than a month into the term, Wayne still appeared to have difficulty relating to the other students and staff members. He'd bump into people in the halls while his head was buried in a book or a journal. At my seminar, he would deliver long monotonous monologues unmindful of the give-and-take process of discussion. Carl may have been right about Wayne's ability as a researcher—he had published six articles in peer-reviewed journals, one of which had been nominated for a national student award—but the big question for me was, could he work with people as well as with mice and see patients as human beings rather than statistics?

"Wayne," I said as he and Kitty sat down, "let's start with your patient. Tell us what the presenting complaint was and what you've learned so far."

"Sure," said Wayne, flipping through a small leather-bound notebook that he always carried in his breast pocket. "Patient is a twenty-one-year-old female senior at Hunter College, referred for evaluation by the walk-in clinic."

We provide psychotherapy for many college students in the area.

"Major in education, minor in psychology," Wayne droned on. "Presented with a constellation of symptoms, difficulty sleeping in both getting to sleep and waking too early, eating disturbances in both directions, missing meals but also bingeing, ruminative thoughts around the issue of postcollege career, lying in bed during the day, missing classes, lack of energy, et cetera. I'm to rule out depressive reaction, psychotic symptoms, et cetera." Kitty gaped at Wayne as he raced through his presentation.

He turned the page. "Patient's problem seems to be a conflict regarding vocational plans. Although she is an ed major, now doesn't want to teach and worries that she has wasted the past four years of her life. At the same time she has no idea what she would do if she didn't teach. At this point, patient appears to be more confused than depressed. My treatment goals are as follows . . ."

I held up my hand. "Whoa, Wayne. Before you get to that, tell me about the patient. What's her name? Gina?"

He nodded, a brief smile flickering across his face.

"Good. Tell me about Gina. What's she like as a person?"

His eyes darted quickly from Kitty to myself, finally settling on a point somewhere behind my head. "Well, she's real smart. Straight-A average, dean's list, honor society, et cetera. She's got a real personality, vivacious, popular with the other students. Goes out a lot. That kind of thing."

"Wow," said Kitty, smoothing the pleats of her skirt across her knees. "She's a grind *and* she's popular. It's so hard to be both. I got the grades but I had no social life."

Wayne glanced at her appreciatively. "You too?"

"Come on, Wayne," she said. "I'll bet you never pulled an all-nighter in your life."

Pulling at a clump of hair, Wayne said, "I meant I had no social life either."

Kitty covered her face in embarrassment. "I'm sorry."

There was an awkward silence and I jumped in. "Wayne, I still don't have a sense of what Gina's like. Describe her to me. I want to see her sitting here with me. I want to feel her presence in the room."

Puffing his cheeks, he blew out a stream of air. "She's uh . . ."

"She's what? Blond? Brunette? Redhead?"

Blushing to the roots of his bangs, Wayne sputtered, "She, um, has black hair like her," he said, pointing to Kitty's pageboy.

"My hair's not really black. More like medium brown."

"Well, Gina's hair is . . ." And then his voice took on a distant tone unlike anything I had ever heard from him. "It's jet black like the sky on a moonless night."

Jet black like the sky on a moonless night? My antennae went up. "Wayne, what color eyes does she have?"

Another blush. "Um, also black."

"Is she pretty?"

He jerked his head "yes" rapidly several times in succession.

"What about her figure?"

Beads of sweat started to form on his face. "I . . . I . . . don't know."

"You don't *know?*"

"I mean, it was hard to tell. She wasn't wearing, I mean, she was wearing a sweatshirt and some old jeans with paint stains on them."

sex, drugs, and other addictions

It was the first semicoherent sentence he had managed to get out. "Good. You noticed what she was wearing."

This seemed to give him courage to go on. "She complained that she was gaining weight, which, of course, is part of the depressive symptomatology."

"How much did she gain?"

"Only three pounds. But it seemed like the end of the world to her."

"I know how she feels," said Kitty.

"Wayne," I continued, "right now, what I'd like you to do is put aside your textbooks and your notebook and just find out what's happening with this young woman. Find out what's going on in her life, what her relationships are like with men, other women, her family. Find out if she has a job. If so, what and where? Where does she live? At home? With friends or by herself? What are her living conditions like? I want a wealth of details. I really want to know this woman. Don't be afraid to ask questions. This is the time to really indulge your nosiness. That goes for you, too, Kitty. And, Wayne, listen to Gina when she talks. Really listen. Just take it all in. Don't diagnose anything yet. Just be there in the moment with her, as fully as you know how."

Wayne was really listening now, his small green eyes fixed on me through his thick lenses. Maybe, just maybe, I thought, he could pull it off. But I was very worried.

When the session was over, I knew who Brenda's intended victim would be. Me. I wanted a cigarette *bad*. But unless I went to the entryway on the ground floor, there was not a single place in the entire hospital, including bathrooms, lounges, or cafeterias, where I could indulge my habit.

A few years ago, the Health and Hospitals Corporation instituted a smoke-free policy in all member hospitals—a reasonable enough edict considering the preponderance of evidence that tobacco harms both the user and innocent bystander. But the unintended result was the creation of a new criminal class made up of patients' families who smuggle in cigarettes and matches and the patients who stash them away, use them as legal tender, or sell their bodies for a pack of Camels or Marlboros. We have created a new drug war at the hospital and the drug is nicotine. Even the staff is not immune, sneaking smokes in their offices. One addicted psychiatrist has set up office on a garbage can outside the hospital so he can puff away undisturbed as he does his paperwork.

It was now two months since I had quit, although quitting for me, in all honesty, means not buying cigarettes, rather than not smoking them. Every day was a struggle to fight that impulse one more time. In the smokeless air of Bellevue, surrounded by fellow sufferers, I was able to contain myself somewhat, but come nightfall, I lost whatever scruples I had about begging from absolute strangers. I have been known to stalk my fellow diners in the smoking section of restaurants to bum a cigarette. My nicotine fix is followed by an immediate low wherein I confront my guilt and anger at my total lack of self-discipline and willpower. It confirms my belief that without a deep-seated commitment to change, insight and understanding are useless. I can analyze my need to smoke back to thumb sucking in the womb, yet I continue. But in one respect my struggle helps—I can appreciate and identify with the difficulties all sufferers have in curbing their own demons.

Carrying the report I had been working on when Kitty interrupted me, I walked into the secretarial area. Lucy was out for the morning having the third quadrant of her gums remodeled, but the patient/typist replacement for Yolanda/Josephine was there, busily wiping down her typewriter with a washcloth. Covertly, I glanced at her desk. No cigarettes in sight.

"Hi, Dr. Covan," she said smiling.

I smiled back. "Hi, Millie." She was a grandmotherly woman in her mid-sixties, her thin gray hair pinned into a bun with what looked like a million hairpins. "Do you think you could have this typed up for me this afternoon?"

She took the report from me. "Oh sure. No problem." Great, I thought as I watched her put a clean sheet into the typewriter. Maybe this one will work out.

Millie stood up, cleaned her chair with her washcloth and, removing a Kleenex from the box on her desk, toweled it off. Then, as I watched, fascinated, she washed off the plastic pencil holder and wiped off every pen and pencil in it.

"Aren't you going to wipe off the paper?" I asked.

"Don't be silly," she said. "No one's touched it before me."

"Millie, have you talked to your doctor about your obsessive-compulsive disorder?"

She was now rubbing the washcloth across her fingertips.

"What obsessive-compulsive disorder, Dr. Covan?"

"This cleaning of everything in sight."

She gave an exasperated sigh. "Really, Dr. Covan. Didn't your mother ever teach you about germs?"

God, I thought, walking out of the office. And I'm supposed to get through the day without a cigarette!

The next time I saw Wayne it was with both Kitty and Elizabeth Driver. I wanted Wayne to have the normalizing influence of his peers, particularly women.

Elizabeth had been an outstanding internship candidate but her selection had been the subject of fierce debate. Rhoda had admired Elizabeth's feistiness, her background in women's studies, her work with battered women and victims of date rape, but Carl saw her as a radical feminist who talked in clichés like "patriarchal society" and "empowerment." Mike Warner complained that she had no sense of humor. Maria Santiago finally swayed the group by pointing out that Elizabeth had guts and passion, and that empowerment was not a bad idea at Bellevue, where so many female patients feel they have no options in life except to have children and go on welfare or take drugs and sell their bodies.

"Have you found out any more about the sources of Gina's conflict and depression?" I asked Wayne.

"Well, we talked about her not wanting to teach. She says majoring in education was really her father's idea. But she really thinks teaching is a woman's thing."

Elizabeth perked up. "What does she mean by that?"

"It's low paying, low status, and it's traditionally been a female profession. She thinks that with all the expanded opportunities for women, she ought to do something else."

"Good for her," said Elizabeth. "What does she want to go into? Law? Medicine?"

"That's just it. She doesn't know. But right now, she's really upset because she gained a pound."

Kitty looked concerned. "Another pound? That's awful."

Elizabeth looked at Kitty with disgust. "You don't really believe that, do you?"

"But last week, Wayne told us that she had already gained three pounds. Is she getting fat, Wayne?"

I had been marveling at just how well Wayne had been doing, actually talking like a human being rather than a computer, and not once consulting his notebook, but now he reverted to his old self. A blush spread across his face and he blew out a stream of air.

"N-N-N-No. She's . . . um."

"Thin?" I suggested.

"Thin is really a political formulation," said Elizabeth. "It's a value judgment, depending on who's doing the judging, which is usually the dominant group in the society: white men."

"I don't really think that's what Wayne had in mind," I said. "Is it?"

"She's just fine," he said, intently rubbing his finger across his chin. "She's perfect."

"You see what I mean?" said Elizabeth. "Women are always trying to fit into men's fantasies of them. They distort their bodies to fit the prevailing fashion, reducing or enlarging their breasts. They'll even risk their lives to fulfill the male agenda. Just look at the silicone fiasco."

"Elizabeth," I said gently. "I don't think that's the therapeutic issue here."

She turned toward me. "It's always the issue."

"We're talking about an eating disorder relative to depression."

She laughed, embarrassed. "I guess I get carried away; I've been reading *The Beauty Myth*. It's all about how women, even those who consider themselves feminists, spend so much of their time and money dieting, wearing the right clothes, buying and putting on makeup in the pursuit of some unrealizable ideal."

"I'm sorry?" said Kitty. "But I think that nice clothes and wearing makeup are important? I don't feel right about myself if I don't look good?"

"And how does your husband feel?" Elizabeth asked.

Kitty pulled her knees together and tucked her legs under the chair, a clear indication that she was feeling uptight.

"He likes me to look my best."

"How does he feel about your not wearing makeup?"

"He thinks it's . . . it's unfeminine?"

Elizabeth folded her arms. "I rest my case."

A shadow fell across Kitty's face. I thought about her marriage and wondered what was on her mind. But right now Wayne was my top priority.

"We were talking about Gina's weight," I said. "Why is she gaining weight so quickly?"

"She calls herself a chocolate addict," said Wayne. "She eats all kinds of chocolate. Hershey kisses, Mallomars, fudge, Hostess cupcakes, Devil Dogs, chocolate-filled Dunkin' Donuts." He colored again, this time a modest pink. "I kind of like chocolate myself."

"Me, too," Elizabeth admitted.

"Gina says she's thinking of abstaining entirely from chocolate."

"I admire people who have the discipline to give up things that are bad for them," Kitty said. "I've decided to give up drinking coffee. I'm afraid of turning into a caffeine addict."

"Caffeine addict? You only drink one cup a day," I said.

"That's true. But I really feel it if I don't have it."

Give me a break, I thought. Here I was struggling with tobacco, cholesterol, fats, and the calories in a bottle of fine wine, and she was talking about a cup of coffee a day. "Kitty, this wouldn't have anything to do with Brenda's threats, would it?"

"No," she said. "Well, yes. I mean, maybe."

The session was almost over. "You're off to a good start, Wayne," I said encouragingly. "I think that what you need to do now is try to get to the thoughts that underlie Gina's conflict and depression. Try to get some more background on her home life, what her parents are like. Maybe you can start with her remark that studying education was her father's idea. See if there is any anger there. After all, there must be some anger, since she was forced into studying something that didn't interest her. The anger could be a key to unlocking some of the buried feelings and help her resolve her conflict."

The next session with Wayne went even better than I expected. He showed up looking more presentable, his pants pressed, his hair freshly washed and combed. "You're looking good," I said. "Got a date?"

Blush. "Not really."

He looked a bit disappointed when I told him that Elizabeth was busy and Kitty had an emergency appointment with Brenda and it would be just the two of us.

"So what did you find out about Gina?" I asked.

"Well, I found out that she has a job. She's a waitress."

"What kind of restaurant?"

He frowned. Wayne didn't like not having answers. "What do you mean?"

"A coffee shop? A bar with tables? An upscale yuppie place with linen tablecloths and baby veggies? Details, Wayne."

"Okay, I'll find out. I think it must be a nice kind of place because money is very important to her. She's always talking about how she never has any money. She lives with a girl and a guy in this two-bedroom apartment in the East Village and there's always somebody sleeping on the couch. And she just hates it. I think she's hoping to save up enough money so she can move out. But it's hard because she's still in school."

"Where does she get money for school?"

"Well, first of all Hunter's a city school, so the tuition is lower. Also I think she gets financial aid and her father gives her some money. And, Fred, I think I got a handle on why she went into education even though she didn't want to be a teacher and why she's now upset about it."

"Really? That's great. Tell me."

Wayne tapped his knees a few times, obviously pleased. Now I understood why he wanted Kitty and Elizabeth—a bigger audience.

"Well, we were talking about how she comes from a poor family in the Fort Greene section of Brooklyn. Her father's a construction worker but he's out of work a lot because he drinks or maybe he drinks because he's out of work—Gina really doesn't know. But he sounds to me like an alcoholic. Gina says that he's angry a lot of the time. He gets into fights a lot. Gina says he's a real animal."

"Are there other children?"

"A brother five years older. He left home to join the army when Gina was thirteen and he's hardly ever been back since then."

"What about her mother?"

"Her mother's a housewife. Gina doesn't have a lot to do with her. She says she's really quiet, keeps to herself. Gina thinks she's afraid of her father."

"What about Gina? Isn't she afraid of her father?"

He bit his lip and frowned. "I don't know. Her mother sounds beaten down. But Gina isn't. She really worked hard in high school, studying every night, bringing home A's to show him. He really liked that and bragged to everyone about how smart his daughter was. But when she told him she wanted to go to college, he had a fit. He said no one in his family ever went to college and he didn't see any reason why she should go either. She begged and pleaded with him and finally he said the only way he would let her go would be if she became a teacher. Get it? That was why she was so upset about teaching. She was doing it for her father, not for herself."

"That's good, Wayne. That's really good."

He grinned broadly. "I never asked that kind of stuff before," he admitted. "I mostly worked with mice. Even when I worked at the college counseling center, the students I saw never talked about serious problems. I never really had the sense of what it was like to find out something about a person. It's kind of like being a detective."

"It is like detective work, only better. They only get to do it after there's a crime. Tell me, how did she feel when she talked about what her father said?"

"Real angry, just like you said, Fred. I kind of know how she feels.

My father wanted me to be an engineer like him or a chemist like my mom."

"What did your father think about your becoming a psychologist?"

"He thought psychology was . . . well, you know. We're from Omaha. You're not supposed to go for help unless you're crazy or an alcoholic or something. And you certainly don't do that sort of thing for a living."

We both smiled. "Okay, let's wrap this up," I said. "Now that we know what Gina doesn't want to do, let's see if we can help her find out what she does want. Teaching might still be an option. She might even like it if she weren't so angry at her father for forcing it on her. But it sounds like it's going well so far, Wayne. You're really getting a sense of her."

He smiled shyly, lips together, and looked me squarely in the eye. "Thanks."

I opened the door to let him out and saw several of the staff members huddled in the corridor. Curious, I walked over.

"She sponged off everything I touched," Maria was saying. "The IN box, the keys, the phone. She wiped off her hand after she accidentally touched me."

"You're right," said Barry McKuen. "She wiped her lips after I kissed her."

Maria did a double take. Barry, a psychologist on our staff, was openly homosexual.

"Only kidding," said Barry. "But I did see her wipe off the doorknob after I walked in."

"Maybe she's the wife of a career criminal," suggested Mike.

"Does she do windows?" Rhoda yelled from her doorway.

"C'mon guys," I said. "She's the replacement for Yolanda/ Josephine. We're coming up in the world."

Carl leaned close to me. "Oh yeah? I wouldn't be so sure about that. Depends on how long she takes with her cleaning rituals."

"Carl's got a point, Fred," said Maria Santiago, as usual trying to mediate our differences. "I'm treating an adolescent girl who's chronically late for school because she takes three hours every morning to braid her hair into corn rows."

sex, drugs, and other addictions

"One of the students I'm supervising," said Mike, "is seeing a patient who can't bear to deposit his bodily wastes into anything but his own toilet. So he gets up at five thirty to get to the office at nine because once he leaves the house he immediately thinks, What if I have to go when I'm at work? So he returns home, goes to the bathroom, leaves the house, and the whole thing starts all over again. It's getting so bad he's thinking of getting up at five."

"Okay," I said. "I hear you. I'll speak to Millie's doctor and see if she needs her meds adjusted."

A few days later, as usual I was dying for a cigarette and decided to substitute one drug for another by getting a cup of coffee from the coffee shop on the ground floor. The three takeout lines were doing a brisk business with people standing outside the door. I joined the shorter express takeout, where the mammoth Greek counterman was shouting orders into the kitchen in his operatic voice.

"One lentil soup, two bean and barley. How are you, Dr. Covan? One coffee, dark. Need a sugar fix? I got fresh cinnamon rolls."

The world is full of temptations. "No thanks, George. I'm on a diet."

George patted his mountainous stomach. "I always say, if you can't eat the things you love, why live?"

"You're right, George. You'll probably live to a hundred and ten, while dieting will be the death of me."

George's guffaw was followed by a bellow. "Next."

"Um . . . a coffee," said a barely audible voice.

"Coffee," George boomed. "Regular?"

"Make that a lentil soup."

"Hold the coffee. One lentil," yelled George.

"On second thought, I'll have the coffee."

I turned around to see Wayne. George leaned over the counter. "Kid, I got an idea. Take both."

"Hi, Wayne," I said. "Why don't you join me for a cup of coffee?"

"Good idea," boomed George. "You both sit down and I'll have the waitress bring you some coffee."

What a place, I thought, smiling. Even the counterman is nur-

turing. As soon as we sat down at the booth, Wayne started looking around, scrutinizing the plastic seats, the Formica tables, the
acoustic ceiling with its fluorescent light panels, the industrial-
tile floor, the fifties-style counter where a man in a tank top with
tattooed arms, chest, and back sat listening to his earphones. The
constant clatter of dishes and diners filled the air.

"This place is okay," he said, "but it could use softer lighting.
And a different color on the walls, like pinky orange. Like salmon.
That's it, salmon."

I looked at the walls and then at Wayne. "Since when have you
taken up interior decorating?"

"Well, like at the place where Gina works, the walls are—"

"You went to the restaurant where Gina works?"

He nodded happily.

"Why?"

"Therapy is an artificial environment and I wanted to see what
she was like outside of it."

"Why?"

"Well, you said to find out what was happening in her life, and
you wanted to know what kind of restaurant. 'A wealth of details.'
Those were your words."

The waitress deposited two cups of coffee and asked if that
would be all. I nodded her off, too stunned to speak.

"I mean, I think it's really important to see a patient in her environment, see how she functions. You learn so much more that
way than just talking. You remember, you said, 'Be there in the moment with her'? Well, I was there in the moment. I saw how she
talked to customers, how she took their orders down. I learned so
much about her just by watching her body language, how she
smiled at the customers. How she turns her head a little to one side
when she talks to them. It's kind of a submissive gesture, like what
animals do when they're in a subordinate position to a dominant
animal."

I was becoming concerned. "Look, Wayne," I began, "I'm getting
the sense that there is more than a professional interest in this
young lady."

He shook his head forcefully. "Oh no."

"Are you really certain that there isn't something outside a professional concern?"

Loosening the tie at his neck with quick jerky movements, he said loudly, "What do you mean? What are you talking about? I thought you would think that was a good thing to do."

"You really thought that because I said I wanted a wealth of details and I said that you should be there in the moment, that I meant you should start following her around?"

"You're always telling us that you don't believe in that analytic distance stuff. And you've criticized me in the past for being too detached. You've said I'm too distant, that I intellectualize too much."

He was red-faced, fighting tears. "I thought you would like this, Fred. I thought this would be a good thing to do. You're always saying that I should use more of myself. And then when I do . . ."

"Which part of yourself do you want to use, Wayne?"

He stopped. Then he stood next to my seat and regarded me coldly. "Dr. Covan, you totally misunderstand me. And frankly, I am beginning to resent this whole line of discussion."

Oh shit, I thought.

"I know that I'm the therapist and she's the patient. I know that. What do you think, I want to sleep with her or something? That's ridiculous." Heads popped up over the partitions separating the booths around us.

Taking a deep breath, I beat a tactical retreat for now. "Okay, Wayne. Just make sure that you maintain a proper therapeutic distance between you and Gina. You hear me?"

"Yeah, sure," he said, backing away from the table. "It was just a misunderstanding."

As I watched him rushing out the door, I thought I'd better keep a close eye on this kid and check with his other supervisors.

David was waiting for his supervisory session when I got back. Following the session where David had successfully gotten Matthew to talk about why he had cut off his penis, his patient had started to improve. They worked on getting Matthew to accept his thoughts and see that he didn't have to act on them. He was no longer considered a danger to himself, his hands had been untied, and their next session was to be the last before he was sent home.

"What's going to happen to Matthew when he leaves here?" David asked.

"In your report, you'll recommend that he continue on an outpatient basis. But since he lives in Staten Island and only came to Bellevue because of our expertise in microsurgery, he'll be seen by a therapist in his area."

I sensed that my answer didn't quite satisfy him. "What's up?"

"I feel so up in the air. Like I've been left hanging. It's all so unresolved."

"I understand," I said. "With so many of our patients, it's treat and release or diagnose and refer. And often we're left wondering what's happened to them. It's like starting a project and having to leave it half done."

"Do you ever do any follow-up on these people?"

"No. Sometimes you really want to. And occasionally it happens that someone comes back to visit and closes the loop for you. But most of the time you're just too busy taking care of the next patient that comes along."

My little chat with Wayne in the coffee shop seemed to do the trick. There was no more talk of seeing his patient outside his office, no more twisting of my words or rationalizing the therapeutic process to suit his own purposes, no inappropriate blushing at every mention of Gina's appearance. Even Kitty remarked on how well Wayne seemed to be settling down, looking people in the eye, socializing with the other trainees. "I gave him a short course in small talk," she said, "which is kind of like my specialty. I gave him assignments—like finding an interesting item in the newspaper or on TV to talk about and paying attention to how the Mets were doing. We also talked about how he could improve his dress."

Wayne was a very willing pupil, she said, immediately putting all her suggestions into practice. She had even taken him on a

sex, drugs, and other addictions

shopping expedition to get him a mix-and-match wardrobe of shirts, pants, and ties. Matching was very important to Kitty, who accessorized every outfit with precision. I noticed at their joint supervisory sessions that Wayne had taken to copying her gestures, keeping his elbows at his sides while making flowing movements with his hands. If there was something parrotlike and faintly comic about his attempts, at least he was trying to relate to other people. And I could only hope that, by getting closer to his fellow students, he would pull away from his overinvolvement with his patient.

Wayne reported that Gina was starting to come out of her depression. She no longer stuffed her mouth with chocolate, had lost the four pounds she had gained, and was paying attention to how she dressed. For the first time, she spoke about taking charge of her life and deciding on what to do after graduation. At my suggestion, he had her make a list of things that were important to her and then, being Wayne, he added the idea of her assigning a numerical value from one to ten to each item on the list so that "it could be properly weighted." With a small Kitty-like flourish of his fingers, he produced the list.

> Making money—10
> Having nice clothes—10
> Having a good figure—10
> Being popular—10
> Having friends—10
> Going out to nice places—10
> Having a beautiful apartment—10
> Driving a nice car—10
> Owning a fur coat—10
> Meeting interesting people—10

Kitty stared at the list. "It's so superficial. What about having a relationship? Love? Doing interesting work? Using her mind?"

"The thing that disappoints me," said Wayne, "is that she gave a ten to everything, so there's no way of assessing the relative value."

"Apparently, they're all equally important," I observed. "Obviously making money heads the list and in the right quantities that would guarantee five of the other items. According to her value system, she should either be a top-flight model or a movie star. Does she have any talents?"

"I asked her that and she said that the only thing she was really good at was people. Not children, which is why she doesn't want to teach. But she really gets along with adults. She says she likes to make people happy." Wayne gave one of his rare, open-mouthed smiles, looking pretty happy himself. I felt a small twinge of queasiness, but at least he wasn't blushing.

"Well, if she wants to make money, gets along well with people, and makes a good appearance, maybe she should go into public relations," offered Kitty. "Or even some managerial position. You said she has a good mind."

"Or sales," I said. "She'd probably be good with customers. Something where she could use her personality."

Wayne raised his head at each suggestion, copying it into his notebook. Then he looked up and removed his thick glasses. For the first time, I could see his green eyes clearly. "Gina knows it's a bad job market out there," he said. "And she hates being a waitress. She says it's demeaning, waiting on people. She feels like she's their servant. And the guys are always hitting on her. She says she has to find some other way to make money or she'll go nuts. I'm worried that she'll slip back into her depressed state just when it looks like she's coming out of it."

"Why don't you explore other kinds of career possibilities with her?" I suggested. "Discuss with her some of the ideas we came up with. It's true that she may have to hold on to her job while she thinks about doing something else. But it sounds to me, Wayne, like you're developing a real rapport with her, which will make it easier for her to deal with some of the underlying issues, such as her relationship with her father. At the same time you work on her career choices, you can also start to probe a little under the surface, find out what makes her tick. Explore why a relationship is not on the list. At some point, you will have to go for the pain. Because it's the pain that's driving her depression and her indecision."

Replacing his glasses, Wayne peered at the notebook in his lap. I could see him writing in his cramped script, "Go for the pain."

I was still unsure about him. It was his emotional distance that made supervision so difficult. You could get only so close. He said he was worried about Gina, but there was no worry in his eyes. Even when he looked at you, as he consciously tried to do these days, his face was opaque. I had never had a student like him and he made me uneasy. So much of my work is based on empathic connection with patients, particularly with their pain. I can relate to their pain, because I've felt my own. But with Wayne, I doubted that he had ever been in touch with his own pain, much less deeply felt it.

So, following my own philosophy, I should have been more cautious. I'm always spouting that emotions driven underground may suddenly erupt. But I failed to keep as sharp an eye on Wayne as I had promised myself, with results that were soon apparent.

I was standing in the doorway of Barry's office, talking about the latest crisis with his live-in lover. "Scott will just never clean up after himself. I can come home, go shopping, make a really spectacular dinner—last night we had lobster ravioli with a velvety cream sauce and a really good chablis—and he'll walk away leaving every dish on the table. It's the way he was brought up. Maids and his mother always picking up for him. But I'm not his mother and I'm certainly not his maid."

"You guys sound just like all the straight couples I know."

"The odd couple," he laughed. "That's us. You know I always wondered if anything was going on between Felix and Oscar."

Just then the door across the hall opened and a beautiful woman about five feet eleven with long black hair walked out, wearing a tight black dress with dark stockings. As Barry and I watched transfixed, Wayne appeared behind her. She turned back to him, displaying a rear view quite as attractive as the front. He took her hand in his and she reached up with her other hand and stroked him gently on the cheek. "See you next week," she said in a soft, seductive voice. Wayne continued to hold her hand and gaze at her.

Finally, he let go, his fingers slowly sliding between hers. She turned and left, a sweet scent—orange blossoms maybe—following in her wake.

"What was *that*?" Barry marveled. "Wayne has a girlfriend?"

"*That,* I'm afraid, is his patient."

Barry rolled his eyes. "Uh oh."

Wayne walked by us completely oblivious, his face bedazzled, his feet somewhere above the floor. Oh my God, I thought, now what do I do? Wayne's in love.

The next morning I waited for Wayne alone, having postponed other appointments until the afternoon. I had decided what I would do—take it slowly, question him more closely about what Gina was like, get him to describe her to me more fully and in concrete terms. By using his own words back to him, I hoped to get him to see that he was acting out his erotic feelings, that it wasn't therapeutic, and he had to deal with his countertransference. It was a good plan, but somehow events conspired against me.

Wayne burst through the door in a state of high agitation. "Have a seat," I said. He went to one of the chairs against the wall, then turned on his heel and began to pace my cubbyhole of an office, four steps in all, between a small round table filled with papers on one side, my desk, three tubular chairs, and the wall.

"It's Gina," he said, his voice rising. "I just got off the phone with her. I was on for more than an hour. She's decided what she wants to do with her life and it's all my fault."

"Wayne, it's hard to listen to you while you're pacing. Why don't you just sit down and tell me what happened?"

He pulled up short in front of my desk and leaned over me. Beads of sweat were on his forehead. "She wants to become a prostitute. A call girl," he said intensely. "It's that list that did it, that list *you* told me to have her write. Gina said that when she looked at it, with all those tens, only one thing made sense. She said that money is the most important thing in the world to her, that she's always been poor, and the only way that she's ever going to get the things that she wants in this world is to sell her body. Because her body is the only thing that she has that is a marketable commodity."

Exhausted, he slumped into a chair. "I tried to argue her out of

sex, drugs, and other addictions

it logically." He held up a fist and began counting out with his fingers. "First, I told her how she was throwing her life away, how she had a brain as well as a body, how she would soon be graduating from college and would have a degree and could do anything, go to graduate school, become a psychologist like me."

Right, I thought.

"Second, I told her how it made no sense from the health point of view. I said she would be exposed to every kind of disease—AIDS, syphilis, gonorrhea, herpes, chlamydia. But she said she knew all about protecting herself. She said that all her customers would have to wear condoms with Nonoxynol-9.

"Third, I told her that her, quote unquote, customers would be the worst kind of people. They could be sadists, sex maniacs, anything. I asked her, 'Haven't you read those stories about prostitutes being beaten up, knifed, killed?' But then she tells me, 'I'm not going to be a streetwalker. I'm going to be a call girl. I know someone who can put me in touch with a woman who runs a really high-class service. It's like working for an agency. They screen all the customers. They're like important businessmen, doctors, lawyers, judges. My friend says I can make up to a thousand dollars a night. So it's like everything on the list, making money, having good clothes, going to nice places, meeting interesting people. And the way I figure it, if I invest my money right, I can retire in a few years.'

"Finally, I tried to argue it from the moral point of view. I asked her what her priest would say about it. That made her blow up. She said, 'I haven't been to church since I was thirteen and the priest told me that sex was a sin.' And then she says, 'That goddamn priesthood is made up of a bunch of skirt-wearing old men who pull their pricks, feel up altar boys, or get young girls pregnant, and then they have the gall to tell the rest of us not to fuck.' So it's like nothing I said made a dent."

"Wayne," I said, "if you're insisting that she doesn't do what she appears to be hellbent on doing, then you are showing less intelligence than my psychotic friend Greenblatt does when he directs traffic. At least he has the sense to go with the flow."

"What do you mean?"

CRAZY ALL THE TIME

"You just don't launch a frontal assault against where she is headed. You find out why she wants to go that way. This isn't a reasoned, vocational guidance decision on her part. Get enough information to find out why she's doing it. Is it just the money or something else? What kind of sexual experiences has she had in the past? What have her relationships with men been like? Try exploring with her the idea that if all your values are material ones, you'll look at your body as a commodity. Stop acting like a preacher and start behaving like a psychologist."

"But if I don't do something to stop her, she'll become a prostitute. She'll ruin her life."

"You *are* doing something. You're getting her to look at the reasons why she does what she does. But she may become a hooker anyway. All you can do is help her to see the consequences of what she is doing and where it is coming from."

"I'm sorry," he said, "but I can't accept that. Gina is a wonderful, beautiful girl and she is about to ruin her life."

"Wayne," I said, as gently as I could, "I get the sense that you are overly involved with your patient."

He glowered at me. "Why do you keep saying that? It just isn't true."

"Look," I said, "this is a tough business. It takes a lot out of us. It brings up all kinds of feelings and reactions, and if we're not aware of them, they will interfere with and destroy the therapy along with our own professionalism. You strike me as a guy who is incredibly bright but incredibly out of touch with your feelings. So what I want you to do is to go into therapy."

As I talked, his hand had crept over his face until it formed a fence over his mouth up to his nostrils. His entire body had stiffened. His shoulders were hunched, elbows drawn tight against his sides, knees pressed together. The only sign of life was his chest, which heaved with every breath.

"*Feelings!*" he spat out suddenly. "If you ask me, feelings are counterproductive. You know where they come from, don't you? They are remnants of the limbic system, the old mammalian brain. Human beings are supposed to be more evolved. We have cerebral cortexes to deal with life. We have reason, intellect. What use are *feelings*?"

He sprang to his feet, moving at me so rapidly that I wheeled my chair backward into the corner of the room. There, in front of a paper target of a torso riddled with bullet holes—my trophy from a day spent on the firing range with New York City fire marshals—he extended his arm and aimed his index finger at my chest. "I'll tell you about feelings. Feelings keep you from seeing things straight. Feelings interfere with the logical progression of the intellect in problem solution. Feelings are untrustworthy. In fact, if you think about it, almost all human error is the result of people not thinking things through and blindly following their feelings."

"For someone who doesn't believe in feelings, you seem to *feel* pretty intensely about what you just said," I pointed out.

Momentarily, I had stopped him in his tracks, but to tell the truth, Wayne's behavior had shaken me. At any given time, the line between being the therapist and being the patient is a tenuous one, but he had definitely crossed to the other side. I wrote down the names of three therapists on a piece of paper and handed it to him. "Here, call all three and choose one. That's not a suggestion, Wayne. That's an order. I'm speaking with your other supervisors and I may take you off the case."

I met with Maria, Rhoda, and Carl, who also supervised Wayne. "I think Wayne is losing control," I told them as we gathered in my office. "He appears to be sexually infatuated with one of the patients. How is he doing with all of you? Is he meeting deadlines? Getting reports done? Is he having problems with testing patients? How is he handling the other therapy cases?"

As I suspected, each of them had noticed changes in behavior but had attributed them to inexperience, stress, or the rigors of working at Bellevue. Rhoda, who supervised him on his primary rotation assessing the psychiatric status of medically ill patients, noted that in recent weeks he often seemed to be drifting off. He would lose the thread of their discussion and would have to be brought back. "He seems to be walking around in a fog," she said.

Maria reported that at first she had been impressed by his treatment of a highly intelligent twelve-year-old boy who was having problems in school, but then Wayne seemed to lose interest and was "just going through the paces."

Carl admitted that his protégé was not doing as well as expected. "He's awfully erratic in his interpretations of psychological tests. He sees sex in everything. Everything. One of the patients was looking at card one in the TAT," he said, referring to the Thematic Apperception Test in which patients are shown a series of pictures and asked to invent stories about the thoughts, feelings, and actions of the people depicted. "So the patient looked at the little boy with a sad expression holding a violin and said it was a story about a young boy whose mother insisted that he play the violin when what he really wanted to do was shoot basketball with his friends. A very common projection. But Wayne insisted to me that the patient was covering up his masturbatory fantasies and that the violin really represented his penis."

I couldn't quite resist rubbing it in. "Well, Carl, he was your baby."

Tilting his chair back, Carl put his hands behind his balding head. "He's immature; give him time. His gonads need time to catch up with his intellect."

"Right now I'd say that his gonads are far out in front," I said.

"It's not entirely the kid's fault. Did you see that patient? She's what fantasies are made of."

"The problem," said Maria, "is that Wayne doesn't have a life. And he's trying to use Gina to fill that void. I have my husband, my kids, my friends, my church. I don't need my patients to give me what I don't get from the outside world. It's a real therapist trap, your patients becoming a substitute for your social life."

"You're right," I agreed. "Many of our patients seem to idolize us. We all need to be loved. It's an intoxicant. And if we didn't have loving relationships in our life, we might look for it in our patients and become afraid that they will stop loving us. We'd avoid saying things that might make them angry at us. We might not point out a patient's lateness or acting-out behavior. We'd end up colluding with the patient rather than confronting so that he or she would continue to adore us."

Maria smiled. "It's funny how patients always talk about becoming dependent on therapy. But what they don't realize is that if we don't watch out we can become dependent on the patient's dependence."

"It's the old transference, countertransference issue," said Rhoda. "You did the right thing, Fred, getting that boy into therapy. He needs to get an analytic handle on his unconscious projections."

"Yeah," said Carl. "But a woman like Gina severely tests the bounds of countertransference."

Maria, Rhoda, and I exchanged glances but remained quiet.

The next week I saw very little of Wayne, who seemed to be keeping a low profile. According to Maria and Rhoda, he was back to his subdued, remote self, mumbling replies, and burying himself in his notebook. "But something is definitely going on with him," Maria insisted. "He's like a duck on the water, unruffled on the surface but underneath he's paddling furiously."

Wayne looked anything but unruffled when he came in on Friday morning for our supervisory session. In fact he seemed to have completely unraveled. He appeared to have dressed in his sleep, not even noticing that his thoroughly crumpled shirt was unevenly buttoned. His shirttail, which he had been managing to keep stowed for the past two weeks, sailed over the back of his trousers. Most alarming was his face, haggard and haunted-looking with puffy bags under his eyes and a stubble of a beard.

Before I could open my mouth, he raised his hand. "I know I look like a wreck," he said. "I stayed here last night and only got an hour of sleep when I stretched out on the couch in the reception area."

"You slept where?"

"I worked all through the night, writing down everything I've been thinking about for the past week."

"Didn't the hospital police—?"

His voice was hoarse and ragged. "I have given this more thought than you'd believe, Fred. I read everything I could find on the subject. I researched the literature, looked up every reference, every journal article, every book." Words tumbled out of his mouth. "I don't think anyone could have been more thorough. And then I wrote it all down, everything I could think of. I wrote and wrote through the night. I can show it to you, all my notes. Everything. There's so much there, there's enough there for ten papers. Twenty papers. So I don't want you to be upset with me because I have really thought this through and I think I can make a difference in Gina's life. I think I can really help her."

"Wayne, what are you talking about?"

"I just know you will understand, Fred, because you've never been one of these traditional analysts. And you know how you always say we should really use ourselves, be in the moment with the patient? Well, I've got it now. I've really got it."

What next? I wondered. "Why don't you start from the beginning, Wayne?"

He shut his eyes and took a deep breath. "Well, first I did what you said. I tried to get her to talk about why she wanted to be a prostitute. I asked her about her sexual experiences. She said she was a real slut in junior high. All the girls talked about her, but she figured they were just jealous because she was so popular. She said it wasn't the sex so much that she liked but the way the attention made her feel. She loved it when the guys whistled at her in the halls and made sexy remarks. It made her feel good. Like she was really beautiful. Really wanted. It made her feel special."

Pausing a moment, Wayne wiped the palms of his hands on his pants. His eyes took on a faraway look which matched the wistful tone in his voice. "Gina said that she had had a dream about me. I figured that it was going to be one of those really disguised dreams with lots of symbolism, but it was really straightforward. She dreamt that she came to see me for therapy and as soon as she walked through the door we started kissing. And she began taking off her clothes and we kept kissing all the while. She took off her jacket and her blouse and her bra and her panties and we just kept kissing and then when she was naked she undressed me from head to foot. And there we were making love on the floor behind closed doors and nobody knew what was going on."

Wayne began breathing harder, his voice taking on a new urgency. "Then I asked her if she ever had any fantasies about me when she wasn't sleeping. And she said, yes, that she thought about me a lot. That I really turned her on because I looked studious and shy and she liked men who were studious and shy. She said she thought a lot about how it would be fun to make love to me just like in the dream, at Bellevue, in the psychology department, while all the shrinks were at work and there was always the possibility that someone could walk in on us. 'Imagine,' she said, 'if someone walked in and caught us naked, fucking.'"

"Wayne, wait a minute—" I began.

But he rushed on. "And then I tried to talk to her again about her determination to become a prostitute and to really think about what she was doing. I know you said not to preach, but the hour was coming to an end and I thought I had to stop her, at least for one more week. So I told her again how she was throwing everything away, her life, her career, her chance to be a happily married woman. I told her that I would help her, that she shouldn't do anything until we had a chance to talk again. She said I wasn't going to be able to talk her out of it, that I was just being puritanical and narrow-minded. But she agreed to hold off doing anything until our next session. So after she left I just couldn't think about anything else. I canceled all my appointments—"

"Wayne, wait—"

But it was useless, he couldn't stop. "And I took the afternoon off. All I could think about was her dream and her fantasy of me and how she was throwing her life away. I went to the library and ran everything I could think of through the computer on sexual fantasies, sexual dreams, psychological studies of prostitutes. There must have been hundreds, thousands of references. I speed-read my way through abstract after abstract, taking notes on everything I read. Then I went to the cafeteria and got some coffee and a sandwich and I came back to the office. It must have been about six in the evening. And I just kept thinking and writing, thinking and writing. The hospital police did walk in several times and I told him I was working. I wrote everything down, everything that had happened between me and Gina since I first saw her. I really tried to get it clear. I must have written about a hundred pages. Maybe more. I looked at every possibility. I remembered what you said about going with the flow, not against it. I charted it out. I made diagrams. And then I came to the conclusion about how I can help her. How I can keep her from destroying her life."

He paused dramatically and then like an actor delivering the curtain line, he declared in ringing tones, "I'll have a sexual relationship with her."

"Wayne," I began and then stopped, groping for the exact words that would convey what I felt. "This is *crazy*."

He cringed as though I were about to hit him.

"You've lost it. Not only do you have the incredible, distorted notion that your sleeping with her can achieve anything positive, but you also tell me about it and think I'm going to approve it. Do you want to put it down in your treatment plan in her chart? Treatment goal: stop patient from becoming a hooker. Technique: therapist should have intercourse with patient."

I watched him bite first his lower and then his upper lip.

"Wayne, have you ever slept with a woman?"

There was a long silence.

"That's what I thought. Do you have a girlfriend?"

"There are girls I like."

"Do you remember last week when I told you to go into therapy? Have you done anything about that?"

He was doing away with what little remained of his pinky nail. "Right. Yeah, I meant to do it. I'm going to do it right away. It's just that I've been busy trying to work out Gina's problems . . ."

"Wayne, you're in terrible shape. You're obsessed with Gina. You're totally out of touch with your feelings and your judgment is grossly impaired."

I walked over to where he was sitting and stood over him, while he tried not to cringe. "Let me put this to you straight, Wayne. Listen very carefully to me," I said, saying each word slowly and dis-

sex, drugs, and other addictions

tinctly. "Unless you go into therapy immediately, we are going to suspend you from the program. Because you have lost your therapeutic perspective with this woman. I can see why. She is a very attractive woman. And she is very confused. But you are bordering on gross malpractice and you are about to destroy your career. I'm calling an immediate supervisors' meeting to recommend that Gina be assigned to someone else."

Penne's never looked so inviting to me as it did after the grueling session with Wayne. It was a really good group. Barry McKuen, Maria Santiago, Rhoda Schlossberg, Mike Warner, Parnell Walsh, and Jenny Noh, who only last year had herself been an intern at Bellevue. I could pick their brains about this problem. A large antipasto platter filled with prosciutto, pepperoni, provolone, caponata, hot peppers, and stuffed mushrooms was making the rounds.

Jenny had just finished regaling us with what Parnell called the latest episode in "the long-running soap opera—Dr. Noh's Search for a Significant Other" when I said, "There's something I need to talk about. One of the interns is in trouble." The mood at the table flipped 180 degrees.

I told them the whole story—Wayne's growing sexual attraction for his patient; Gina's desire to drop out of college and become a prostitute; Wayne's off-the-wall plan to save her. "Have you ever come across anything like this?" I asked them.

"Well," said Rhoda, rearing back in her seat, "I'm treating a hooker who wants to stop being a prostitute and go to college."

"I'd say that's more the norm at Bellevue," observed Mike, reaching clear across the table with his knife to harpoon a mushroom.

Rhoda slapped his hand. "You had seconds on mushrooms the last time, Mike."

"That woman keeps a ledger," growled Parnell.

"Anyway, as I was saying," continued Rhoda, "my patient, who is the kind of woman I planned on looking like until I stopped growing at five foot two, says that what really got to her about the life was hanging out with all the stupid streetwalkers. It got so bad that when she got an intelligent John she'd spend her time trying to talk rather than screw him.

"It wasn't funny," she said when we all laughed. "The poor woman was going broke. So that's when she decided that she really had a mind and should go to college."

"A body is a terrible thing to waste," sighed Barry.

"But getting back to our problem," I said. "The truth now, have any of you ever been really attracted to a patient so that you wanted to have sex with that person?"

"Not in my wildest fantasies," declared Parnell ringingly. "And I do have wild fantasies."

"Doing therapy with someone is a real turnoff," said Barry. The others agreed, murmuring, nodding their heads.

"I should be so lucky," said Jenny with a dimpled smile. "All my patients are under sixteen or over fifty. Even fantasy is out of the question."

Rhoda gave me one of her withering looks. "Really, Fred, I'm even surprised that you asked the question. I should have thought that questions of countertransference would have been long since resolved by people in our position."

"Well, I was attracted to a patient as an intern here at Bellevue, just like Wayne," I said. I hadn't thought of the parallel until that moment. "She was a beautiful Eurasian woman. And I was really turned on."

Mike leaned forward. "What did you do?"

"Just what any of you would have done. I recognized the attraction and the fact that, objectively speaking, she was beautiful, but I knew that I wasn't going to do anything about it. I was aware of my sexual feelings and they were under my control. Now I find that even if a patient is sexually provocative, I'm not attracted to her."

Parnell, who had been listening to my confession intently, said, "But unfortunately, as we all know, some therapists are."

We all leaned in a little closer as Parnell took a long drink of his Perrier. "One of my dear friends," he began in his full-throated baritone, "a prominent psychiatrist, a man of great talents, told me

sex, drugs, and other addictions

the most hair-raising story recently. He began by saying that he was unhappy in his marriage, that his wife was an Ice Queen who wielded sex like a weapon and was highly critical and difficult to please, just like his mother. Although he recognized that this was no excuse, the only way he could deal with his feelings of castration was by having affairs with other women. The first time he picked up a woman in a bar and went to her home, he felt great guilt, he said. But it was also a tremendous feeling of power, knowing that he charmed and seduced a woman, that she was 'under his spell,' so to speak. He began picking up more and more women, almost like an exercise, to see if he could do it. Sex became a powerful stimulant to him. The more he had, the more he wanted. He began frequenting massage parlors, picking up hookers, indulging his every sexual fantasy.

"Then the inevitable happened. Just the kind of patient you were talking about came into his office, a confused, vulnerable, but sexually provocative woman. Now my friend is a very good-looking man in his early fifties, cleft chin, graying at the temples. Up until then, he had managed to erect a barrier between his professional life and his sexual urges. But now the little devil in his ear spoke to him. 'Go ahead, it'll be good for her. She needs it. It will give her self-esteem, self-confidence.' And the walls came tumbling down.

"After that," he continued, "it became even more of a thrill to seduce patients rather than other women. Even more of a power trip, because his hold over them was twofold, as therapist and lover. These were high-level achieving women, often at the top of their professions, but who had a particular vulnerability to being seduced by an authority figure. And as an exceptional reader of people, he knew just where the greatest area of susceptibility lay. So successful was he that each patient felt that this was her secret alone, that he really loved her. And they loved him, all of them. Now he is facing ruin. His wife has filed for divorce. His license was revoked and he is being sued by five of his patients who were only too willing to come forward once they learned that his love for them was nonexclusive.

"When I asked him how he could ever let himself do such a thing, do you know what he said? He said, 'I really couldn't help it. I was totally out of control. It was just like an addiction, an obsession, a drug. The first time with a patient, when I would lock the door to my office and she would know why I was doing it and made no move to stop me, it would give me such a rush like nothing else in the world. I knew that I was the most important person in the world to her, that she would let me do anything to her, that she trusted me utterly. And she was only too happy to pay my two-hundred-dollar fee as she left. Afterward, I would feel such disgust at myself, such horror at what I had done, that I had abused the person's trust and taken advantage of someone who had come to me for help. But that, too, became a drug, like the self-loathing of the alcoholic or the junkie, which can only be assuaged by another drink, another shot of heroin.' "

A deep silence followed the end of Parnell's story. I thought of Wayne and was glad our meeting about pulling him off the case was tomorrow morning.

My students never knew what hit them when I went straight from lunch at Penne's into their weekly seminar on psychological testing. But I was determined to make sure that what Parnell had recounted would never happen to any of them. Putting on my most authoritative voice, I admonished all of them, wagging my finger: "Don't you dare ever have sex with your patients."

That night, I went to my private practice office on the other side of town, where one of my patients told me about his own sexual practices. It involved the nineties safe-sex solution, phone sex, but with a twist. The man, who spent in one month on phone calls what most people pay on their mortgage, would call bakeries all across the country. If a man answered, he would hang up and begin again. Once he got a woman on the line, he would ask if they had any pies. Of course, she would reply. What kind of pies? Could she describe them? While she spoke to him of lemon meringue, of Key lime, or banana cream, chocolate pudding, New Orleans pecan, Boston cream, Nesselrode, he would masturbate. Quickening the pace, he would press her for details. Were they creamy? Gooey?

Chocolatey? Was the filling warm and runny? Did it melt in the mouth? Then, when he could feel that he had reached the point of no return, he would ask the question that so obsessed him and allowed him finally to obtain release: "Would you throw the pie in my face?"

Walking out of my office, it occurred to me that just as there is a continuum of normality, there is a range of human sexual expression from slapstick comedy to appalling tragedy. All the way from my patient masturbating to the images of pies in his face to the most sadistic rape. And what lies at the bottom of this? Unacknowledged feelings, the very things that Wayne found of so little use.

Reality Testing

Chapter 4

Nothing is more rock-bottom fundamental than the need to believe in reality. I think, therefore I am; I perceive, therefore the world is. But reality is often more complicated than that. At Bellevue, reality can be up for grabs—and not just for the patients.

Brenda Coleman, the patient I had assigned to intern Kitty Webster, was a paranoid schizophrenic who had come to Bellevue twelve years earlier when she was hospitalized for a psychotic episode. After she had been stabilized on drugs, she was discharged to the Mental Hygiene Clinic for outpatient treatment. The clinic psychiatrist dealt with her medications and her psychotherapy was assigned to an intern. Although she continued to have delusions, successive interns year after year managed to keep her out of the hospital and functioning in the outside world. Brenda welcomed each new intern, seeing herself as helping to "train" them even as they helped her cope with her illness.

I thought Kitty would be a good match for Brenda. One of the things that had clinched Kitty's selection as an intern for me was a recommendation from a former supervisor who noted she "has a remarkable ability to work effectively with our most disturbed patients." Brenda would be a real test of that ability and I had hoped that her celebrity-filled, sexually charged delusions would shake up Kitty's neatly packaged version of reality, making her stretch and grow in the process.

In my first supervisory session with Kitty, she told me what it had been like meeting Brenda. For the first half hour of their initial session, she thought that Brenda would be a no-show. Then the door had stirred, soundlessly, moving so slowly that Kitty imagined it was being opened by a butterfly. And Brenda did resemble a fragile insect as she entered. The chart said she was fifty-one, but she looked ageless, with fuzzy, tangled, gray-brown hair. She has crazy eyes, thought Kitty. The two raspberry-red smears on her lips seemed to have been applied by a trowel. Tidier than a bag lady and more mismatched than Wayne, she wore a blue-and-yellow-striped man-tailored shirt and a flowered, garishly colored skirt. Above her clunky black pumps, her dark pantyhose were wrinkled into tiny accordion pleats as though she had tugged down rather than up. True, she would have stood out in Kitty's hometown in rural Illinois, she thought, but Brenda looked like many other people who wandered around Manhattan.

Peering nervously about her as though she were being followed, Brenda reached behind the door and wheeled in a shopping cart. She inched her way cautiously into the room and sat down in the chair closest to Kitty. For a minute she almost disappeared into the shopping cart, emerging with the largest, bulkiest, reel-to-reel tape recorder Kitty had ever seen.

"Um, excuse me," said Kitty. "What are you doing?"

Brenda stared at her uncomprehendingly. "I'm taping the session, of course."

"Taping the session? But . . . but . . . if anyone's supposed to do that, I am. I mean, you're the patient."

"Oh, you're the new one. I forgot."

Kitty got up from behind her desk and walked toward Brenda, who shrank back as though she were about to be hit. "I'm sorry, I completely forgot to introduce myself. I'm Kitty Webster."

Tentatively, Brenda grazed Kitty's outstretched hand. Her fingers were clammy. "How do you do, Miss Webster," she said politely. Touching. Surprising. She doesn't seem all that crazy, thought Kitty.

Brenda turned on the tape recorder. "I completely forgot there was a new one. Mr. Grossman was nice, but he was Jewish. I have nothing against the Jews, but they know nothing about the New Testament. What religion are you?"

"I'm Christian."

"Christian? That's wonderful. What denomination?"

"Quaker."

"A Quaker. Then you don't believe in killing things."

"Well, I am a pacifist, if that's what you mean." She wondered if she should be sharing such personal information with the patient, but then decided that establishing a connection was paramount.

Brenda's blue eyes blazed. "I mean killing things. Like those women who wear fur coats. Or scientists who cut up little animals. And people who eat meat. Do you eat meat?"

"Actually, I'm a vegetarian."

"Are you? So am I." Kitty was rewarded by a genuine smile that lit up Brenda's deadpan features. Feeling good about the way things were going, Kitty sat back in her chair. They were getting on well and Brenda seemed a lot more coherent than Kitty's predecessors had made her out to be. Now, maybe the thing to do was give her a little dose of reality.

"I noticed you were kind of late this morning."

"I'm sorry about that. I woke up late and I was really rushing around. It's because I got to bed so late," said Brenda.

"Really? Why was that?"

Brenda covered the side of her mouth with her small blue-veined hand. "I was up until four in the morning watching *Casablanca,*" she whispered.

"Oooh, that's one of my favorites," Kitty enthused.

Brenda looked at her with derision. "Really? Well, you know, Ingrid didn't actually get it right."

"No?"

"I stayed with Rick. I didn't go back to my husband."

Rick? Kitty was momentarily lost. "Oh, you mean the Humphrey Bogart character?"

"Now Bogey was a nice man. It was really his story that Ingrid was playing. Because he went back to Bacall even though he loved me."

"So," said Kitty brightly, happy to have caught on so fast, "you think that *Casablanca* is about you."

Kitty was rewarded with a look of amazement as though she was the crazy one. Then Brenda exploded with delight. "Oh, you're the new one. I keep forgetting." Her voice took on a new liveliness. "There's so much you'll want to know about me if we're going to work together."

As if to impart a great secret, she leaned forward confidingly, imparting a smell of mildewed clothing and musty attics. Kitty revised her opinion. Maybe she is crazy.

"I guess you know that the CIA and FBI are after me. They know that I know too much," Brenda whispered. Her eyes widened. "I know things before they happen. Like I knew what was going to happen in Dallas. I wanted to tell JFK but Jerry Ford told me not to. Because he knew what would happen later, that Lyndon Johnson would be president and then Richard Nixon and then his turn . . ."

Breaking off in midsentence, she gaped at a point just above Kitty's breast. "Is that Satan sitting on your chest?" she demanded.

My God, Kitty thought, she sees things too. No one had ever noted that before. "Where exactly do you see Satan," she asked.

"There!" Kitty peered in the direction of Brenda's quivering finger to where a gold brooch, about the size of her thumb, was pinned.

"Brenda, that's not Satan, it's a cat. See," she said, taking it off and showing it to her, "it has pointy ears and whiskers. You said you liked animals."

Like an actress in a B movie, Brenda shielded her face with her upturned palm and arm. "The Antichrist comes in many forms," she rumbled ominously.

Kitty didn't like the turn things were taking. Remembering that schizophrenics were easily distracted, she said cheerily, "Brenda, you were telling me about Jerry Ford and how he warned you about what was going to happen to JFK."

It worked. Brenda sat back, amiable, chatting as if about old friends. "I knew Jack and Jackie because of my father who was a rear admiral in the navy, but I didn't sleep with Jack, because I was too young. Johnson would have been my first president instead of Nixon, but Jerry told me I shouldn't get involved with him. Jerry's always looked after me just like Jeannette MacDonald and Nelson Eddy do."

"I'm sorry. Jeannette MacDonald and Nelson Eddy?"

"Don't you know who they are?"

"Not really, I'm afraid."

Brenda shook her head disbelievingly. "They're my advisors. They told me, 'Stay away from Lyndon Johnson. He's not good for you. He's only out for himself.' And it's true," she said, her voice rising. "They all are. All my so-called friends, Liz Taylor, Joan Collins, Liza Minnelli—she's no better than her mother was, you know—Barbra Streisand. I see them night after night telling stories about my life on TV and half the time they don't get it right." Agitated, her fingers fluttered. "I saw *Three Days of the Condor*, Robert Redford and Faye Dunaway hiding out from the CIA, because he knew too much. He saw the dead bodies. But it wasn't him. It was Faye. *Me!* I saw the bodies. You remember the scene when the door opens in response to his voice? It was *my* voice. I walked in. I saw all the horror. People sitting at their desks, talking on the telephone, typing memos, going to the bathroom, drinking from the water cooler. All of them dead. *Dead, dead, dead*. That's why the CIA and FBI are after me."

Now Kitty told me, "The main problem is sometimes I have a problem telling what's real in her life from what's delusional." Part of Kitty's confusion stemmed from the fact that Brenda was functional, working part time as a secretary in a stockbroker's firm, maintaining her own apartment, supporting various political and social causes, studying opera, even occasionally socializing with a small group of friends from her church choir who managed to put up with her despite or even perhaps because of her eccentricities.

"I mean, I know she didn't sleep with all those presidents," said Kitty.

"Five, right?" I asked.

"Six," said Kitty. "She's just gone to bed with Bill Clinton."

"God, it's hard to keep up with her."

"And I know," Kitty continued, "those old movies aren't about her life, but was she really the daughter of a rear admiral? It says in her case file that she was a navy brat and grew up on various bases. It's possible that she may have even met one of the presidents. She also complains that her coworkers sometimes make fun of her and talk about her behind her back. So maybe it isn't all paranoia? I mean, they would talk about her, wouldn't they, if she told them the government was after her and she personally knew all those celebrities?"

"But she might not talk about those things at work," I suggested. "She's much more apt to get into an argument with her fellow workers because they're wearing a fur coat or they wipe their noses with paper tissues rather than handkerchiefs."

"You know what I find strange?" asked Kitty wonderingly. "She's like me and my friends in so many ways. She's spiritual, she's a vegetarian, she cares about the environment and animal rights."

"We're all more alike than we are different."

"But, of course," Kitty reassured herself as much as me, "Brenda goes to extremes. She actually feeds the cockroaches and mice because, she says, 'They have a right to live too.'"

"About her spirituality, has she told you about being a prophet, yet?"

"No, wow," said Kitty. "I've never worked with a schizophrenic before. I hardly know where to begin."

"Well, you might begin by reminding her to dress more carefully and watch how she puts on her makeup. And tell her she has to take a bath every day because that smell you detected could end up costing her her job."

"Right," said Kitty. "I already did that. I told her she has to look in the mirror before she goes to work and make sure that her clothes match and her makeup is on straight. I said I would help her with her appearance and she seemed happy with that."

"That's good," I said, feeling pleased about the assignment. Kitty's need to put the world in order might actually be of benefit to Brenda. "And you could suggest that by taking the garbage down to the basement of her building, she could feed far more cockroaches and mice than in her apartment."

"Good idea. I even introduced the idea that at some point in the future I might stop by her apartment and help her get it into shape, which she liked. But, Fred—" She stopped abruptly, as though unsure whether to continue, and then plunged ahead. "These are such trivial matters."

"Kitty, they're fundamental, if we're to keep Brenda going. Our job is to keep Brenda out of the hospital."

"I'm sorry."

"Yes?"

"I'm sorry, Fred."

Suddenly I felt exasperated. "Kitty, quit saying 'I'm sorry.' Just tell me what's on your mind."

"I'm sorry." She hesitated. "It's just that here we're talking about Brenda putting on a matching blouse or skirt, or sweeping her floor, when her real problem is she thinks people are acting her life on TV."

"So you would try to take away her delusions?"

"Yes, yes," said Kitty passionately.

"How would you do that?"

"I don't know. Psychoactive drugs? Thorazine? I know there are some medications."

"And what if she won't take the medication, or does only on an occasional basis?"

"Then maybe she should be admitted and given injections?"

"Kitty, you are talking about taking a woman we have managed to maintain on an outpatient basis for twelve years, who shows up for work, even if she is often a half hour late, who keeps her own apartment even if it's a haven for bugs, and putting her in the hospital? What would that accomplish?"

"I'm sorry. I call that getting in touch with reality."

"Getting in touch with reality," I repeated. And then I dropped what I knew would be a bombshell. "It doesn't matter if it's real or not."

Kitty nearly jumped from her chair. "It doesn't matter?" she cried. Then catching herself, she said calmly, "Fred, are you really saying that it doesn't matter if you can't tell what's real from what's not?"

"Whose reality are we talking about here, Kitty? Brenda's or yours?"

She thought for a moment. "There's only one reality, Fred, the fact that she's a paranoid schizophrenic with delusions."

"That's right," I said. "So her reality is that presidents and Hollywood actors are her friends and lovers and the CIA and the FBI are her enemies. Do you know why she focuses on these people?"

"I guess it's because they're people she reads about in the paper or watches on TV?"

"So?"

"So her identification with these important people makes her feel important?"

"That's right," I said. "The specifics of her paranoid ideation are determined by the culture. So here she worries about the CIA, governmental plots, food contaminants. In the former Soviet Union, it would be the KGB. In an African village, it would be the tribal chieftain. That's the reality of a paranoid schizophrenic. And to change that reality we might have to medicate her into Zombiedom."

Kitty nodded, but I could see she was not convinced.

"Brenda takes her medications on a very irregular basis. Do you know why?"

"They make her sick?"

"She has some side effects, but that's not why. The reason is that she likes her delusions. She leads a mundane, drab, cramped existence and the delusions make her feel important, sexy, sought after, admired. The delusions can also be terrifying and scare her half to death. But they make her feel alive."

Kitty stared at the floor for a long minute. When she looked up again, her brow knitted, her mouth tightly drawn, it was as though a small crack had appeared in her stewardess persona.

"Then what you're saying is that my job is to help her live in a world of delusions? I'm sorry, but I don't think I can accept that."

"I'm saying that your job is to help her to function to the best of her ability. You need to teach her to deal with the fears that torment her and to help her have as much happiness and satisfaction in her life as she is capable of. Even if it means living with her delusions."

She nodded hesitantly.

"Did you have some other treatment in mind?" I asked.

"Yes. Yes, I do." Her hands were tight fists and I knew it was taking every ounce of her courage to disagree with me. "There's a person there, a human being at the bottom of this. I can feel it. I want to sort out what's real from what's not. I want to help her find out who she is and teach her to learn to live with it. I want her to know that fantasies and delusions are just that, that they will never by their nature be satisfying. That the world can be a good place and not something you always have to run away from."

I had great respect for Kitty at that moment. I admired her passion and her idealism. But I knew that she was seeking an impossible result. Like a good parent, I had to let her find that out for herself. "Why don't you start by taking a detailed history and see if you can figure out what's real?" I suggested. "You can present it as a therapy case in seminar and we can talk about your ideas of how to reach Brenda."

"Great," said Kitty, her face glowing again. "I just know there's something I can do if I try hard enough."

After her next session with Brenda, Kitty told me that it wasn't until the last fifteen minutes of the session that she was able to make any progress with her history-taking. To her gratification, Brenda had shown up in a scooped-neck purple dress with large yellow flowers that hung like an awning on Brenda's slight frame, but at least it was clean and pressed and there was an approximation of a part in her flyaway hair. She had also showered—that accounted, she said, for her lateness of twenty minutes. Kitty waited until Brenda finished talking about the complications brought on by the fact that George Bush, her latest ex-presidential lover, was also the former chief of her enemy, the CIA.

"In the time remaining, Brenda," said Kitty, opening her steno pad, "I'd like to work on getting to know more about your past, who you are and what your background is. For instance, where did you grow up?"

"My past?" said Brenda, bobbing up and down in her chair with excitement. "I've been thinking a lot about that."

"Good," said Kitty encouragingly. "What have you been thinking about?"

"About my being raped when we lived on the base."

Kitty could feel her skin prickling. Brenda's symptoms had a cause, childhood sexual abuse. Real abuse. If she could uncover it and get Brenda to work through her feelings about it, maybe she could get her to give up her delusions. "Brenda," she said, as non-threateningly as she knew how, "you were raped? Tell me about it."

With a slight upward nod of her head in the direction of the fluorescent light panel in the ceiling, Brenda whispered, "Is that bugged?"

"No," Kitty assured her, adding quite cleverly, she felt, "all therapy rooms are routinely checked for bugs."

"Well," said Brenda, "you're not going to believe what I am about to tell you. But I assure you that each and every word of it is true. And I have never told a single soul about it." Her manner took on the stagy emphasis of a speaker addressing thousands. "Between the ages of eighteen and twenty-four, when I lived on the base, I went through death-defying experiences. Death-defying! In those years I was always under the threat of rape. Every day. And I didn't have it half as bad as the daughters of the other admirals. They had no sons, you see, only daughters. The sailors kidnapped and raped us because they wanted revenge for what had happened following World War Two."

Her eyes danced, she gave a high and excited laugh, almost a whoop. "They were demoralized, you see, because the United States had become an imperial power just like Germany and the Soviet Union. And they remembered a time when America was altruistic, interested only in helping others."

Energy surged through her frail body as she sat upright and shook her fists at the ceiling. "But don't think we were helpless," she shouted in apparent defiance of her CIA listeners. "We were strong, we knew how to defend ourselves. Even when there were gang rapes, we fought back with knives and guns. And we had no compunction about killing them. I, myself, must have killed a dozen or more. But it was an awful bloody battle. Many of the women were left with broken bodies, arms and legs torn off in the heat of battle," she cried, her hand swiping the air. "Some were left with holes where their wombs ought to be, their babies ripped out and stomped on. And do you know who was responsible for the worst of this?"

"No," said Kitty slowly.

Brenda beat her breast with her small fists. "*I* was. It was *my* father who fired the other high-ranking officers, thus unleashing the jealousy and the intrigue in the navy, which made the sailors *crazy,*" she yelled. Returning to a whisper, she cupped her hands around her mouth. "All this was and still is very secret. We girls were never able to talk to anybody about these things, forbidden to have any contact with each other, for reasons you can well understand. All of our fathers were in competition with one another and they didn't want this kind of gossip and intrigue spread around. So this was all hushed up, even to this day. I don't even know if our fathers really knew what was going on. But let me tell you, it was clear to all of us that the navy was not going to protect us. That we were completely on our own and had to defend ourselves. But very slowly and with great secrecy, we did manage to seek each other out. And I remember . . ."

She glanced again at the fluorescent light and moved closer; her fuzzy gray-brown hair was brushing Kitty's. "I remember," she whispered directly into her ear, "there was this dance when I met two daughters of admirals and we began to talk. And then for the first time we found out that we had all had the same experience. We had all been kidnapped and raped and had fought back and killed our attackers. And then, you're not going to believe this, one of the girls opened her pocketbook and showed us what was inside. And the other girl and I just looked at each other because we all carried the same things inside our pocketbooks—a gun, a knife, and a poison capsule. If we could not stab him or shoot him to death then the poison capsule would be our last resort. We would stuff it into his mouth."

Brenda sat back, her arms folded, waiting for Kitty to say something.

"That's an incredible story, Brenda."

"Incredible, but true," said Brenda. "This is really my life. This happened to *me*. And now you can see why the government is following me, why they try to listen to everything I say."

"That must have been a terrible time for you," said Kitty sympathetically.

"It was terrible," Brenda agreed. "But it was also exciting. It was real. I was strong and could defend myself because of my military upbringing. But now there's no place for me to have real power and force. That's why I study opera. I want to sing about it. I can play Tosca and kill Scarpia, my attacker, because I am Tosca. I have lived Tosca."

"Well, at least I know one thing for sure. Brenda was raped," Kitty said as we rode the elevator down to the cafeteria."

"Raped?"

Elizabeth, who was two people away from us, sharply turned her head. Rhoda, Barry, David, and everyone else on the elevator also looked in our direction. It was twelve thirty and the lunch rush was on.

"How do you know that?" I asked.

"She told me."

"When did it happen?" yelled Elizabeth over the heads of a young woman in a suit with a stethoscope around her neck talking to a young man in a lab coat and jeans. "When she was in the hospital?"

"Someone was raped in the hospital?" asked Barry in horror.

Suddenly the whole elevator was abuzz with people talking excitedly. "Did anyone notify security?" called someone from the rear.

The door opened and an Indian aide I recognized from one of the wards stopped Weenie, who was getting on. "Mr. Weiner," he shouted. "I think you ought to know, someone's been raped in the hospital."

Weenie rushed past him onto the elevator. He acknowledged me with a lift of his eyebrow. "It's really not my department," he said, shrugging.

Several weeks later, I had a joint supervisory session with Kitty and Wayne. After Wayne had told me about his decision to go to bed with Gina, I had met with his three other supervisors to talk about how we should deal with his countertransference. Rhoda agreed with me that Wayne should be taken off the case. Maria was worried about Wayne's continuing with the patient but at the same time pointed out that the young man had a strong sense of responsibility and was terrified of failing himself and his patient. Carl was adamant that I was overreacting. He said Wayne had just made an appointment to see one of the therapists I recommended and that we should try less drastic measures. After a long discussion we reached a compromise that was acceptable to everyone. Wayne would remain Gina's therapist but he would meet with her only at the Mental Hygiene Clinic, was to have no contact with her outside the hospital, and was to tape-record the entirety of every session. We would supervise and watch him very closely.

Kitty told Wayne and me more about Brenda's problems on the naval base, a recurring theme in their sessions. "I realize that not everything Brenda says is true, but there is an underlying theme. It must have been because of the abuse on the naval base that she became psychotic."

"Whoa, wait a minute, hold on," I said. "We don't even know for sure whether Brenda was a navy brat. We've never been able to contact her family, which is not uncommon with schizophrenics. All we know is what she tells us. We're not even sure if Brenda Coleman is her real name. She's used aliases from time to time."

Kitty listened, nodding politely, but I could see that she remained unconvinced. "Fred, I'm sorry, but I've read every report by every trainee and staff member who's worked on her case and she's always talked about growing up on a navy base, although having been raped was never mentioned in her chart. She says I'm the first person she's ever talked to about being raped. Maybe it's because I specifically asked her about her past or maybe she just feels a certain identification with me that she hasn't felt with any of the others?" She turned to Wayne: "What do you think, Wayne?"

Wayne had the startled look of a schoolboy unexpectedly called on. "What do I think?"

"Was she raped?" asked Kitty.

"By the sailors?"

"Yes."

"Well," said Wayne, furrowing his brow, "I know that sailors do that kind of thing. But what about her and the other daughters killing the sailors? I mean, how could they hush up that kind of stuff?"

"Come on, Wayne," I said, "we all know that the CIA hushes up things."

"That's true," he said.

"Let's think about this," I said. "If there were sexual attacks on innocent young women on a naval base by young men in uniform, it would certainly be a tremendous scandal and might even affect national security. It would be even worse if it got out that in some cases the women were the victors, shooting and stabbing and even forcing poison capsules down the sailors' throats. Wouldn't you expect the CIA to cover up this kind of thing?"

Kitty's mouth hung open. Wayne looked perplexed.

"Come on, both of you," I demanded. "It's called schizophrenic thinking. You start with a basic fact, apply some delusional logic, and all of a sudden you're in Wonderland. We go from A to B to Q."

Kitty smiled. "I'm sorry. But don't you think that some details might be true even though others are clearly delusional? I mean, mustn't there have been some abuse in her past?"

"No," I said, "there *might* have been. But you know that abuse alone is not enough. There has to be a genetic predisposition."

"It's a biochemical disease," stated Wayne flatly. "It runs in families."

"But it doesn't *always* manifest itself, right? What Kitty's trying to find, Wayne, is the stressor that triggers the illness, usually when the person is in their late teens or early twenties. But it is almost impossible to identify, not only because of the delusions but because almost anything could have pushed her buttons, from psychological or sexual abuse to getting bad grades in school. Even something as simple as doing poorly on an important exam can shove someone who is genetically vulnerable over the edge. And then the person has what is popularly called a nervous breakdown. But it's really the first episode in the continuing deterioration that is caused by schizophrenia."

"At what age did Brenda have her first breakdown?" Wayne asked.

"We don't know. When she first came to us twelve years ago, she was completely nonfunctional. She couldn't sleep or eat because she thought the government was putting poison pellets into her food and booby-trapping her bed. She told us that she had been hospitalized before and that her voices told her to go to Bellevue because it was safe there. We hospitalized her then and she was put on antipsychotic medication. But as Kitty knows, she won't take enough, or on a regular basis, when she's an outpatient."

"There is a kernel of reality operating inside Brenda," Kitty insisted. "It's what told her to go the hospital. Now if we could just figure out which part of her story is real and build on that?"

"Kitty, you're going to make yourself crazy trying to figure out the truth. You just have to accept the fact that you're probably never going to know. The best way to look at what Brenda says is like a kind of Rorschach response to her hurt, disappointment, terror, and guilt. There is no external corroboration."

Kitty wiggled her navy-blue patent-leather pump impatiently. "I'm sorry. Those are all feelings. What about content? I mean, here I come up with something that might be at least partly real and you're ready to dismiss it?" Kitty's natural tendency toward Valley-speak became even more pronounced under stress, as now when she felt she was questioning my authority.

"What's real?" I asked her.

"What do you mean, what's real?"

"Well, you're always talking about reality. What's real?"

She made a sitcom gesture, head to one side, eyes popping. "Duh," she said.

"Really. I mean it. What's real?"

"I am? You are? He is?" she said, waving airily at all three of us.

"How do you know?"

"Well, for starters, I can see you? I can hear you?"

"What if you were blind and deaf?"

"Well, I might not know you were in the room but you'd still be there?"

"What if someone told you the room was empty? Someone like Dr. Mike Warner, whom you respect?"

"I'd probably believe him, but his saying it wouldn't make it so?"

"If you believed it, it would become your reality."

"But it still wouldn't be true?" insisted Kitty, her voice almost cracking with strain. "Wayne and you would still be here?"

"Yes, but you would act as if we weren't here. Look what happened on the elevator this afternoon. Everybody was running around as though a rape had just occurred. I'll bet some women are going to leave early tonight. It might even make the evening news. 'Unknown Rapist Ravages Bellevue Hospital.' "

"Was there a rape? Really?" asked Wayne.

"See what I mean?" I said, emphasizing with my hands.

Her hands twitched as she snatched her shoulder bag from the back of the chair. "Really, Fred, I'm not a child. And I'm not in Philosophy 101. Just saying something is real will never make it so."

The next morning as soon as I parked my motor scooter and walked through the door, I knew something was up. A handful of hospital police carrying walkie-talkies were doing broken-field runs across the lobby toward the elevators. Scurrying out of their way, doctors, nurses, visitors, patients, streetpeople, asked one another what was going on. "Go get 'em," a grizzled man with the face of an alcoholic urged, his wiry arm waving them on as he stood on a couch. The homeless who regularly gathered in the lobby took up the cheer.

As a young female officer I knew ran by, I could hear the words "twentieth floor" crackling over her radio. My floor. I felt my heart jump. "Conchita," I yelled as she swept past, "what's going on?"

"Elopement," she shouted over her shoulder. One of our patients had escaped.

Pulling off my ID badge and holding it in front of me, I barked, "Coming through, coming through." It worked; waves of people fell back as I made my way toward the elevator corridor. There I was stopped by a cop guarding the empty hall, while a group of hospital police surrounded one of the elevator doors. Suddenly a cry went up from someone behind me. "He's naked." The news flowed through the crowd.

reality testing

"Who's naked?"

"The person they're after."

"A naked patient?"

"How could a patient be naked?"

"I'm Dr. Covan, chief psychologist," I said to the burly carrot-top young sergeant in front of me.

"Come on in," he said, escorting me through the police line. "We're going to need you."

"Where's the patient?" I asked, looking around the corridor, which was empty except for the police.

"On elevator three. Everyone got off the elevator when he got on and someone called us. We got him now."

"How did he elope?"

"Slipped out when a crowd of bigshots were being shown around."

"Oh no," I groaned, wondering which heads would roll.

"Ain't it awful?" he said. "First a woman gets raped in the hospital and then this."

"Raped?" I gasped. "When did that happen?"

"We're still investigating it. Occurred near the elevators yesterday, lunchtime. But we don't have the perp and the victim hasn't come forward."

Whoops, I thought. "What about the guy? Is he really naked?" I asked.

"No. Just bottomless. Not his doing, of course, since they stopped issuing bottoms to men on the psych ward this week in order to save money." I started to reply but he held up his hand as the elevator indicator showed it was about to touch down. "Get the camisole ready," he yelled to his troops. "He's here."

Suddenly a tremendous whoop went up as the elevator door opened and a bearded man, wearing a blue Bellevue Hospital pajama top and nothing else, shot like a bolt past the momentarily stunned cops into the middle of the corridor in full view of the crowd. Suddenly everyone was quiet, waiting to see what would happen next. Catching sight of his large audience, the man grabbed his crotch. An attendant ran up to the nearest cop and handed him a hospital blanket. The hospital police rushed into action, threw the blanket over the man, and led him away. As the crowd started to melt away, a pediatric emergency room physician I was friendly with spotted me and walked over.

"So tell me, Fred," he asked, "what was a psych patient doing running around Bellevue with just his jammie top on?"

I shrugged. What else could I say? "Budget cuts."

"So what's real?" I queried, looking at each one of the interns as they turned toward me. I really wanted to know. Word was still out that a rapist was on the loose in the hospital, even though I had re-counted the entire elevator dialogue for security and anyone else who would listen. Die-hard conspiracy theorists insisted that a rape had indeed taken place but had been covered up—the inevitable outcome of an overheard conversation that had mutated into rumor and from there into irrefutable fact.

Kitty had just finished a masterful presentation, in which she not only gave the full flavor of her patient's delusions but acted them out for us, her voice an uncanny imitation of Brenda's as it slid from whisper to full-throated roar.

"Kitty feels that the only way she can treat Brenda is by getting her to separate what's real from what's not. So what we are dealing with here is the nature of reality. How do we know what is real?"

"What kind of question is that, Fred?" said David Anderson. "We all know what's real."

"You mean you're a believer about reality?"

David scratched the short thatch of hair above his forehead. "Well, yeah," he said, looking puzzled.

"I'm an agnostic about reality," I said. Everyone laughed. "No, I mean it. Prove to me that reality exists."

"Well, this table exists." He banged it hard with his fist, making his notebook jump up. "See, it's solid. It's there."

I turned to Wayne. "David says this table is solid. What do you think?"

Wayne tapped his cheeks. "Um, well, on one level it's solid. But on the submicroscopic level, it's molecules, and on the submolecular level it's quarks and gluons with mostly space in between. And quarks and gluons are themselves not real in the sense that no one's ever seen them. And what do we mean by 'seen'? We know that the observer affects the thing observed. So can we say that a thing is really solid?"

"Okay, we've done away with solidity as reality. So how do you know what's real?" Elizabeth was running her hand through her blond hair, peering disdainfully over the top of her rimless glasses. "What do you think?" I asked her.

"I think that's kind of a trick question, Fred. I mean, reality is culturally determined. In order to understand a thing, you have to deconstruct it by knowing where the person is coming from. For instance, how you perceive something is going to be colored by whether you are a man or woman, black or white, gay or straight. In the end, the way in which you identify yourself is going to determine your reality."

"Do you agree with Elizabeth, Kiesha, that reality is different for blacks than it is for whites?"

"Look, I've read Plato, Aristotle, Locke, and all those other Western philosophers and I can spew out this intellectual stuff as well as any one here," said Kiesha. "But I've got to tell you even a discussion like this is a self-indulgent luxury. You want to know what reality is," she said dryly, "just ask the people on the wards here, or the homeless in the old Bellevue building, or the families in the projects who worry when their kids are late that they've been killed in a drive-by shooting," she said impatiently. "I'll tell you what reality is, it's one quarter of all black young men getting killed or ending up in jail. That's reality in America."

"But that's not the whole picture and you know it," said Ginger Baron, who had been following the discussion with her usual intensity.

"Then what is?" I asked her.

"Kiesha's right in one respect," Ginger said. "It's the interactions between people that make our reality. Sartre said that 'Hell is other people.' But then so is heaven." She leaned forward, "And that's where we come in. To show people that the way they currently interact is not the only way of living in the world. Sure, the world can be a violent, ugly place. But we can coexist in other ways that are caring and loving and help people change and grow. Kiesha knows this. Otherwise why would she be here?"

Kiesha's eyes darted toward Ginger and then quickly away. "I'm here," she murmured almost to herself, "because I want to help stop the killing."

"Now you're getting to what I was talking about." But before I could finish my thought, Garrison Bernstein spoke up. Garrison, or Gary as he preferred to be called, was the son of a renowned psychoanalyst.

"The interpersonal is only one aspect of reality," he said, looking at each of his classmates in turn like a practiced lecturer. "We're leaving out the entire *intra*personal dimension. I mean, if you think about it, for each person, there is not one reality, but three. The id, the ego, and the superego," he said as the class groaned. "And all of these are in conflict. So at any given time, we see things through three sets of eyes, the unrestrained infant, the reasonable adult, and the moralistic parent. And each part of this psychic trio is trying to define reality for the other two."

"There goes Freud Junior again," said Nick Torres. "So, Professor, you vant to know vhat I tink about reality? Reality is a belch after a good meal. It's the way your girlfriend's body moves under you when you're making love. It's the kick you get when you arc the ball over the head of that tall guy right into the basket. Shall I go on?"

"We get the picture, Nick," I replied quickly. "So summing it up here, Nick thinks reality is sensuous experiences. Ginger says it's other people, while Gary says it's the different parts inside you. David thinks reality is solidity while Wayne tells us solidity is just an illusion. Elizabeth says reality depends on culture and Kiesha says this whole discussion is irrelevant, that reality is getting your teeth kicked in. So far, reality is something none of us can agree on."

"So, Professor, tell us. What is reality?" asked Nick.

"I think you've shown it by our discussion here," I said. "In my opinion, there is no absolute reality."

"Spoken like a true psychotic," Gary laughed.

"Well, it helps to have a flexible view of reality in dealing with someone like Brenda. I'm a constructionist. I believe that our reality is constructed for the most part by what we say about it, how we construe it. For example, we can all consensually agree that this is a table. What we fight over is the adjectives. Is it a pretty table or an eyesore? An indispensable or useless table? A unique or a common table?"

"Wait a minute, Fred," said Nick, sitting down on the table. "What do you mean, we all agree it's a table? I say it's a chair."

"You're right," I said, joining him on the table. "It's a chair."

"I'm sorry," said Kitty, throwing up her arms in exasperation. "If you all get up and sit on this table, does that make it a chair? I mean this idea that everything is a matter of your conception and that there is no reality outside your own construction . . . well, I feel like Samuel Johnson two hundred years ago when Berkeley argued there is no reality outside of your perception. Johnson kicked his foot into a rock and hopped around with the pain and said, 'Thus, I refute Berkeley.'"

I pressed on. "But what is the reality? The reality of the pain? The reality of the stone?"

"The reality is that you stub your toe against reality? The reality is that there is something out there beyond your perception?" offered Kitty.

"What if you're a leper and you have no pain receptors in your toes?" I asked. "What if the world is only made up of lepers?"

Ginger stamped the floor with her heel. "How do I know the floor isn't made of sponge cake or chocolate pudding instead of concrete?"

"Well, you could try eating it, Ginger," said Nick as everyone laughed.

"The fact is," I said, "we do make assumptions that we don't question. We do a lot of 'as ifs.' When I get on my scooter, I act as if the trucks and cars and buses will crush me if get in their way. For me that is a reality."

"Why do you make that assumption?" challenged Gary. "Wayne says there's a lot of space between those atoms. Why don't you assume that your molecules and the bus's molecules will intermingle and you'll beam right through the bus like in "Star Trek"?"

"Okay, okay," I said, holding up my hands in surrender. "I'll give you the buses. The point is, it's what we say and believe about the buses that's important."

Ginger started counting on her fingers. "That they're late. That they always come in threes or not at all. That they always pull out of the bus stop just as you get there."

I charged on, determined to make my point. "According to Gregory Bateson, the psychologist and philosopher, there is no such thing as a problem. For some people getting up in the morning is a problem. For others it's their job or their wife or their husband. When you label something as a problem, it becomes like a magnet, a shit magnet. All kinds of bad, painful things are attracted to it. And then it becomes your reality. It's like that saying that an optimist sees the glass as half full and the pessimist as half empty. I think that saying the glass is half full or half empty is a judgment call. But, it is that judgment that will determine your reality and how you evaluate all your experiences.

"As therapists," I continued, "this is always going to come up for you. A patient tells me, 'My wife is abusive and hates me.' Then it turns out that she criticizes him sometimes and has a painful yeast infection. So what is the reality? Is she just critical at times and has a vaginal infection that turns her off sexually? Or is she abusive and hates him? These are very different realities and they have very different consequences. The first reality allows him to take concrete steps to improve the situation. The second one turns him into an embittered complainer who creates the very reality he most fears. 'My wife hates me. Nobody loves me. I'm a totally unlovable human being.' You go through life thinking that and it'll become true."

I turned to Kitty, who was resting her cheek on her fist, deep in thought. "Has any of this been helpful to your work with Brenda?"

She smiled, but her hazel eyes were grave. "I'm sorry, Fred. I still think there's a difference between someone who thinks his wife hates him and Brenda, who thinks that all the movies are about her and that the CIA and FBI are after her."

"That's right. That's why we call her a schizophrenic and label her beliefs delusions. Because we can consensually agree that she's crazy and we're not. But Brenda and we are still connected." Addressing the whole group, I said, "Remember that continuum of normality we spoke about? There is a reality continuum that stretches from the moment-to-moment truth of a high-functioning individual to the psychotic delusions of a Brenda. What matters is not the behaviors but the consequences. So you could say I'm a consequentialist. If you think that everyone is out to get you, there will be inevitable consequences. You will avoid people, be lonely, have no relationships. I believe that everyone, no matter what the complaint, can change. Even Brenda to some degree, with our help. But in order to change your circumstances, you have to change the way you think and the way you evaluate your environment. And when you do that, you change your reality."

The seminar had ended and the students began getting ready for their next appointments. "Before you go," I said loudly as some of the students stood up. "There's one final thought about reality I'd like to leave you with." And then I produced my trump card, the one that had stopped me in my tracks when I spotted one of my abashed colleagues reading it earlier that day. I held up the front page of a supermarket-known tabloid and there inscribed in huge black letters for all to see were the words: WOMAN HAS AFFAIRS WITH FIVE PRESIDENTS.

Although several students said the discussion had been fun and that it had given them something to think about, Kitty was not among them. Outwardly, she was still smiling, apologetic, ingratiating. But underneath that sweet exterior, I sensed a new wariness, a wish to keep me at arm's length. All my attempts to probe beneath the surface were met with velvet rebuffs—"I'm fine, Fred. I've never been better. I'm so happy here." But though she continued to do excellent work, even devoting a weekend to cleaning out Brenda's apartment when the neighbors complained about the filth, and had apparently given up the idea of ridding Brenda of her delusions, I was still concerned. Despite what she thought, my point about how we create our own reality was not intellectual nitpicking. Paradoxically, it was very real. Her reality was that she had a need to be perfect whether that meant not having a hair out

CRAZY ALL THE TIME

of place or ever making a mistake—a recipe for disaster at Belle-vue particularly and in the world generally. How could I make her see that perfection, itself, was a flawed ideal?

I was just finishing up another "list" Weenie needed immediately when Mike Warner knocked at my door. Tall, slightly stoop-shouldered, balding, and clean-shaven, Mike, the psychologist, bears little physical resemblance to the campus hippie and fire-brand he once was. These days, he and his striking-looking Chinese wife, Beverly, a curator of Asian art, lead a quiet, cultivated, bookish life with their two young daughters in their Greenwich Village brownstone. They love to entertain and their parties are known for great food, live music furnished by themselves or friends, and good talk lasting far into the night.

"Fred, last weekend, I had an experience that I just have to share with you." He dragged a chair over to where I was sitting and strad-dled it, leaning over the back. "There's a drug called *ayahuasca,* which is used by some Brazilians as a sacrament in their church. The other day Beverly and I took it for the first time."

"What is it? A hallucinogen?" I asked.

"Kind of. I'll tell you about it and you decide for yourself. Tra-ditionally it's done in a ritualized setting. So there we were in a room in someone's loft with about thirty people, all dressed in white, men on one side, women on the other, seated at a long re-fectory table with only candles for illumination. And the candles are making the light and shadow dance across each of their faces and the whole scene looks medieval with all its mystery and spir-ituality. Then an attendant brings in the *ayahuasca,* which looks like dark green tea, in a glass pitcher. Each person walks up to the end of the table to receive a cup, a man serving the men and a woman the women. The stuff tastes god-awful. There are buckets next to your chair where you can vomit. Then you sit and wait to do the 'work' and experience whatever comes your way. And come it does. Let me tell you, you meet all your demons and you get to know them," he said with a soft laugh. "God, was it painful work."

He paused, his warm gray eyes looking off into the distance, and then continued in his deep, vibrant voice. "I began by thinking about a problem Beverly and I had been having for the past few months. I don't know whether you've noticed it, I've been rather irritable, although I've tried to hide it. Beverly's way is to appease and make nice, but I was keeping it going and I wanted to understand why I was being so stubborn. I wanted to get behind this anger, see what it was made of. There I was waiting for a revelation while all around me people were puking their guts out and I remember thinking I can handle this.

"And then, whammo, it hit me," he said, his sinewy body jerking backward as though it were still coming. "It was like the gods were getting me for my hubris. For the next three hours I was lying on the floor, sobbing my heart out. I was in touch with so much sadness. Pain like I had never felt before. I felt so sad, so hurt. There was a tensor lamp on the floor next to me and I put it over my heart as though I could absorb heat from it. The sadness was overwhelming. It was like a line stretching back to my childhood. I felt my mother's indifference, my father's anger. I went through the breakup of my first marriage, my heartache over my daughter's rejection of me, and then all the pain from my patients, which surprised me because I thought I didn't take that in. But it obviously had seeped in over the years. And I cried and cried it all out. It was such an incredible, cleansing, cathartic experience."

His eyes glowed. "The whole experience had the most profound effect on me. I got to the source of my anger. I really located it in my childhood and saw how it had grown. I reexperienced each episode. I understood why I was so insistent and I knew that it was over. That I no longer had to protect myself in this way. That I could really allow the loving side of myself to come through."

"That's amazing," I said.

"Sometimes I think that as a society we have the most puritanical attitude about drugs," he said thoughtfully. "It's even worse than it used to be with sex. It's not that I think we should all take heroin or crack. It's just that at least for me, mind-altering drugs have given me a window on other realities that I never otherwise could have had. They have put me in touch with the deepest levels of my being. Awakened me to ways of thinking and seeing and experiencing the world that I might not have found otherwise. I think the right drugs if used in the right way might help people to reexperience the delight and appreciation of life that we all once had, even if briefly, as children. Just imagine what controlled, clinical use of a drug like *ayahuasca* or Ecstasy could do for people who are depressed."

Interesting, I thought. Although Mike would have never talked in front of Kitty, I wondered what she would have thought about what he had gone through. Mike had certainly experienced another reality when he took *ayahuasca*.

At my next joint supervision session with Kitty and Wayne, he asked quite uncharacteristically if he could speak first. The threat of being thrown out of the program had concentrated Wayne's mind wonderfully. He had cleaned up his act, taking himself seriously as an authority figure. He had even taken to dressing like one. Similarly, he had pointed out to Gina that she ought to take herself more seriously, starting with attire that suggested she was something other than a plaything for men. As his supervisors had demanded, he was tape-recording every session, playing excerpts during our meetings.

In their last session, Wayne told us, Gina had taken his advice with a vengeance, showing up in a dress that reminded him of the Mother Hubbard nightgowns his mother wore, with a high ruffled neck, sleeves down to the wrists, and a ruffled hem that almost scraped the floor. "And that's how she opened the session," said Wayne, turning to the tape recorder.

Gina: "So, Wayne, what do you think? You like this outfit?"

Wayne: "Um, yeah . . . What do you think of it, Gina?"

Gina: "Don't give me that psychological answer-a-question-with-a-question bullshit. Just tell me what you think. Do I look like a nun, or what?"

Wayne: "Is that what you think? You look like a nun?"

Gina: "Yeah. My mom would love it. That bitch would love it if I became a nun for real."

Wayne: "Your mother's very religious?"

Gina: "She's a damn saint."

Wayne: "And you're the sinner?"

Gina: "You got it. I fuck my brains out and she goes to church and says novenas for me."

Wayne pushed the pause button. "At that point, Gina got real silent. She just bunched herself into a ball on the chair and she kind of went away. I just didn't know what to do, Fred. Whether to call out her name, ask her what was the matter, or say nothing. I decided to wait her out. I felt like she was on the verge of something and the less I said, the better."

"Good move," I said. The kid was showing signs of intuition.

Wayne fast-forwarded the tape. "Now listen to this part."

Gina: "You know what, Wayne? You're no fun anymore."

Wayne: "What do you mean, Gina?"

Gina: "You used to get more excited when I came in. You'd kid around more. You know. Like you'd flirt. I thought you and I were getting it on pretty good."

Biting his upper lip, Wayne hit the pause again. There was a worried look in his eyes. "Here, I don't know whether I did the right thing or not, Fred. But you said we should model our behavior for our patients."

Oh no, I thought, he's doing it again, using my own words against me.

"So I felt I had to be absolutely, scrupulously honest with Gina, or how could I expect the same honesty from her?"

Kitty shot an alarmed glance in my direction. "Go on," I said.

Wayne hit the play button.

Wayne: "Gina, I have something I've got to confess."

Gina: "A confession? Great! Just like in church."

Wayne: "When you first came here, I was tremendously attracted to you. I thought you were the most beautiful woman I'd ever seen."

Gina: "Oh my God? Really?"

Wayne: "Really. I was so drawn to you physically, I forgot the most important part of therapy."

Gina: "Which was?"

Wayne: "That you were my patient. I was here to help you with your problems, your depression, not to get you to like me. And certainly not to have sex with you."

Wayne hit the pause button again as blotches of red appeared on his face.

A sense of doom was starting to envelop me.

"This part's really embarrassing, especially in front of her," he said, indicating Kitty.

She took his hand in hers and said with unalloyed sweetness, "We're all just learning, Wayne."

"Me too," I said.

"Okay," he said, grimacing. "Here goes."

Gina: "Wayne, tell me the truth. Are you a virgin?"

Wayne: "Um, I don't think I ought to answer that question."

Gina: "You *are,* aren't you? Look at you, you're red as a beet."

Wayne: "I haven't had a lot of sexual experience."

Gina: "I figured. It's really a pity that you think you shouldn't go to bed with me. I could really help you, you know. More than you could probably help me."

Oh please, God, I prayed, listening to this exchange. Don't let it be.

Wayne: "Well, Gina, one thing I can tell for sure. You're no virgin."

Gina: "You bet."

Wayne: "How old were you when you had your first experience?"

Gina: "Guess."

Wayne: "I have no idea."

Gina: "Just take a guess."

Wayne: "Seventeen?"

Gina: "What do you think? I was an old maid?"

Wayne (tentatively): "Fifteen."

Gina: "Come on."

Wayne: "I don't know. Fourteen?"

Gina: "Twelve. I was twelve years old. I was a baby, just beginning to get tits. I wore a training bra."

Wayne: "You were twelve years old. How old was the guy?"

Gina: "How old? Let me see. I'm twenty-one, so he'd be forty-three then."

Wayne (incredulously): "You went to bed with a forty-three-year-old man when you were twelve years old?"

Gina: "Sure. It happens all the time. Don't you know anything? Don't you watch the talk shows?"

Wayne (long pause): "Is that why you can't go back home?"

Gina: "You catch on fast for a shrink."

Wayne: "How could he?"

Gina: "Very easily. He was what? Two hundred and fifty pounds? A construction worker with stone-crushing arms? And me who didn't yet tip the scale at a hundred pounds?"

Wayne: "What happened, Gina? Do you remember?"

Wayne hit the pause button. "Gina got real quiet here. Then she suddenly jumped up and started walking around the room. And I knew it was like she was trying to decide. Tell him or not tell him. Tell him or not tell him. I said, 'Gina, tell me. I've been there. I haven't gone through what you have but I know what it's like to suffer.' And then she looked at me. But it wasn't like she was looking *at* me, but through me. Her voice was like coming from far away."

He hit the play button.

Gina: "I was standing naked in front of the full-length mirror on the back of my bedroom door. Just looking at myself. You know, the way girls do. I was curious. I wanted to see how my body was developing. It was so innocent. I never noticed that the door was ajar. I've gone over and over it in my mind a thousand times. I don't know. Maybe I wanted him to see me. But I was innocent, innocent. I mean it."

Wayne: "Gina, you were twelve. You weren't responsible for what happened."

Gina: "I know, I don't know. He pushed open the door and he said things, called me a slut, asked me what I was looking at, my titties? My cunt? I didn't even know what a cunt was. He said something about having a gift for all the boys between my legs. A gift? What kind of gift?" Her voice was quavering. "I don't remember," she shouted.

Wayne (urgently): "Think, Gina. Remember. It's important."

Gina: "I can see him in the room and he's shutting the door, standing in front of it. And I feel small, shrunken. And he's walking toward me. And . . . I can't. I can't."

Wayne: "You can, Gina. He's not here in the room. He's not with us now. You can go on."

Gina: "I don't remember what happened next. Oh yes, yes. I was afraid he was going to hit me. Whack me, like he did to my brother all the time. But he had never laid a hand on me in my life. And I didn't know what I did that was wrong. But maybe being naked was a sin. And he was going to punish me for it. But instead he picked me up in his arms like a baby, and for a moment I thought it was all right. He's just worried about me."

(A long silence.)

Wayne: "He picked you up and then what, Gina?"

Gina: "He picked me up and put me on the bed. Then he undid his belt and started pulling at his pants. Clawing at them, like he was on fire. And he was making sounds I never heard before. Like ugh, ugh. Grunting like an animal. I was so terrified. I pulled the bedspread over my head, but he yanked it off and he got on top of me. And I yelled, 'DADDY DADDY DON'T DON'T YOU'RE HURT-ING ME PLEASE STOP PLEASE PLEASE OH STOP STOP.' But he just kept going, pinning down my legs with his huge thighs. I thought he was going to *kill* me. 'I can't breathe,' I said. He got up on his elbows and he pushed even *harder*. The pain was so, so aw-ful. I hurt so much. I started screaming, 'MOMMY, MOMMY, HELP ME.' And then he put his hand over my mouth and then I knew. I knew there was nothing, nothing, nothing I could do. I just had to lie there and pray it would end soon."

Wayne: "Oh, Gina. I'm sorry."

Gina: "Finally he stopped, collapsing on me, so I had to push against his shoulders just to breathe. And when he got up, his come was all over me. I didn't know what it was. It was so thick and gummy. My first thought was he had vomited on me. And then I saw it dripping from his penis. He took a tissue from a box on my dresser and wiped me. Tenderly, like I had hurt myself. And then I noticed the blood all over the bed. He saw me looking at it and he said, 'You're all right. It just happens the first time. You won't bleed again. I promise you.' I was holding my stomach. I hurt so bad inside and out. He just sat down on my bed and said, 'Gina, this is just between you and me. Don't tell anyone. Not even your mother. You hear?' I remember shaking my head, yes. But then he grabbed me by my shoulders and said, 'Say, "I hear you, Daddy."' I said, 'I hear you, Daddy.' And he said, 'Good. Because I wouldn't want to hurt you.' Can you imagine? That's what he said. 'I wouldn't want to hurt you.' "

The whole room was filled with her sobs. Aching, throbbing, high-pitched wails that went on and on. We all sat, looking at the tape recorder as if it were doing the crying. Then Gina's voice was back on, wrenching, her words sounding ripped out of her. "He told me . . . it all happened . . . because I was a . . . *whore*. He said . . . I had . . . seduced him. He said this . . . over and over again . . . every time he did it to me . . . that I was just a *whore* . . . that I would never amount to anything."

Wayne hit the stop button. "She cried like that, it seemed for hours. I never heard anyone cry like that," he said. "It was unbearable. I just sat there, holding her hand and she squeezed my fingers so tight they hurt. And then when she had finished she thanked me. And I told her, 'I'm going to help you, Gina. We're going to get you through this together.'" He stopped, brushing his eyes under the rim of his glasses, unable to continue.

Kitty was wiping away her own tears. I felt exhausted from Gina's intensity and pain but elated by Wayne's incredibly sensitive handling of it, by his own redemption as a person and as a therapist. I looked forward to telling Carl how well Wayne had done.

"Fred," Kitty said suddenly, "would you see this as another example of 'creating your own reality'?"

I smiled. "Exactly."

"What?" asked Wayne.

"When Gina's father told her she would never amount to anything, that she would always be a whore, he created her reality," explained Kitty.

"That's what I think," said Wayne. "It's why she couldn't decide what she was going to do with her life. For years he had given her this message, 'You're nothing but a goddamn whore.'"

"But he also told her that if she went to college she had to teach," I said. "So on the one hand she subconsciously acted out her father's message by sleeping around and on the other hand she was the good little girl, going to school, getting good grades, studying education. So now the two lines are coming together. What is she going to do as a career? She doesn't want to teach. That's what *he* wants. She thinks, I'll become a hooker. You ask her where she gets this idea and she gives you ten good reasons, starting with money. But you're both right. The unconscious seed for this idea came straight from the message he had planted a decade ago. And he had made her a whore by abusing her and by telling her she was one."

Kitty winked at me. "I think I got it now, Fred."

Love in the Time of AIDS

Chapter 5

The inevitability of death is what makes us value life. And though in the end we cannot prevent our deaths, at least we can chose how we live and how we die.

Working with AIDS patients had been a turning point in intern Nick Torres's life. Nick came from a middle-class family, where his father was a musician, his mother an art teacher, and his sister a dancer. A talented painter, Nick started out to get a fine arts degree from Queens College. But in his junior year, two of his friends became ill with AIDS. Devastated, he dropped out of school to take care of them. After they died, he became an AIDS volunteer and found that the rewards and the relevance offered him more gratification than did the abstract world of art. Returning to school, he switched his major to psychology. I took advantage of his experience when I assigned him Inez Ramos, a twenty-eight-year-old woman dying of AIDS—the same disease that had killed her husband. She had become depressed and unable to care for her three daughters, who were now in three different foster homes.

Nick described his first meeting with his patient at our supervisory session. He had peeked into the room through the small observation glass panel. Inez appeared to be asleep. Her face was slim, her cheekbones etched under teak-colored skin. She had yet to display the skeletal thinness that so often accompanies AIDS. He walked into the room, studying her as she slept. The veins under her eyelids were like markings in fine china. Her reddish brown hair, limp and matted, hung in clumps. She opened her eyes. They were dull, he thought, the color of dried mud. She gave him the briefest of smiles.

"I'm Nick Torres," he said, extending his hand. "I'm a psychologist in training here and I'd like to talk to you."

"Torres," she murmured. Her mouth moved, tasting the word. "You Spanish?"

Nick sat down, pulling the chair next to her bed. "I'm the product of an intermarriage," he said pleasantly. "My mom's from Puerto Rico, my dad from the Dominican Republic."

Inez took this in silently, unsmiling. Then she said, "Ray was from Ponce, like me."

Nick glanced at the chart in his lap. "Ramón, your husband?"

"Mi esposo," she said softly, nodding.

"You miss him?"

Tears welled in her eyes. Abruptly, she turned away, burying her face in the pillow.

He waited while she cried silently to herself. He glimpsed her narrow wrist and hand reaching out of the bedsheet toward the nightstand. Raising himself slightly in his chair, he saw she was holding a small silver frame that enclosed a photo of two figures, one much shorter than the other.

"Is that Ramón?" he asked.

"See for yourself," she answered, handing the picture to him.

The man in the snapshot was bare chested, with rippling muscles, a firm midsection. About thirty, Nick guessed. His hair was short, marine style. He sported a well-turned mustache and a cocky smile. Tightly enclosed in his right arm, her face half hidden by his chest as she looked up at him, was Inez. She was wearing a gaily colored sundress. She looked young, girlish, happy—light-years away from the woman in the bed.

"When was this?" Nick asked her.

"Just after Luz was born. We were so happy."

He glanced at his chart. "That was eleven years ago."

love in the time of AIDS

Taking the photo back, she looked at it for a long minute before replacing it on the nightstand. "You see what a man he was?"

Nick didn't know where to begin. "That was before he got sick," he said tentatively, hoping to leave her an opening.

"Before AIDS," she said bitterly. "Before I had ever heard the word."

"He was a good-looking man."

"He was . . ." She looked at Nick for the first time since he had come into the room. "Look, Mr. Torres. You seem like a nice guy. Leave me alone, okay? I'll be all right."

"You'll be all right? Inez, you are very depressed. That's why you're in the psych ward."

"I'm depressed. So what?" She lay back on her pillow, staring at the ceiling. "I'm dying of AIDS. My kids are in foster care. My man is gone. You want me to celebrate?" All this was said flatly, almost chanted.

"Inez, let's take this one thing at a time. You're in the first stage of AIDS and your thrush and vaginal infection have been cured. Doctors are getting better and better at treating AIDS and the illnesses that people get from it. No one can say for sure how long you'll live. Second, your kids are in foster care only because you're in the hospital for depression. As soon as you're able to function, you'll get them back. It's true that Ramón is gone. But don't you feel the slightest bit of anger toward him? It says on your chart that you got it from your husband."

Her delicate fingers plucked like bird talons at the blanket, pulling it up to her chin. "You don't understand," she said. "I loved him."

"But he sold drugs, heroin," Nick persisted. "He gave you AIDS."

She shook her head sharply and raised her finger. "Ray never shot up."

"Then he did other things. Think about it, Inez. He *gave* you AIDS."

Her eyes brimmed again. "He loved me. He never wanted to hurt me. He was my husband, the father of my children. I forgive him for whatever he did. My life's over now. Don't you understand?" She turned on her side, away from him, pulling the blanket around

CRAZY ALL THE TIME

her like a shield. "Now, you go away," she whispered hoarsely.

After recounting that meeting with Inez, Nick said, "Man, I just don't get it, Fred. Why isn't she angry with him?"

"You're the one who's worked with AIDS patients," I pointed out. "How do men react to their lovers who give it to them?"

"Well, they go through stages. Usually they reach some kind of peace and acceptance and forgiveness, because they've seen their lovers' suffering and dying. But at first they *are* angry. Angry at getting the disease. Angry at their lovers for screwing around. Inez said Ray didn't shoot up. So either he was lying or he was messing around."

"Did you explore that with her?" I asked.

"Yeah," he said. "I've been back two times, now. And every time I bring it up, she says things like 'I don't want to talk about it. What does it matter now? My life is over. Ray's left me.' But she doesn't admit to any anger. I just can't help feeling that if I could get at her anger I could use that energy to help her out of the depression."

"Yes," I said, "but don't forget realistically her situation is pretty desperate and she's lost the man she loved."

"How could I forget?" he asked, the frustration evident in his voice. "No matter what I say, if I try to talk about her kids and how much they need her, it's always, 'Ray's gone. What do I care now?' I mean, she's an intelligent woman. She was a full-charge book-keeper before she got sick. She's struggled to raise her three kids and now they're going to be orphans. She's *got* to feel something against the man who did this to her. It just doesn't seem normal not to," he said.

I reached over and gently tapped his clenched fist. "Nick, I understand how upsetting it is to see Inez going down the tubes."

"It bothers me," he admitted, "maybe even more so because I'm Hispanic. Hispanic women—not all of them and certainly not my mother—tend to be on the passive side. Unfortunately, a lot of the men like them that way. It's cultural, but I still think it's unhealthy."

"Doesn't this go beyond culture? I assume that anyone would be angry about being infected with a terminal illness. But just like we can't tell people not to feel what they're feeling, we can't tell them to have feelings they don't have."

love in the time of AIDS

"My gut tells me that she's denying her anger and has turned it inward. And that's a major contributing factor to her depression and hopelessness."

"Maybe there *is* no anger, as strange as that sounds. But you should try to find out how he got the disease. Because if he got it from being with other women, it seems to me that culture or no culture, whether she's passive or not, it would be difficult not to be angry at his infidelity."

"Great," said Nick sarcastically. "It's okay for him to give her AIDS but it's not okay for him to fuck around."

"*And* give her AIDS."

The next week, Nick told me that when he went in to see Inez for their session, he found her sitting up in bed. "Hey, Inez," he said cheerily, sitting down next to the bed. "You're looking better."

When she turned to look at him, he saw that her eyes were still dull and lackluster. She took his hand and looked him firmly in the eye. "I've decided what I want to do," she said quietly. "And I need you to help me. Please help me?"

"Anything," said Nick sincerely. "You name it."

"I want you to help me die."

Nick felt his heart thud. "Inez, what are you talking about?"

"I want you to help me commit suicide and tell the kids that I died in the hospital because I was sick." She squeezed his fingers. "I've thought about it and I don't want to live this way. I've got nothing to live for. Ray died a terrible death and I don't want the kids to suffer watching me die like they did watching their father. So if you really want to help me, Mr. Torres, that's how you can do it. And you'll not only be helping me but you'll also be helping my kids."

Nick was as surprised and worried by her clarity and calmness as he was by her decision. He sandwiched her frail hand between his large hands. "I understand what you're going through. Believe me. But we have to talk about this."

She shook her head emphatically. "There is nothing to talk about. You're a good psychologist and I like you. You're *simpático*. But I don't need therapy. I need a way to *die*."

"Inez, I'm not an executioner."

"You work in the hospital. You must have friends. People who are sympathetic, who'd help you get pills, tell you how to do it. I heard about some doctor on TV. Call him."

"Inez, you're depressed. That's why you're thinking about suicide."

She pushed her blanket away revealing a white nightgown trimmed with hand-embroidered flowers at the neckline. "If you won't help me, I'll do it myself. I have Ray's gun from when he was dealing."

"Inez," Nick persisted, "instead of all this talk about suicide, why don't we get to what's really going on? Your anger at Ray for leaving you and for getting you into this terrible condition in the first place."

"Why do you always say that?" she snapped. "Why do you keep telling me I'm angry at Ray when I'm not? How can you know what I'm feeling? You're not me."

Well, at least now she was angry, thought Nick. "Inez, it's not me you're angry at."

"Okay," she said sulkily. "Don't help me. I'll do it myself with the gun."

"And you claim to be worried about your kids? They'll forgive you for dying of AIDS, but they'll never forgive you for blowing your brains out. They'll hate you forever and they might even kill themselves. Don't you know that the children of suicides often commit suicide themselves?"

"They'll forgive me," she said, staring straight in front of her. "Just as I have forgiven Ray. I just want to join him in heaven. That's it," she said, pointing her finger at him. "Before I do it, I'll write them a letter saying I've joined Papa in heaven."

Nick grasped at his last straw. "Inez, you're a Catholic. Like me. It's a mortal sin to kill youself."

"And you need to commit mortal sins to get AIDS. So what's the difference?" she shot back.

"You did not sin. Ramón's sins gave you AIDS. This sin will be yours alone," said Nick sadly.

Nick had told me about the session in the staff cafeteria. It's not my usual hangout. The cuisine is institutional and the coffee a notch above industrial runoff, but it's only eight floors down from my office and it's cheap—free for students. Without asking, Nick had sat down in the chair opposite mine, crossed his legs, and leaned back. I put down my tunafish sandwich. "Have a seat," I said dryly.

While telling me what had occurred, he was his usual cool self, except for his fingers, which drummed agitatedly on the table. "Fred," he said, "the bottom line is Inez wants to kill herself. She wants *me* to help her or she'll do it herself with Ray's gun."

"Oh boy."

"Yeah. And you want to know something else? It's really scary because she's so calm and resolute about it. She cried constantly before but didn't shed a tear today."

"That's because she's mobilized to *do* something."

"It's almost like she already died. Like she's crossed some line and she's no longer here and there's no way I can reach her."

Nick stared into the distance. This was one student I didn't have to teach how to "be there" with the patient. His eyes shifted back to me. "Tell me what to do," he pleaded. "I'm scared. This isn't just talk with her."

"If you believe she's really serious, we've got to order a one-to-one suicide watch. Also you've got to talk with her psychiatrist about changing or increasing her medication. But let's think about this for a minute. What about the previous AIDS patients you've worked with? Didn't any of them ever contemplate suicide?"

"Yeah, when they were really sick, they'd talk about ending it all. I remember one guy in particular, Quincy, a narcissistic hair dresser, who'd been really beautiful—long blond curly hair, well built. And he had many lovers and admirers. He planned to kill himself before the disease ravaged his looks so he'd, quote, 'make a good-looking corpse.' "

"Did he kill himself?"

"No. If there's such a thing as a good death, he had it. It was like he discovered a reservoir of love and empathy inside. He dropped all his affectations, laughed at the horrible changes in his body. When he went bald from the chemo for Kaposi's, he said, 'Just what

I've always wanted, the ultimate low-maintenance hairdo.' When he was up to it, he'd visit all the other patients, cut their hair, tell them how good they looked, joke with them in the way that only the dying can do with each other."

He picked at a piece of tuna that had fallen from my sandwich and popped it into his mouth. "Yuck," he said. "No mayonnaise." He sprinkled salt on the remaining half of my sandwich and began eating it. "Mind?" he asked between mouthfuls.

"Speaking of AIDS," I said, "when they first decided to put the AIDS ward next to the staff cafeteria, there was a near riot. Some staff threatened to boycott the cafeteria. Others wanted to stage a protest."

"What happened?" asked Nick, taking a sip of my coffee to wash down my sandwich.

"The administration held an AIDS in-service education for the whole hospital. A medical expert assured us that even if a patient left the ward and somehow made his way into the kitchen and jerked off on the mashed potatoes and you ate it, there'd be almost no chance you'd become ill because the gastric juices would destroy the virus. That's what they *told* us, anyway."

"Uggg," said Nick. "Jerking off on the potatoes. Potatoes au semen."

"So you can see why I don't use mayonnaise on my tuna."

Nick stopped chewing in midmouthful and put down the sandwich.

"Finished?" I asked as I began eating the remainder. "But back to your hairdresser. What do you think made the difference with him?"

Nick thought about it for a moment. "He had a support group. All the people who had lusted after him rallied around him. It was the first time in his life he felt he was truly loved, not for his beauty but for himself."

"Maybe that's what Inez needs," I said. "A support group."

"I've considered that. Her parents are dead and she's an only child. And Ray was one of those possessive, jealous men who resented her having any friends. She only has her children and she'd never complain to them."

He jumped up from his chair. "I've got it. We'll bring in her kids. That's what she needs to restore her will to live."

"Easy, Nick," I said. "They're all very young. If she's scaring you now, what's she going to do to them?"

"Remain a living mother for a while, I hope."

"We've got to get permission from administration because they're under twelve. I'll get on it right away. You call the foster-care agency," I said.

I needed to rush to a meeting with the hospital administrators, but in one of those instances of synchronicity that always seem to happen at Bellevue, we spotted a notice outside the cafeteria of a lecture given by a noted thanatologist entitled "The Right to Die—Civil Right or Moral Wrong."

"A death expert," snorted Nick.

"Want to go?" I asked.

"Nah," he said. "I know where I stand."

"Where's that?" asked a young Indian medical student who had been reading the notice.

"I'm pro choice," said Nick. "If you want to take your life that's nobody's business but your own."

"Really?" I asked. "What about the patient we were just talking about?"

"That's different. I mean, well, let me back up a bit. It's all right to take your own life if you have a terminal illness or there's no way out. But if you're depressed, then by definition you're not thinking clearly."

"Let me get this straight," I said. "If your terminal illness makes you depressed then it's not all right to commit suicide."

"Well, no. First you have to treat the depression. I mean, if every time you felt sad you reached for a gun, half the population would kill themselves, and it's normal to feel sad if you have a terminal illness."

"Suicide is never an answer," said the medical student emphatically in his musical lilt. "And euthanasia is murder."

"But what if the patient is suffering unbearably?" asked a middle-aged black nurse. "I work on the oncology unit. Doctors walk in for five minutes but I'm there for eight hours a day. I've seen deaths that were worse than any death in a medieval torture chamber. People who've lost parts of their faces, their stomachs, their intestines. I've had patients screaming with pain after I'd given them their medication. Recently there was a patient on the unit who had an inoperable tumor eating away at his carotid artery. And the only thing the doctors could do was put a plastic tent around his bed so that when the tumor blew out his artery, the blood wouldn't spurt all over the room."

"God," I said, feeling my feet grow cold.

Nick put his finger against the side of his head and went "boom."

"I mean, we put a dog out of its misery. Why won't we do the same for a human being?" said the nurse.

"Because their soul is still alive. Because you can't play God," said the med student.

A young woman in blue jeans standing about a foot away with a stethoscope around her neck said quietly, almost to herself, "I have a cousin who has inoperable brain cancer." There was a sudden stillness. "He's eighteen. He's bright and funny and loves life. He says as long as his brain is still working, he wants to live, but . . ." Her lower lip trembled as she said huskily, "Once that goes . . . no."

Gently, the med student touched her arm. "You must teach him how to die."

Returning to my office, I caught sight of Ginger moving down the hall at a clip. "How's it going in the psych ER?" I called after her. She had started that rotation a week earlier.

She turned and gave me a dazzling smile, her eyes shining. "It's great. I love it."

"What do you love about it?"

"The fact that I'm seeing psychotics in the raw, so to speak, before their reactions have been dulled by drugs. It's a real challenge to interview them. Snippets of real life, free associations, random juxtapositions of time and place and delusion. And I've got to make some sort of sense out of it all. It's a real thrill. Like taking a perfectly risen soufflé out of the oven."

I laughed. Before becoming a psychology student, Ginger had

run a highly successful catering business. "Ginger," I said jokingly, "have you ever thought of combining cooking and therapy?"

"You mean put aprons and toques on the patients and have them work out their aggressions by pounding chicken breasts into supremes? Yes, it's a real fantasy of mine."

In some ways Ginger, who tended to take everything to heart, seemed more fragile than the other interns. Yet here she was, not only coping with one of the most difficult student assignments but eating it up.

"Is there anything you don't like about working in the ER?"

She nodded. "Admitting them against their will. The idea of having that kind of control over their lives. It's such a monumental decision. It's like, who am I to have the right to take away a person's freedom?"

"Most psychologists have problems with being an authority figure," I said. "Especially since all our training gears us to be understanding and empathic. But it's an integral part of our job. If admitting a patient means depriving that person of the opportunity to hurt himself or others, then you have to be the bad guy for the patient's own good."

"Thanks, Fred," she said. "I needed that."

That brief encounter left me feeling pretty good. Ginger may have had her problems with being an authority figure, but Nick had his problems with authority and I was having problems with Nick because of this. It was looking like any rule that came his way, good or bad, sensible or stupid, he had to test.

The first time I noticed his defiance was when he handed in his chart on Inez. In the section on diagnosis, he had written one word: "Depression." And under treatment goals, he had noted: "Patient will become less depressed."

I called him into my office, waving the chart at him. "Nick, this won't do."

He leaned back and grinned cockily. "What's the beef, Fred? I was concise. Inez is depressed and my goal is to make her less depressed."

"We went all over this during orientation," I said. "Charts have to follow SOAP—Subjective, Objective, Assessment, Plan. Patients aren't just depressed anymore. You have to accurately describe their state. They are dejected-looking, expressing feelings of hopelessness, making self-deprecatory statements, have slowed-up motor behavior, sleep disturbances characterized by early-morning waking. And then when they're discharged, the chart gets SOAPIER—Implementation, Evaluation, Recapitulation. Got it?"

"In other words I've got to copy from *DSM*-III-R," said Nick, referring to the bible of workers in the mental health profession, the *Diagnostic and Statistical Manual,* third edition, revised.

"You *will* selectively use *DSM*-III-R as a basis for your charts."

Nick pushed back the fingers of his left hand and cracked the knuckles. "The patient is depressed. I know what it means. You know what it means. Even Weenie and his cohorts know what it means. Hell, they're *chronically* depressed."

I wanted to laugh but I wouldn't let him get away with it. "I know how you feel, Nick. I'm not crazy about spending fifteen minutes writing a description of a patient when one word will do, either. Especially if I have thirty patients to write up. But I'm not going to waste my time and energy fighting battles that I can't win."

Working his way down his fingers, he cracked them one at a time. "Fred," he said, "I got to tell you. This is a load of shit. I'm here to help people. And I don't want to spend my time doing this."

"Then get a job in a homeless shelter. Because if you're going to work in a hospital, this is the name of the game."

"This is bullshit. I'm going to spend more time writing up the patient than treating her."

"It may be bullshit, but it's a fact of life. Hospitals in this country now are controlled by bureaucrats and by survey teams. And if we don't play by their rules, then we get closed down or the hospital doesn't get reimbursed. And who winds up suffering in the end? We all do. We lose our jobs and the patient has no place to get treatment."

Nick scowled. "I'll go along with this asinine nonsense because I work here. But let me tell you, if I ever get a chance at running things, there'll be some real changes."

"You got my vote. But first do this," I said pointing to the chart.

• • •

The next day, Nick's rebellious behavior got him into trouble with the law. I received a copy of a ticket he got from a hospital police officer. Not only had he broken the hospital rules by not wearing his ID badge but he had also given the hospital police grief when asked to produce it.

"Goddamn it, Nick," I said, waving the ticket at him. "Don't you have better things to rebel against? I've given you a lot of responsibility to take care of patients and here you do something stupid like getting into a fight with the HPs about not wearing your ID."

Nick looked up from his notebook, whose margins he had elaborately decorated like an illuminated manuscript with surreal ink drawings of birds and animals. He picked up his pen and tapped it on his desk. "Something on your mind, Fred?"

"Cut the crap, Nick. You know what I'm talking about. The hospital rule is to have your ID visible at all times and the HPs are just doing their job when they check it. And they don't need some young wise-ass kid making their job more difficult."

He leaned back and put his feet up on the desk. "Come on, Fred. So I keep my ID in my pocket. What's the big deal? Why is this cop asking for my ID, anyway? It's like a police state."

"Look, there is a good reason why you're supposed to be wearing your ID. So we don't have Charles Manson doing surgery on the patients or staff."

"Yeah? Well, if you left it up to HP, they'd give him a royal welcome if he had a good jacket on. I've watched the guard at the entrance to the elevator, and half the time he looks everywhere but where the ID badge is. Especially if you're white and look like a doctor."

I sat down on the chair next to his desk. "I do stress-management workshops for the hospital police, and do you know what they say is the most stressful aspect of their job? It's not homicidal maniacs or raving patients or outraged family members but dealing with staff members who refuse to show their IDs. Putting up with abuse from doctors who are supposedly their colleagues and whom they are trying to protect. Arrogant coworkers who say, 'Why should I have to show *you* my ID. Who are you?'"

"Yeah? Well, maybe that's what they told you. All I know is

they're much more apt to go after someone like me. They look at the color of my skin, that I wear my hair in a ponytail, that my ear is pierced. They're selective. That's why I do it."

I knew all of this was just rationalization. I held up my hand. "You made your point, okay? Now stop."

Taking his feet off the desk, he swung around in his chair toward me. "What are you saying? That I don't have a choice?"

"You got it. And the fact is that most HPs are black or Hispanic themselves."

"Still," he jumped in, "they're just power junkies. They're just tripping on me."

"Listen," I said, "if you don't have enough real battles to fight, just let me know and I'll give you some more patients."

"Okay, okay. I'll wear my ID."

"Good. Thank you."

"You're happy?"

"Yes. And you can keep your ponytail."

"Oh thank you," he laughed. "As long as I can keep my pontail."

As usual, I was mentally ordering my lunch by the time Nick and I had threaded our way through the maze of diners and wait staff at Penne's. To my surprise, Wayne was there, seated next to Pam Wyatt, a young psychiatric social worker who often joined us. On her right sat Rhoda, smiling maternally at the two of them. Suddenly I put the whole thing together. Rhoda was combining her two favorite activities, supervising and matchmaking. On the one hand she was picking up on Maria's idea that Wayne needed a social life to protect him from projecting his sexual desires onto his patients and on the other hand she was arranging a *shiddach*—the time-honored Jewish practice of bringing together Ms. and Mr. Right.

"Sit down, Fred. You're just in time for the latest episode in 'Jenny Noh's Search for Love,'" boomed Parnell after everyone almost sat on one another's lap in order to make room for us.

Jenny laughed. "There's this guy Dave in my apartment building, and for the longest time I thought he was a letch. He's married and has two kids but he's like this very touchy-feely person, always giving me big hugs. For the last month or so, he's been after me to have a drink with him and I always turn him down. I mean he's kind of cute in a way, but I'm no homewrecker."

She took a breadstick from the basket on the table and went on. "Anyway, yesterday he rings my doorbell and tells me he has to talk to me and please would I just this one time have a drink with him? He looks so down in the dumps that I say yes. He takes me to a local pub, where I sometimes go after work. We sit down in the dining area, and I'm silently practicing my 'I'm sorry but I don't date married men' speech. We order drinks and Dave just sits there not saying a word. Finally, after the drinks come, he leans over, takes my arm and looks deep into my eyes. 'Jenny,' he says in this really serious voice, 'I've got to tell you something.' And I think, uh oh, here it comes."

She paused dramatically. "And then he says, 'I'm *gay.*' The funny part is the guy *was* after me. But not as lover, as a mother. And that was why he always wanted me to hug him."

"Maybe he'll sleep with you anyway?" asked Parnell.

"Right. And give me AIDS too. I can't believe he's putting his wife at risk like that," she said.

"Ah, what ever happened to the good old days?" sighed Parnell. "Recreational sex, threesomes, group gropes." He reached across the table and took Jenny's hand. "You poor young thing. I bet you know nothing about a quick roll in the hay. Now, it's sexual history-taking, certified proof of being HIV-free, condoms greased with Nonoxynol-9, dental dams."

"People should ask other people if they have practiced high-risk behaviors or been involved with those who have," said Pam solemnly. "I know I do." Wayne looked at Pam with new interest.

Rhoda beamed at the two of them. "I don't know," she said—an expression I had never heard her use—"it sounds like a prudent course, but when a guy's mind is in his pants, can you really believe anything he tells you?"

"Of course you can," Parnell insisted. "I've never slept with anybody but you, dear. Well, I did once, but I used fifteen rubbers and three dental dams and did a retrograde ejaculation into myself using centuries-old tantric sex techniques."

"Uh, what do you call someone who has AIDS, herpes, gonorrhea, and syphilis?" asked Wayne, who up to now hadn't said a word.

"An incurable romantic," said Wayne happily as Pam laughed so hard she had to take off her glasses to wipe away the tears.

"Inez has stopped eating," Nick said.

"Oh God. When did that happen?" I said.

"Yesterday. She started refusing all food. All she'll take is a little water." It was two days after we had talked in the cafeteria. Without asking if he was interrupting anything, Nick walked into my office and sat down heavily.

"Did she talk to you about it at all?"

"Oh yeah. She said she was taking things into her own hands."

"What did you say?"

"I told her that starvation was a terrible, painful way to go, that it would probably make her sicker. So she said, 'Then get me some pills.'"

"She's blackmailing you."

Nick rubbed the back of his neck where it joined his shoulders. "That's just what I said to her. She just looked at me and said, 'You don't know me or you wouldn't say something like that. I'm already thin, so I don't think it will take too long. And they say that after the first few days, you stop feeling hungry. Promise me one thing,' she says. 'Don't let them put a feeding tube down my throat. Don't let them torture me.'"

"It'll be out of your hands. Did you tell her that?" I said.

Nick nodded. He stood, socking his fist into his palm as he walked in a tight circle. "Jesus, Fred. We have to get those kids in. It's our only hope."

The hospital administrator had already decided to make an exception in Inez's case, saying, "Children need to be with their mothers and mothers with their children."

Nick smiled when I said, "She said the rules were there to help patients, not to stand in the way of their recovery."

"Nice," he said.

Now Nick was chafing at the bit, waiting for the appointment at the city-funded foster-care agency. Although he had stressed the emergency nature of his request, the worker had scheduled the meeting five days from when he had called, explaining that she had only been on the job for six months, had a caseload of forty-five patients, and emergencies were an everyday occurrence. And then she had blown Nick's mind by saying, "It's not as though she's immediately terminal."

"It is now," he said grimly, recalling that conversation.

I talked him out of storming the foster-care office that afternoon as he threatened to do rather than wait the day and a half for his appointment. "You're just going to get their back up," I pointed out. "And right now we need their cooperation."

He got up to go, but then stopped at the door, his eyes fixed on me with a mute appeal.

"What is it?"

"Nothing, nothing," he said, turning away. "It's just . . . " He turned and took a few steps into the room.

"Yes?"

"Whew, this is really difficult." Beads of sweat were glistening on his hairline. "It's really embarrassing."

"Hey, Nick," I smiled. "You know as well as I do, when you hit embarrassment, you hit paydirt."

He took a deep breath, exhaling audibly. "The other day, when we did the AIDS exercise?" he began. "And I was in the Don't Know column?" He was talking about an AIDS sensitivity-training workshop the staff and students had participated in where we were each handed a slip of paper on which was written HIV-negative, HIV-positive, AIDS, or Don't Know. We then discussed with the group how we felt about the diagnosis we had been handed.

"Right," I said.

"Well, I really don't know."

"What do you mean?"

Nick toyed with his earring. "It's like that guy Jenny Noh told us about in Penne's."

I had to think back. And then I realized the cause of his discomfort. "Nick, are you trying to tell me you're gay?"

"I don't know."

"You don't know? You don't know you're gay or you don't know whether you're HIV-positive?"

"Both."

"Why don't you tell me about it?" I said, indicating the chair next to my desk.

He sat down, chewing on his lip. "Eight years ago," he began hesitantly, "when I was eighteen, my mother had a radical mastectomy. My father was distraught. I don't know which upset him more, the mutilation or the threat to her life. Whatever it was, he was beside himself. I went to see my mom right after the operation and she looked so awful, lying there with a tube coming out of her arm and my father just crying. You got to understand, this is a man who never cries. I just didn't know what to do. I ran out of the room. And there was a guy, a few years older than me, who was visiting a friend who also had cancer."

He hunkered down, his folded hands between his legs, lost in the memory for a moment. Then he continued. "We got to talking and then we went to the cafeteria for some coffee. We discovered that we had a lot of things in common: a love of opera, painting, literature. He invited me to his apartment to hear some rare records that he had of Maria Callas. I know that sounds corny. But I went. I was feeling so . . ." He hunched his shoulders forlornly. "So fragile. He made some omelets. We drank some very good white wine. And when he kissed me on the neck, I didn't try to stop him. He seduced me really. But part of me wanted it."

"Did you . . .?"

"Oh we had sex, if that's what you're wondering. And no, he didn't wear anything. At least I don't remember him using a rubber."

"Did you have an affair?"

"No," he said emphatically. "I never saw him again. He asked for my phone number and I refused to give it to him. I just put the whole thing out of my mind and became a determined heterosexual, laying every babe in sight. It was never a problem for me getting girls." He gave a beguiling smile that attested to the truth of his words. "But I always had some gay friends. And then being an AIDS volunteer, I thought about it a lot. Was I gay? Was I bisexual?

And in the back of my mind there was always the question. Had I been exposed to AIDS? And had I given it to others? I mostly use a condom, but, well, you know." He threw up his hands helplessly. "Sometimes the opportunity arises with a woman and I just seize it." He looked at me. "What do you think, Fred? Does this change your opinion of me?"

In answer I told him about Roger. "My best friend from first grade was gay. He didn't come out until we were in college. In fact, he dated a woman friend of mine, whom I had introduced him to. He was a talented artist, got involved with the Andy Warhol crowd, and moved in with a well-known drag queen who was heavily into drugs, and was abusive and self-destructive. Roger was an early victim of AIDS."

"Did you go through his illness with him?" Nick asked.

"No. I wish I had. When he got sick, he moved back home and his mother and sister took care of him. I always felt guilty about not seeing him before he died. We weren't particularly close by that time, but I felt a real loss. We had so much shared history together, grammar school, summers upstate together, visiting each other in college. He was like a brother."

Nick listened to my story, nodding sympathetically. And then he said, "What do you think, Fred? I have close friends who are gay. I've been an AIDS volunteer with the Gay Men's Health Crisis. I've had sex with a man. Am I gay?"

"Well, let's see," I said. "Do you want to have sex with any men you know?"

"No."

"Do you want to have sex with any women you know?"

"Yes."

"Can you think of a man who you'd like to have oral sex with?"

"No."

"Would you like a woman to have oral sex with you?"

"Of course."

"How does snuggling under the sheets with a man sound to you?"

"Not interesting."

"How about under the sheets with a woman?"

"Very interesting."

"Then I pronounce you straight."

"Are you sure?"

"My little test would be simplistic and probably not valid with a lot of people, but for someone who's as in touch with their feelings and is as honest as you are, I think it's proof that you're not homosexual."

Nick laughed. "But about the other Don't Know thing, Fred. What do you think?"

"I think you ought to get tested. You want to know and the doubt will make you crazy."

For a moment he closed his eyes. "I thought you'd say that. Eight years of wondering. Worrying about every cold, every time I woke in the middle of the night feeling warm and sweaty. I'll make an appointment with the doctor today."

In our next session, Nick told me the moment he met Caroline Quinn he knew he was in trouble. She looked like the prim and proper nuns at St. Mary's School for Boys, the ones who had made his early life a misery. Quinn was young, about his age, he guessed, but she already wore her brown hair in a bun and her lips were tightly compressed. If she buttoned her blouse any higher, it would cover her ears.

"I'm sorry," she said calmly after he had spent twenty minutes outlining the dire necessity for the children's visit, "but I can't grant your request."

"Ms. Quinn," he said, doing his best to hold his temper, "their mother is dying."

"But she's not dying right now. You yourself said that she's not even in the last stages of AIDS. She could live another year or two or three."

"Not at the rate she is going with her depression and her suicidal plans. She wants to kill herself. She's stopped eating."

"Mr. Torres, you know as well as I that there are ways to make her eat."

Don't reach for her throat, Nick told himself. "She needs a reason to live. And she has. Three of them, in fact. Luz, Marisol, and Ramón junior."

Quinn folded her hands and gave him a clenched-jaw smile. "Now, Mr. Torres," she said. "You know what you're asking is not in the children's best interests. Seeing their mother so ill in a hospital could prove traumatic."

"You think that's traumatic?" he asked. "What do you think it's going to be for them when their mother dies? Especially if she kills herself."

"I would say that it's up to you to see that she doesn't commit suicide. That's why she's hospitalized, isn't it?"

Gritting his teeth, Nick said as calmly as he could, "Who is your supervisor?"

"My supervisor. You wish to speak with my supervisor?"

"I do."

"Why don't I make you an appointment to see my supervisor?" she said, all sweet reasonableness. "I'll give you her name and number. But I know she's very busy and won't be able to see you until next week."

"How about today? I am not going to leave until I have an appointment with your supervisor for tomorrow at the latest. I am just going to sit here. You will have to forcibly eject me. So how about it? Do you give me an appointment or do you call the security guard and I make a scene?"

As he guessed, Quinn would rather die than cause a scene. Before Nick's eyes, her steely reserve gave way to a jittery nervousness. "Two o'clock tomorrow. Okay?"

"Thank you, Ms. Quinn," said Nick, bowing as he left.

Having stood for his reenactment of his meeting with Ms. Quinn, Nick threw himself into a chair and asked, "How can people act this way, Fred? Doesn't she understand that a person's life is at stake?"

"Nick, part of being a clinician is dealing with the nonpatient patient. Because everywhere you go you are going to run into these people who are well intentioned but devoid of common sense."

He put his face in his hands. "What do I do if the supervisor says no?"

"Use some strategy. Quinn may be a narrow-minded, rigid, well-intentioned rule follower who's only doing what she thinks is her job. So the best way to work with her or her supervisor is to appreciate what she is doing and then point out that what she is doing may not be consistent with what she is *trying* to do, which is look out for the children's best interests."

"That's just it," Nick charged. "They're looking out for the kids' worst interests."

"Nick, I know you have trouble working within these systems. But you'll never get anywhere with the bureaucrats of the world until you learn to make the system work for you. And there are a lot of Quinns out there. Unfortunately, they may not all have your wisdom and brilliance about what is the proper thing to do. And they might even believe that they are right as strongly as you believe you are right. But just remember, whenever a situation like this comes up, you don't want to fight. You want to win."

"Okay," said Nick, looking a lot more subdued. "I'll go home, put on a CD, cool down, and I'll think about it."

The next afternoon, Nick told me about his meeting. Wearing his only suit, a conservative dark blue, he went in to do battle with the supervisor. She was Mrs. Marjorie Elliot, a tough-looking gray-haired woman. Quinn was also there, the two of them standing shoulder to shoulder.

"Good morning, Mrs. Elliot, Ms. Quinn," said Nick, smiling disarmingly as he extended his hand to each of them. "I can't tell you how grateful I am that you have set aside time from your busy schedule to meet with me."

He sat down with his legs crossed, his hands folded over his knee, his head tilted in what he knew was an endearing pose. "I'll come right to the point," he said. "I really appreciate how much you want to protect Inez's children, who have already suffered so much by being taken out of their home after the tragic death of their father and are now separated from their mother and from each other. And I know how concerned you are that going to the hospital would upset them and make their adjustment to the foster homes that much more difficult. But I am also convinced"— and here he touched his heart—"that their mother will die, either by committing suicide directly or starving herself or simply depleting whatever resistance she has to the disease, if she isn't given a reason to live. And the only reasons she has are these beautiful children. Unless she *sees* them, she will die very soon, perhaps within a week, and that, I think, would upset the children a lot more than a supervised, therapeutic visit to the hospital."

Quinn started to speak, but Elliot stayed her with her hand. "You've made your point, Mr. Torres," she said crisply. "We're prepared to make arrangements to have Luz go to the hospital as soon as we can work it out with the foster parents."

Wow, thought Nick, stunned that the resistance had crumbled so fast. "That's wonderful," he said. "I really appreciate it. But what about Marisol and Ramón junior? Think what it will do for Inez to see all three children, her family, together."

Elliot smiled, and then, to his immense surprise, winked. "You got one, okay? In this world you take what you can get."

The following day we met in the secretarial area to wait for Luz. Although it was only early December, Lucy, our secretary, had already set up her annual display on her desk of a foot-high plastic Christmas tree surrounded by a tiny electric train that choo-chooed noisily and rang a bell every time it completed a circuit. The annual display was giving the staff its annual headache. There were times, and this was one of them, when I was convinced Lucy was nuttier than the succession of patient/typists that graced our office that year. The door opened and in walked a woman of about forty holding the hand of a delicate, almost ethereal child with black ringlets that fell to her shoulders.

Inez didn't even stir as we opened the door to her room. A tray laden with food was next to the bed, obviously untouched.

"Mama," cried Luz as she ran to the bed.

Inez turned as if in a dream. "Luz, is that you? Is that really you?"

CRAZY ALL THE TIME

"Yes. It's me."

Trembling, Inez touched her daughter's hair cupping the soft ringlets, then stroked her cheek silently.

Luz took her mother's frail hand into her own and kissed her palm. They hugged tightly. She looked at her mother and then at the bowl of soup on the bed tray.

"Mama," she said, picking up the spoon, "open your mouth."

"The Worst Faggot in the World"

Chapter 6

Garrison Bernstein, like many of our students, chose Bellevue because he wanted to be where the action is. But unlike the others, he was an insider, the son of Milton Bernstein, M.D., a major player in the small world of orthodox Freudian psychiatrists, senior member of a prestigious psychoanalytic institute, and the author of several influential books on transference neurosis. Garrison grew up in a sprawling Fifth Avenue co-op famed for Milton's Sunday brunch, where he and his colleagues rehashed theoretical battles over a lavish buffet of New York Jewish delicacies.

For a city boy, there was something of the hothouse plant about Gary. His early years were in private school, his adolescence in a New England prep school, his undergraduate years at Yale. As predestined, he enrolled at Harvard Medical School to follow in his father's footsteps as a psychoanalytically trained psychiatrist. But then he abruptly changed course, dropping out of medical school and entering a Ph.D. program in clinical psychology. Since he came from such a protected environment, I expected that Bellevue might give him a real taste of the "challenging problems" he so wanted.

It was January and Gary was just assigned to a new rotation in the Mental Hygiene Clinic where he would evaluate new patients.

During our next supervision session, between the usual phone in-teruptions, Gary told me about his first meeting with patient Paul Trent.

The first thing Gary noticed about Paul Trent, age sixty-six, was his long, supple fingers, which seemed to have a life of their own as they grazed the lapels of his gray flannel jacket, delicately ad-justed his rimless glasses, straightened his tie, and groomed his well-trimmed mustache.

"What brings you here, Mr. Trent?"

His fingers folded themselves on the knee of his crossed leg. "Well, I, um . . ." He cleared his throat and began again. "Well, I have not been sleeping and I've been worried sick, a regular wreck, and I've been crying a lot. Well, you know, it's been just such a mess." His voice was deep, cultured, lightly tinged with a southern accent.

"Tell me about that," Gary prompted.

"It's really ironic, you know. I came to New York to get away from the stifling small-town atmosphere and then something like this happens to me. I thank the Lord in His mercy that my father never lived to see this day. All he ever wanted was for his son to be strong, make a good living, get married, have children who'd carry on his name. And when I think"—his fingers fluttered to his thin chest—"when I think how . . ." He looked away quickly, his voice break-ing as each word fell like a blow: "I let him down."

This is good, thought Gary. Very good. "How did you let him down, Mr. Trent?"

"By being the vile, disgusting, hateful creature I am. By being a homosexual."

"Uh huh. Tell me more about that."

Trent shook his head, confused. Gary's phone rang. Trent bolted from his chair, his fingers swooping above his head, face white, eyes wide with terror.

"Mr. Trent, it's all right. It's just the phone."

Trent eased himself onto the edge of the chair, his chest still heaving. He blotted his forehead with his handkerchief.

"It's been like that ever since they came for me. They burst into my house with no warning—fifteen of them, police officers, postal

"the worst faggot in the world"

inspectors, both male and female, at eight o'clock in the morning, like storm troopers battering down my door while I searched frantically for a robe. So there I was, naked, while they"—his voice shook with anger as he pointed a trembling finger at his invisible tormentors—"violated my home, shoving a warrant in my face, tearing everything apart, sweeping my papers off the desk, emptying the drawers and closets onto the floor, and all the time screaming at me, *'Where are the pictures?'* They called me a child pornographer, a sexual abuser of little boys—I, who never touched anyone underage in my life. One of the officers held up a magazine that they had tricked me into sending for and said, 'You little cocksucking, slimeball faggot, I ought to cut off that little dick of yours.' I ran into the bathroom and locked the door while that same man yelled, 'Don't even think of trying anything.' And I got down on my knees and threw up into the toilet. And do you know what I thought? I thought, he's right. I am a creepy, slimy faggot."

Gary could feel the blood pumping through his veins. This is great, he thought. I can work with this.

When he described the scene to me, I told Gary that he had a right to be excited. Mr. Trent would be a very interesting patient to work with. Gary agreed and said that he was still feeling pumped up when his next patient came in later that afternoon. An Orthodox Jew was his first thought because she was so modestly dressed. Gloria Nadler was covered up from her neck to her wrists to the top of her ankle-length boots. Her clothes were so bloused out and loose-fitting it was impossible to tell if she was fat or thin. She wore her dark brown hair in a knot at the top of her head. Large brown eyes dominated her oddly ageless face. She looked like she might be anywhere from twenty-five to sixty years old.

From the forms Gloria Nadler had filled out, Gary knew that she was a dermatologist whose postresidency work had lasted only four months before she was "let go for medical reasons, specifically acute panic attacks." She had come to Bellevue's Mental Hygiene Clinic rather than a private therapist because she had no savings, no income, and no medical insurance.

"When did you first start having these attacks, Dr. Nadler?" Gary asked.

"About six months ago when I started working at the DermaCare Clinic on Park Avenue," she said. "During the first few weeks, they happened infrequently. After a while they happened every time I saw a patient. I got fired two months ago. I can't blame them. I got to where I couldn't touch or look at anyone's skin. How could I work?"

"It only happened when you saw patients?"

"Yes," she said. "I was fine until the moment they took off their clothes and then I broke into a cold sweat and my heart started racing like a car engine and the walls of the examining room started to close in on me, and I'd think, oh my God, I'm doing to die."

Gary sat back, fascinated. Incredible, he thought. A dermatologist with a panic reaction to the sight of skin.

"That's very sad. Poor woman," I said. "You've got two really challenging cases now, Gary."

"I know. I'm really going to like working with them." Gary was slouched in a chair in my office, his right arm thrown nonchalantly over the back.

"Why?"

"They're both such classic examples of unconscious repression of inner drives resulting in displacement and projection."

"Could you be a little more concrete?" I asked.

He leaned forward, his elbows on his knees, his whole body suddenly tightening as though bracing for action. Gary seemed to have two personas—an F. Scott Fitzgerald side, cool and detached, seemingly imperturbable, the other side passionate, as relentlessly argumentative as a Parisian intellectual at a Left Bank café. We were now on the Left Bank.

"Well, look at Dr. Nadler. She's a dermatologist who has repressed her sexual conflicts until they've resulted in a hysterical panic disorder and she now freaks out at the sight of skin. Can you imagine anything more Freudian? And Trent. He has obviously substituted himself as a narcissistic sex object to make up for the fact that he can't have his first choice—his mother."

I held up my hand. "Whoa, Gary. How do you know all of this?"

"Nadler was swathed in clothing from head to foot, so her prob-

"the worst faggot in the world"

lem has to be sexual. As for Trent, the way he described his parents to me, he had the textbook childhood of a homosexual: smothering, doting mother, distant, disapproving father. The works."

It was my recollection from earlier conversations with Gary that his own childhood had that same "textbook" family dynamic, but I didn't mention that to him. Instead, I said, "I grant you that it's a good bet that Dr. Nadler's symptoms indicate some kind of sexual conflict. Although we need to know more. But with Trent, who knows why he, or anyone else, becomes a homosexual?"

Gary resumed his Fitzgerald slouch, flicking a microscopic speck of lint off his sleeve. "Come on, Fred. You know as well as I do, homosexuals aren't born. They're made. His early identification with his mother combined with his inability to relate to the distant authoritarian figure of his father resulted in his own gender confusion and made it impossible for him to resolve the Oedipal conflict, identify with his father, and become a normal male."

"Gary, right now you're dealing with a guy who's been raided, indicted, and is facing fifteen years in prison. He's so freaked out he has to be peeled off the ceiling every time the phone rings and he is so depressed he's a suicide risk. His being a textbook case is interesting but, to me, you've got more urgent things to deal with here. So why don't you tell me what your treatment plans are?"

"Well," said Gary, "he is in a lot of distress and I would like to see him five times a week. And my goal is to help him understand the roots of his homosexuality so that he can work on resolving the conflict surrounding it and either accept or change his sexual orientation."

"Change his sexual orientation?" I asked.

"Fred, he's an ego-dystonic homosexual. He hates himself for it. He thinks he is the worst kind of human being. Even the psychiatrists who lobbied to get homosexuality declared an alternative life-style recognize ego-dystonic homosexuality as a pathological condition that requires treatment."

"You're right, Gary. He appears to be a self-hating homosexual. But you don't have enough data to support that conclusion. You know very little about his life, and the fact that you can declare him ego-dystonic at this stage shows that you're more wedded to the classic psychoanalytic theory that all homosexuals are basically unhappy, abnormal, and in conflict with their sexual orientation than to helping this patient."

"Fred," said Gary, leaning forward intently. "I don't think all homosexuals hate themselves. That's not fair. But with Trent, there's evidence for it. Why else would the raid and arrest have driven him into such a deep depression? Don't you see, the trauma upset his delicate defense system? He's always hated himself for his homosexuality, and unless we get to the root—"

"Great, Garrison. You're going to turn this sixty-six-year-old gay guy into a lady's man."

"Why not?" he kidded. "He looks good, goes to the gym three times a week. He can enjoy a happy life."

"You mean a happy heterosexual life."

"Okay, a happy heterosexual life."

"Wouldn't it be more realistic to work toward Trent having a happy homosexual life?"

Gary folded his hands behind his head and stretched out his legs. "Tell me the truth, Fred. You really think any homosexuals are happy?"

"Many of them, yes."

"Even in our society, where there is so much prejudice against them, you think that two men or two women can have a mature, developed relationship?"

"I've seen many healthy, mature homosexual relationships," I said.

"Yes," he said hesitantly, "but a lot of the literature assumes that part of maturity is the capacity to have a physical, emotional, intimate relationship with a member of the opposite sex."

"Yes. I've read that," I said. "And those guys who stand on the street corners and whistle and hiss at women are mature?"

"Sure," he grinned. "And I'll defend them and their infantile sexist behavior to the death," he proclaimed, punching the air with his fist. "But, really, Fred," he said seriously, "we both know intelligent people who believe that any man who has to make it with another man is basically afraid of women. And I've known gay men who were not happy people, who believed they were missing out on a great deal."

"True, but there are also a lot of miserable heterosexuals around and their heterosexuality is no guarantee of emotional maturity or psychic health." My phone rang again. It was a ward unit chief, telling me that I was needed in Ward 21 South right away.

"I've got an emergency," I said. As we walked down the corridor, I said, "In my opinion, no one knows the etiology of homosexuality and every theory that has been advanced has either been shown not to be true or is far from being proven. We don't know where Trent is going to be three months from now let alone the decades you'll need to do enough analysis to get him to appreciate tits like we do. I suggest that you try to find out what this case means to him. If the trauma really just uncovered his preexisting homosexual self-hatred, don't you want to know why or how it did that? You need to know everything you can about this man. Try being more interactive. But don't just collect data. Let's see if you can do something to help him right now. And Nadler too. We can treat her panic attacks while you explore her sexual conflicts."

Gary nodded. Before turning to 21 South, I added, "I'll give you some references on relaxation training that will be useful for Nadler in dealing with her anxiety. And I'll give you some readings on short-term therapy for posttraumatic stress reactions to help Trent get over the trauma of the raid and arrest."

Gary was a lot less sure of himself than when he came in. But his eyes lit up when I mentioned references. "Okay, Fred."

I was impressed by Gary's courage and his willingness to question the beliefs that were the religion of his father. He reminded me of myself twenty-five years earlier, when I was an intern at Bellevue. My supervisor was a traditional analyst, a withholding, non-responding, nonreacting, nit-picking authoritarian. At all of our sessions, he would chide me for my "mistakes," like interacting with my patients, responding to what they were saying, talking about my own experiences, confronting them with the paradoxes and consequences of their behavior. After several months of trying to do it his way, I told him in no uncertain terms how working like that felt to me. "It's like wearing a straitjacket over a corset. I can't breathe. I can't do it. It's just not me." For years afterward, as I was exploring techniques and developing my own style of doing therapy, I had a gnawing fear that I had failed by not being able to adopt the classic approach, and I wasn't even the son of the eminent Milton Bernstein.

After dealing with the problem in Ward 21 South, I met Rhoda in the hallway and walked back to our office area with her.

"Rhoda, how well do you know Milton Bernstein?" I asked her as we entered her office. On her wall was a painting of Freud's couch in Vienna where his celebrated patients freely associated. She perched her small frame on the top of the desk so that one shoe scarcely grazed the floor.

"I've been to Sunday brunch at his house a few times. That's about it. Why do you ask?"

"What's he like?"

"A giant generator giving off waves of power. He absolutely dominates any conversation. And not just by his intellect, which is formidable, but by his physical presence. He's tall, like Gary, but more powerfully built. But maybe it just seems that way because he's so . . . " Her hands groped for the right word.

"So . . .?"

"Intimidating." She laughed. "I think it has something to do with his cold Germanic temperament. He has such an icy reserve. It puts people off, which, of course, may be just what he intends."

"Isn't it wonderful," I mused, "how people who are cold, withdrawn, and emotionally ungiving become psychoanalysts? It's type casting. They act out their withholding personalities and call it technique."

"Fred," said Rhoda, as if chiding a naughty child, "you're not being fair. Analytic technique has a lot to offer. Properly done, it allows the patient and the analyst to journey into the deepest reaches of a person's psyche."

"It's fine for a patient who can spend an hour a day and lots of money for at least the next five years. Speaking in a strange tongue called free association to someone who responds only with 'uh huh' or 'tell me more about that.' Frustrated in every request for support, opinions, or advice and made to feel so childish and helpless that he inevitably experiences resentment, which the analyst then calls the transference neurosis. The analyst actually creates the transference neurosis, which is supposedly a recreation of the patient's feelings toward his own parents, which in turn is based on the assumption that these parents are as withholding and mean as the analyst is."

Rhoda looked at me, shaking her head. "Fred, you're raving."

"No, I'm teasing you," I chuckled.

That afternoon, as I was quickly walking to the elevator, I bumped into Nick, who was rushing by.

"Hi, how's it going?" I called out as we passed each other.

"Great," he yelled back, then stopped and walked over to me. "I had the AIDS test done," he said quietly, glancing about nervously at the small crowd waiting for the elevator.

"Good. Have you gotten the results?"

"Yes and no."

I raised my eyebrows quizzically, waiting.

"Yes, they got the results back. No, I haven't gone for them."

"So you're still stuck in the Don't Know column?"

He touched my arm lightly and lowered his voice even further until he was almost whispering. "It's been eight years and I know the chances that I got the disease from one encounter are extremely small. But I'm seeing someone now and it's getting pretty serious."

"Nick, I know this is difficult for you. But the longer you wait to get the results, the longer this is going to gnaw away at you. If you put it off too long, it may even affect your relationship with this woman."

He gave a wry smile. "I thought you'd say something like that. By the way," he said, returning to his normal tone, "Inez is eating again. Crying a lot too. It's really hard for her, but at least she's back with her kids."

"Good work, Nick."

The elevator door opened and people began squeezing into the small space available. I jumped on and gave him a thumbs-up sign as the doors closed.

• • •

When Gary appeared at my door for his supervision a week later, he held two big books under his arm. "I've been doing a lot of reading—Freud, Socarides, some of the other classics. They all conclude that homosexuals become so due to"—he opened one of the books and read to me—" 'the inability to form a healthy sexual identity in accordance with their anatomical and biological capacities.' " He was smiling broadly.

"Ah, the divine gospel, as spoken from God to Freud and interpreted by Socarides," I responded. "Now let's bring in one of my authorities." I opened the door and yelled across the hall. "Barry, could you spare a minute, please?"

"You called, Fred?" asked Barry, leaning his head through the doorway.

"What do you think of this book?" I asked, brandishing Socarides's *Homosexuality*.

Barry's eyes widened in mock horror as he held up his fingers in the sign of the cross warding off Dracula. "Back, begone," he intoned. "Seriously," he said, as Gary and I smiled, "that guy is from the Dark Ages. The idea that homosexuality is a form of arrested or inhibited development should be exorcised along with other Freudian bugaboos like clitoral orgasms representing an immature level of sexual functioning in women. Kinsey found that four percent of the men he interviewed were exclusively homosexual but thirty-five percent reported some homosexual experience."

"Kinsey?" snickered Gary. "Isn't that kind of ancient history?"

"And I suppose Freud isn't? But if you want more up-to-date information, a recent study found that ten percent of the male population is exclusively homosexual, while up to sixty percent of men surveyed have had at least one homosexual contact. Hard to believe, huh, that you're actually a member of a sexual minority?" Barry kidded.

"Kinsey's work," he continued, "which is still a classic of its kind, showed that there is range of sexual behavior from men who are exclusively homosexual to those who have had at least one heterosexual experience to those who are bisexual to men who are heterosexual but have had at least one homosexual experience and finally to men who are exclusively heterosexual."

"Wait a minute," said Gary. "I just read a study funded by the National Institute of Mental Health that found that only one percent of their sample population was homosexual."

"Well, let's see, if that's true and there are about two hundred and fifty million people in the United States, then two hundred and fifty thousand people in the U.S. are gay," said Barry. "That must mean that *all* of them live in Greenwich Village."

"Whatever the numbers," I said, "in my experience, like everything else in life, there's a continuum—in this case, stretching from the Arnold Schwarzeneggers to the Liberaces."

"Well, put me in the Schwarzenegger column," said Gary, flexing his arms and puffing out his chest.

"I'm more like Ozzie and Harriet." We both looked at Barry. "Make that Ozzie and Ozzie. Say, I've got a great idea, Gary. Why don't you and your fiancée come to dinner at my house this Sunday night? Get some idea of how the other sixth or twelfth live?"

"Thanks, Barry. I'll check with Maggie. She's our social secretary. Can I let you know tomorrow?"

"Sure. We're that way too. If Scott didn't keep tabs on things, I'd never know what our plans were. But, I'm warning you, I'm a great cook. Just ask Fred."

I patted my stomach. "The last time Diane and I were there he made venison pâté followed by roast boar. It was incredible."

Barry chuckled. "That was in my wild-game period. I have a new recipe for crown roast of lamb with a garlic crust I'm dying to try out."

"Let's start with Trent," I said after Barry had left. "What did you find out?"

Gary had gleaned a lot more from his patient. From the age of six, Paul Trent had felt different from other boys. He hated sports, rough play, teasing girls. His best friend was Abbie, a girl his own age who lived next door with whom he played dress-up. When his father caught him wearing Abbie's mother's dress, carrying a purse, and prancing around in high heels, he dragged his son away, gave him the only beating of his life, and told him he was never to play with Abbie again. From then on, Trent never played with another girl. It wasn't until after World War II, when he was discharged from the navy and had moved back home, that Trent discovered his "true nature," as he put it, when a total stranger gave him his first orgasm in a bus-station bathroom.

"Trent flipped out immediately," Gary said. "His father put him into a private psychiatric hospital, where the psychiatrist told him his problem was that he was homosexual and couldn't accept it. He advised him to leave the hick town he was living in and go to New York where he could find people like himself. So he starts a new life in Greenwich Village, gets an accounting degree, finds some gay friends, and joins a local Catholic parish headed by a renegade priest who welcomes homosexuals. Eventually he became an active member of the gay community. But all of his relationships have been platonic. His sex life has consisted of brief, anonymous encounters with men he never saw again. He also told me he was never into young boys or even young men. Then with the raid, the whole thing blows up in his face."

"That's good, Gary," I said when he had finished. "You found out a lot about him."

"Yeah, I feel sorry for the guy. Always being an outsider like that, never feeling like he fits in. I remember when I first went away to school how I felt, a middle-class Jewish kid surrounded by all these rich Protestant boys. I really had a rough time in the beginning until I learned to, you know, talk the right way, even imitate their body language."

"Did you find out anything about how he feels about his current situation?" I asked.

"Not much. All he talked about was how unhappy he was that he couldn't go to church anymore."

"That's interesting. Did you ask him why?"

"It was because he couldn't take Communion. He said, 'I've lost the real support that the church has given me.'"

"I don't get it. He used to take Communion, now all of a sudden he doesn't. Why? What's changed?"

Gary sat back in his chair, poker-faced, looking at me with his head half cocked. "Fred, I still think to understand his present situation, we have to go back to his past, particularly his early pre-Oedipal and Oedipal conflicts."

"I understand what you're saying and I, too, want to get some more history. But right now we don't have a good sense of the present, why he has stopped going to Communion. We need to get a better understanding of his current pain. I want you to consider the possibility that the thing that turned his situation into a problem was his current set of attitudes, beliefs, and judgments, regardless of where they came from. And that, if he changes those, he automatically changes the way he sees himself."

Suddenly I had an idea. "You consider yourself a scientist," I said. "Let's put it to the test. Find out why Trent won't let himself go to Communion any longer; what he's saying to himself. Let's see if by changing his thinking, we can also change his behavior in some specific way, for example, by his going back to church or by alleviating his anxiety and depression."

"Okay, I'll try," he said, but there was doubt in his voice.

My phone rang and I said to Gary, "See you tomorrow. You're doing good work."

No sooner had Gary walked out of my office than he was almost knocked off his feet. "Excuse me," he said.

"Sorry, Gary."

"Sorry, Gary."

It was Wayne and Pamela, still holding hands after their collision with Gary. He stared at them. "What's with you two? You both look different."

He was right. Maybe it was the fact they were wearing their hair at identical lengths, just at mid-ear.

"Contacts," said Pam, beaming, as two pairs of bottle-green eyes turned in our direction.

"Aren't your eyes . . .?" I began.

"Yep," she nodded. "But Wayne thought it would be cool if we both had the same color. I think green eyes are sexy, don't you?"

"Matching nose rings are next," called Mike Warner from his door.

• • •

At our next session, Gary told me about his recent encounter with Gloria Nadler.

"Come in, Dr. Nadler," said Gary, opening his door.

"Please, call me Gloria," she said. As before, she wore layers of clothing from neck to ankle.

"Okay . . . Gloria. You haven't told me anything about your life. Why don't you . . .?"

"And I'll call you Garrison."

Gary felt that this was unacceptable, even if she was an M.D. ten years his senior. "I think that in order to maintain a professional relationship it would be better if you called me Mr. Bernstein."

"Well, all right, Mr. Snotty Bernstein. Have it your way," she said. "But you can still call me Gloria."

A shiver went up his spine. She was acting very strangely. Collecting himself, he said, "So, um, Gloria, tell me about yourself."

She picked up a pencil from his desk and started twirling it between her thumb and middle finger.

"What is there to tell?" she shrugged, rolling the pencil between her hands. "I have no life anymore."

"Tell me more about that."

"I hang around my house, read, watch TV, shop, cook dinner for mom and me," she said. "She's seventy-one years old and her arthritis is so bad she can hardly get out of bed. I'm all she's got and now she's got me full time. She's very demanding. She always says she needs me so much because she had me when she was older than other mothers. When she was thirty-five years old, one year younger than I am now."

"So you feel your biological clock ticking?"

"It's one minute to midnight. And then, pouf, it's all over."

"How do you feel about that?"

"How should I feel?"

Gary ignored her question. "Do you ever go out on dates?"

"How am I going to meet anyone? I don't go anywhere."

"Friends? Do you see any friends?"

"No. I'm not saying I don't have any. But most of my close friends are from college and are still in Boston. I don't have too many friends in New York."

"the worst faggot in the world"

"Are any of these old friends men?"

"You mean like boyfriends?"

"Yes."

"What does that matter?"

"I was wondering if you have any boyfriends because you indicated that you want to have children. Obviously, that's more likely to happen if you're sexually active," Gary said gently.

"Sexually active? Well, if you want to know the truth," she said, "I'm not all that crazy about naked bodies. I mean, I saw them all the time in my practice. And most of my patients had rashes or warts or pustules. Their skin was erythematous or scaling or oozing or crusting. Ugly things."

Gary had difficulty imagining that most of the patients in a Park Avenue practice had skin like that.

"It was okay when I was a resident—I mean, I got through it—but lately it's happening even in my dreams. Every night, I seem to have the same dream. A patient comes in, gets completely undressed for a melanoma examination, and at first his skin is smooth and glabrous, then as soon as I reach out to touch something that looks like a mole, lesions start appearing on his skin like cockroaches on a dirty stove."

"Gloria, are you a virgin?"

She flinched. "No. I have had some experience."

"Such as?"

"In college. I just haven't dated since I moved back here for med school." She opened her mouth as if to continue and then clamped it shut again. "Please," she asked in a whimper. "You're sounding like my mother now. Could we talk about something else? Please."

"How'd it go," I asked the following Monday. It was lunchtime and we were both grabbing a bite in my office before I went to a faculty meeting at NYU.

"It was a disaster," Gary said glumly.

I was appalled. "Because you asked him why he couldn't take Communion?"

Gary looked at me puzzled. "Oh, you mean Trent?"

"Who were *you* talking about?"

"Maggie."

"Okay, let's talk about Maggie. What happened with Maggie?"

He gave me a reprise of the evening with Barry and Scott and the fight with Maggie that followed. He said that Maggie gushed over the perfectly decorated apartment and delicious dinner and that Barry and Scott talked "endlessly" about Scott's three kids from his marriage. Then, when they were back in their own apartment, she had implied that Barry and Scott had a better, more communicative, relationship than she and Gary.

"The problem with Maggie is," he said, "she's so impressionable. Barry holds Scott's hand and they look into each other's eyes and she gets all teary. She thinks that it's so wonderful that they have this great relationship and are so open with each other, talking about his kids like that. And while she's getting sentimental, what about those kids? They're certain to be fucked up."

"How do you know that?" I asked, opening a container of strawberry yogurt.

"It's happening already. The older boy keeps making excuses not to see his father, which Scott says he understands because his son, who is now eighteen, is trying to work out his own sexuality. And his nineteen-year-old daughter, who continues to see him, is flirting with the idea that she might be bisexual or gay, even though she told Scott she hasn't yet made it with a woman." He took out a sandwich from a bag he was holding and unwrapped it. "Do you think that's healthy?" he asked, taking a bite.

"Sure," I said, showing him the container. "It's low-fat."

He looked at me uncomprehendingly for a moment. "I don't mean your yogurt. I mean what's happening with his daughter."

"I don't know what's healthy or not healthy for her. It depends on how she works it out. But she's thinking, exploring, examining her life. That sounds good to me."

"But, Fred, what if he is unconsciously encouraging her explorations into homosexuality?"

"Come on, Gary. Lots of teenagers experiment. It's age appropriate. And who knows what we unconsciously encourage our kids to try? Remember, most homosexuals have heterosexual parents."

"the worst faggot in the world"

Gary smiled, then chewed his sandwich for a moment. "We both know I'm upset about Maggie, not about Barry's kids. I mean, the woman I intend to marry spends an evening with two gay guys she's never met before, doesn't know from a hole in the wall, and then says, 'Why can't we have their kind of relationship?' "

"Just tell her it's because she's not a man."

"Thanks a lot," said Gary, reaching in his bag and bringing out a container of coffee. "Maybe she should try being with a woman. Maybe I should try a guy."

I finished my yogurt and started in on a brownie. "Look, good relationships are a lot of work. Now you're starting to deal with the rough stuff. Just try being her friend and lover and stop trying to psychoanalyze her so much."

"You think it's that simple?"

"For you, maybe it's not that simple."

We then went on to talk about Dr. Gloria Nadler.

"I'm worried about her," I said. "Better take it slowly and keep her focused on the reality of her situation. Try telling her that her feelings are to be expected. As a highly intelligent thirty-six-year-old woman whose career is in jeopardy and who wants a child but has a nonexistent love life, anxiety and depression are very appropriate reactions. This allows her to see that her reactions are normal but at the same time lets her know that she has to deal realistically with her situation or it's not going to get resolved."

"Yeah," said Gary, not too enthusiastically. "Stay in the present." Then he brightened. "I've started picking up on her transference."

"Really?"

"Yes. I pointed out to Gloria that when she was talking about her mother being demanding, she was actually experiencing me that way."

"In what way are you demanding?"

"That's just what she asked. I told her that I was demanding that she open up and tell me what was going on. But at that point, she immediately became resistant and disagreed with me. In the same way I bet she does with her mother."

I took a sip of coffee. "Sometimes, Gary, as Freud said, a cigar is just a cigar. Isn't it possible that sometimes when Gloria responds to you, she is just responding to you and not to you as a representation of her mother?"

He looked at me uncomprehendingly. "I thought the whole point of using transference is to get her to see that she's responding to me as a representation of her mother. Only then can she end her resistance."

"Okay. Let me see if I've got this right. If you don't use transference, she'll just see you as a man making demands on her, a woman. But even though you see that her problems—the sex and skin thing and no baby—concern her relating to men, you think you should skip that and talk about her mother?"

"Leave her mother out of it, huh? God. What would my father say if he knew you were implying that I should leave the mother out of it?"

"Garrison," I said, leaning forward conspiratorially, "heresy can be fun."

My phone rang. Gary got ready to leave.

"Before I go," he said, "I thought you might be interested in why Paul Trent can't take Communion anymore."

"You found out? Good. Why is it?"

"He said it was because he was not worthy of God's love. He said, and I quote, 'The raid was a confirmation of everything I've always known about myself.' So in his case, it is his self-hatred—brought on by his unacceptable sexual orientation—which has been there all along but was only unmasked by the pornography raid."

"Not so fast, my friend. Trent has been a homosexual all along and he has taken Communion all along. Now suddenly he no longer feels entitled? Why can other homosexuals take Communion if he can't? How is he different from the other homosexuals in his church?"

"That's what you want me to ask him?"

"That's what I want you to ask him."

When he saw that Gary was gone, Barry stuck his head into my office.

"the worst faggot in the world"

"Boy, is that kid ever uptight," he said. "I can't believe he grew up in New York. Hasn't he ever seen a gay couple before? You'd think we were Vulcans or something."

"Make that Cordon Bleu–trained Vulcans. He did rave about your cooking."

"You know what got me? When he said to Scott, 'You had three kids and you walked out on your wife?' Scott didn't leave Arlene. Arlene walked out on Scott and the kids. Besides, hasn't he ever heard of divorce?"

"Well, he's led a very sheltered life."

"Cloistered is more like it. I find it fascinating that he's the son of an eminent psychoanalyst."

"Come on, Barry. Look at Milton Bernstein's writings. When you translate all his jargon into plain English, he's more bigoted than Archie Bunker."

"Isn't it interesting that psychoanalysis, which is supposed to be a study of the human psyche, ends up reinforcing the most basic prejudices?"

"True," I said, grabbing my jacket and scooter helmet as we walked out together. "And Dr. Bernstein is one of the worst offenders. Did you see that article last month? He called the acceptance by the American Psychiatric Association of homosexuality as a valid life-style choice a 'moral outrage' and recommended returning to the use of the word 'invert.'"

"Well, I guess the old man's a lost cause," he said as we headed for the elevators. "But at least we can educate his son."

A week later, a very upset Gary told me about Gloria's latest revelation, which had happened that morning. She had come into his office, almost bubbling over with excitement. "Hi, Bernstein," she trilled, plopping into her chair with an abandon that was uncharacteristic. The shape and size of her figure were now clearly apparent under her black sweater and her straight black skirt, which came only to her knees. He noted that she wasn't as thin as he thought.

"Well, Gloria," he said carefully. "You seem pretty cheerful today."

"Oh, I feel great," she enthused.

"Really?" he said. "How are you doing with your recurring dreams?"

"Oh, they're gone," she said, flinging her arms out expansively. "Completely gone. You cured me."

"Really?" he said, instinctively worried and afraid to ask any more questions. "How did I do that?"

"Well," she said, moving her shoulders in a flirtatious gesture that seemed copied from a bad late-night movie. "You gave me something else to think about."

Steeling himself for the worst, Gary took a deep breath. "Gloria, what did I give you to think about?"

"This!" she cried. And before he could stop her, she stood up, pulled her sweater up and pushed her skirt down to expose a well-rounded stomach.

He sat there stunned, dumbfounded, paralyzed. Damn, he thought, what the hell is going on? What has Covan gotten me into?

"I'm pregnant," she sang out. "And it's yours."

Gary looked at me now. "Fred, I'm fucked. I'm absolutely fucked."

"You said you wanted to induce a transference relationship? Well, you certainly got it."

"Yeah," said Gary, smiling grimly. "Like be careful what you wish for because you might just get it?"

"Something like that. What did you do when she told you it was your baby?"

Gary covered his face with his hands. "I was terrified," he said, shuddering. "All I wanted to do was get her or me out of the room. I didn't care which one. I finally got her to sit down and cover herself by telling her that I refused to continue if she didn't. Then I asked her how she knew she was pregnant. She said she threw up every morning, her breasts were enlarged, she missed a period, and, 'Anyway, silly,' she says, 'all you have to do is look at my tummy.' So I ask her as calmly as I'm speaking now, 'Why do you think it's mine?' And she says in this breathy, Marilyn Monroe voice, 'I don't know how this happened, but I never felt this close to any man in my life.'"

"What did you do?"

"I said, 'But, Gloria, we didn't do anything. How could I be the father? Have you had sex with a man recently?' And she says, 'Don't be silly.' And then I just wrapped it up as fast I could. So I said to her, 'Let's schedule an extra session for you. Let's see. This is Monday. How about first thing Wednesday morning?' And do you know what she said? 'I'm so glad you feel that way about me.'"

He gripped my wrist tightly. "Fred, what am I going to do?"

The cool Gary and the hot Gary were both gone. And in their place was a young man who looked like he had just had the floor yanked out from under him.

"Just relax Gary. As Aeschylus said, 'He who learns must suffer.'"

"Oh," he said, his voice dipped in irony. "You mean this is one of those goddamn growth opportunities?"

"Yeah," I laughed.

"Well, I'm getting them in spades. Maggie complains that my relationship with her is not as good as Barry and Scott's. My father is after me to be his clone, go back to medical school. 'Get the M.D. and the Ph.D.,' he says. 'People respect that.' And then there's Paul Trent. I'm not supposed to cure him of his homosexuality. I'm just supposed to say, 'That's cool, man. All we have to do is just get you to pray in church. Your whole problem is you can't take Communion.' I mean, this is what I'm here for? So a guy can take Communion? I'm not even sure what Communion is."

"Welcome to the real world," I said.

"This isn't real," Gary roared. "It's crazy. It's true what they say about Bellevue. It's a nuthouse. When Gloria showed me her stomach and said it's my baby, I thought, ethics board, here I come. I'm going to be brought up on charges. She'll claim that I had sex with her, made her pregnant. It's my word against hers. I'm up against a woman who is a physician, for God's sake. Who are they going to believe?"

I patted his arm. "Gary, you're forgetting one thing—"

"Yeah, you're right," he interrupted, almost jumping from his chair. "We could do a DNA test on the fetus, because there is no way that the baby is mine."

"I was going to say that you don't even know she's pregnant."

He shook his head emphatically. "Oh, she's pregnant all right."

"When you were in medical school, didn't you ever hear of a condition called pseudocyesis?"

"Sure, hysterical pregnancy, with all the signs of the real thing." Gary suddenly looked like a drowning man who spies a floating log. "You think that's what's going on?"

"I don't know. But I sure hope so."

"It's true that last week she looked like she had a flat stomach and now she looks like she's about four months pregnant. But she used to wear loose clothes, Fred. So I have no way of knowing without a pregnancy test."

"Now you're talking."

"And if she objects, I could just tell her that as a doctor she knows she has to rule out all possibilities, no matter how remote." He sat back, smiling weakly. The log had turned into a dock. "So you think that her intense desire for a child could have triggered this?" he asked, his professional curiosity returning.

"That, plus your long-sought-after transference relationship developing."

He grimaced. "So she got both her wishes, me and the baby. Is that what you're saying, Fred?"

"You've made her a very happy woman. By the way," I added, "I wouldn't argue with her about . . . I mean, you haven't had sex with her, have you?"

Gary winced. "Fred, give me a break."

"Okay," I said, "then let's assume that she is delusional and is decompensating. Here's what you'll do. You'll keep the appointment as scheduled. Meanwhile, as soon as you leave here, you'll speak to the unit chief of the Mental Hygiene Clinic to arrange a psychiatric evaluation ASAP. Then, depending on how out of control she is, you either bring her into the walk-in clinic for an evaluation or over to the psych ER, because she might have to be admitted."

"Wow," said Gary softly. He got up to go and then stopped. "I forgot, I'm also seeing Trent this afternoon. What should I do about him?"

At that point, I really felt sorry for Gary, who looked wrung out, his blond forelock plastered to his forehead with sweat, his entire body limp.

"What did Trent say when you asked him why he was different from all the other homosexuals who were receiving Communion?"

Gary leaned forward, some of the old fire returning to his eyes. "He said, and I quote, 'It's because I'm the worst faggot in the world.'"

I thought about that a moment. "So Trent is saying he believes he is so sinful and so despicable that he doesn't deserve to take Christ into himself, which is essentially what Communion is. But somehow all the other homosexuals are able to take the sacrament. That's pretty interesting, Gary."

"It is? Why?" he asked, genuinely interested.

"Because it gives us a way into his system," I explained. "What we need here is Snow White's magic mirror."

Gary looked at me as if he hadn't heard right. "As in the fairy tale?"

"Right. Remember when the wicked stepmother asks 'Who's the fairest of them all?' The magic mirror could only answer with the truth. People prefer to think of themselves as victims rather than hear that they are responsible for their situation. But acceptance of that truth is the first step toward change. You can tell the patient the most outrageous things if you are sincere and communicate in a caring and nonjudgmental way. Here's what I want you to say in this case. And here's how I want you to say it."

Gary did exactly as I had advised and told me about the session with Trent later that afternoon. If anything, Gary told me, Trent looked even more down than when he had seen him last week. His eyes, hair, and skin seemed grayed to a kind of prison pallor, although he had yet to go to prison. Even his fingers had ceased their restless roaming and now lay still in his lap.

"Let's pick up where we ended last week, Mr. Trent. You were saying that you couldn't take Communion because, as you put it, you are 'the worst faggot in the world.'"

Trent bowed his head, his hands folded in a prayerful attitude. "Yes," he said sadly.

"So in other words, Mr. Trent"—he paused, waiting for him to look up—"you are the most despicable of homosexuals. So much so that you are undeserving of God's love."

He nodded mournfully, not looking up. "Yes. That's so."

"Well, let's think about that for a moment, Paul."

Trent looked up, astonished to find Gary using his given name.

"Now, as I understand it, you consider yourself a good Christian who follows God's commandments and tries to avoid sin, isn't that true?"

"Yes, it is," he said, his gray eyes questioning, wondering where Gary was headed.

"Well, my understanding of Catholicism is that pride is a sin. A sin that should be avoided. Am I right?"

"Yes. That's true."

"Do you consider yourself a prideful person?"

"Oh no," Trent insisted with a shake of his head. "In fact, I'm very humble. You must have seen that."

"Then how can you say that you are the worst faggot in the world? Because by saying that you are making one of the most prideful statements I have ever heard."

Trent looked at him, perplexed, two long fingers making dents in his pursed lips.

"You are saying that in God's eyes, you are not deserving of God's love," Gary went on, "although all your gay brothers are. But you are more of a faggot than them somehow. You are *the worst faggot* that has ever lived in human existence."

And then he paused, waiting until Trent's eyes were riveted on him. "Where do you get off thinking that you're so special? That you're such an exceptional faggot that you don't deserve to receive Communion? That sounds sinfully prideful to me, Paul."

Trent's gray eyes darted wildly back and forth as if trying to catch something in motion. And then they stopped, frozen in place, as if not seeing at all. He's gone tilt, Gary thought, like a pinball machine.

Gary waited. He looked at the black second hand as it moved spasmodically around the large clock face on the wall. He gazed at the bright optimistic faces of Maggie and himself in the framed

"the worst faggot in the world"

New York Times announcement of his engagement. He glanced at his notebook, which he had yet to open.

Finally, Trent stood. "I suppose it's time for us to stop for today," he said distractedly. "Good-bye, Mr. Bernstein."

"Where are you going? The session isn't over yet."

"Yes. But I'm tired. Good day to you," he said strolling out of Gary's office.

My upcoming week was busier than usual because I had appointments with fifteen candidates for the following year's class of interns in addition to my usual work. I was feeling harried and looked forward to my supervisory session with Kitty. We would be discussing Brenda Coleman, whom I always found fascinating.

Kitty told me that she was worried about Brenda, who seemed to be deteriorating. She was spending less time with her friends and had recently gotten into a physical fight on the street during an animal-rights demonstration.

"Then she called me at eleven last night," said Kitty. "I never thought I'd hear the end of it from my husband, Tom, who had just gotten to sleep after a double shift at the hospital. He was furious."

"Well, I'm sorry, Kitty. But you understand why I have you interns give out your home phone number for emergency calls from patients. Emergencies are something that you'll have to deal with for the rest of your career. Do you have an answering machine to screen your calls?"

"Now you're sounding like him. No matter how hard I try . . ."

"Is there something else here you'd like to talk about, Kitty?"

"I'm sorry. This isn't appropriate."

"It's okay with me. It's up to you."

"It's just that Tom's always wanting me to be more. Be different. You'd never believe how hard I try and he always wants something else."

"Like?"

"Like anything I'm not. Like everything everyone else is."

"If you want a response from me, you're going to have to be a little more specific."

"I'm sorry. I'll try. Well, I'm really organized. I'm really neat. I'm prompt. I'm a good cook. I'm always prepared. We never run out of anything because I've always planned ahead. His clothes are always in perfect order. You know, a place for everything and everything in its place."

"Well, I know you're not describing my wife."

"I'm like June Cleaver except that I've put myself through college and I'm getting a Ph.D. and I'm self-supporting."

"And what else does he want?"

"He wants . . . I don't know what. He complains because I don't do exciting things. That I'm not spontaneous. But . . ." She stopped. "I'm sorry, I'm getting carried away here."

"But what?"

"I just think that if I was those things, he'd find something else I wasn't."

"How long have you been married?"

"Five years. We got married after we graduated from college."

"Was it always this way?"

"Well, when I think about it, yes, it always was. I just didn't think about it. I was very young, insecure, even more than I am now, if you can believe it. I always kept trying to do more, be better. But now I'm beginning to wonder if there's ever any end to this."

I sighed. "Well, I'm not the easiest guy to live with. I can be pretty demanding. I always think I know how things ought to be. Luckily, my wife is strong enough to point out alternatives and stand up to me. You know, once, years ago, we did this really interesting weekend workshop for couples. It was fascinating. At one point, everyone had to write a wish list of the things we wanted our spouse to do differently and then rank-order them, you know, from most to least important. Then we traded lists with our partner and had them rank-order the requests from most to least difficult for them to do. In every case I know about, including both of ours, there was a perfect inverse relationship. The most important requests from my wife were the ones I thought the hardest for me to do, and vice versa."

"What was your number-one request for her?"

"That doesn't matter."

"Come on, you can tell me anything," she smiled, using my words back at me.

"I wanted her to be perfect."

"Yes, but what was your request?"

"My request was that she should be perfect." We both laughed.

"So you're just like Tom?"

"I don't know about being like him, but I've certainly changed a lot during my marriage. And she's convinced me that she is perfect—for me. You know this marriage stuff is not easy, it takes a lot of work. Have you two considered counseling or couples therapy?"

Kitty looked sad. "He doesn't think *we* have a problem. *I* have the problem. Besides, he'd never go. He says he doesn't believe in therapy. He thinks strong people can handle their problems themselves; therapists are just crutches for weak people."

"Do you think he'd read something about couples and improving relationships?"

"I don't know."

"Well, I'll make you a list of some good titles, just in case. It's called bibliotherapy. Sometimes it helps."

The next week, I gave a stress-management workshop for some of the administrative staff. Unfortunately, it was poorly attended because they were too stressed out with work to come. When I returned from the workshop, Gary was waiting for me.

Gary told me that Trent had canceled yesterday's session, then handed me a piece of paper. "I got this in the mail over the weekend. It's from Trent." He watched me as I read the letter.

"I don't know if you really understood what my life was like before," Trent had written. "I was so alone. But now you've made me see that I haven't been alone. My friends have always been there. The Church has been there. It's I who deserted them. I really was being arrogant. I don't want to offend you, but I really don't need you anymore. You've made me see that. And I'll always be grateful to you for that. In two weeks, my lawyer will be arguing to the court that I was the victim of entrapment. He's optimistic and so am I. God bless you. Sincerely, Paul Trent."

"Whew," I said. "That's beautiful. Most cases are not that easily resolved. But at least in this one, Trent got what he wanted."

"That's just what I felt," said Gary. "But I guess not every shrink feels the same way."

"What do you mean?"

Gary then told me he and Maggie had gone to his father's Sunday get-together that weekend. The usual crowd of psychoanalysts were standing around the buffet table, balancing their plates of bagels and nova, and talking. And his father came to Gary, put his arm around him and asked, "How's your case going, Garrison?" Everyone gathered around, while Milton Bernstein filled them in on the case: "Ego-dystonic homosexual whose repressed feelings of disgust and self-hatred enhanced by his activism in gay causes were suddenly unmasked by the trauma of being arrested on child-pornography charges."

Before he knew it, Gary was telling everyone there about his session with Trent, and he was thrilled by the fact that these people, whom he had known since childhood, were now listening to him talk about a case rather than the other way around. He thought they'd be amazed that he was able to deal with Trent's complaint in a few sessions, but the oldest analyst in the group, a man who had actually known Freud, said, "Well done, young Bernstein, it appears that you've taken a patient on the verge of self-discovery and set him back into uncharted waters for years to come."

After that everyone landed on Gary like a ton of bricks, even his father. "At Bellevue's department of *psychology*," he said, hitting the word with heavy irony, "they cure people a bit faster than we do," and everyone laughed.

Later in the afternoon, when the last guest had left, Gary went to the library where his father was working. "How could you allow me to be embarrassed and humiliated in that way?" Gary asked. His father peered at him over his bifocals and said, "You're not going to make it in this field, Garrison. You don't have the stomach for it."

"At that moment," said Gary, "I just saw him for who he was—someone who always had to put me down, make cutting remarks, not laugh at my jokes, cut me off with a look if I dared to question an order of his. And this was one time I wasn't going to let him get away with it. I just said, 'You're wrong, Dad. I may not write books that will become standard texts in the field. Or be the high priest of a psychoanalytic institute and have people fawning all over me. But I will help people to have better lives. This is who I am and this is what I do.' "

Murder and Mayhem

Chapter 7

I was supervising Ginger, who was just telling me about her new rotation in the psych ER and how Parnell was a great supervisor, when Gary burst into the room.

"What should I do, Fred?" he asked, panting.

I was about to ask Gary to wait a minute, when he saw Ginger and said, "Sorry to interrupt, Ginger, but I think I got a real problem."

"What's up?" I asked.

"Gloria's delusional. Thinks we're getting married. She saw my engagement notice, freaked, and ran out of the office."

The phone rang and I ignored it. "Slow down, Gary," I said. "Just tell me what's going on."

He collapsed into an empty chair and related what had just occurred. He had gone into his office at the Mental Hygiene Clinic and was startled by a purring voice. "Hello, sweetheart."

Gary jumped. "What the . . . what are *you* doing sitting in my office?"

Gloria pouted, her lipsticked mouth contrasting garishly with her pale face. Instead of being tightly furled, her hair was loose around her shoulders. "I thought you would be happy to see me, Garrison."

He shuddered. "I am, Gloria," he said carefully, backing around his desk to his chair. "By the way," he said sitting down, "how did you get in here?" The door between the reception area and the therapy offices at the Mental Hygiene Clinic was always kept locked.

"This," she said, pointing to her old hospital I.D., which dangled from the lapel of her dress just above her swollen breasts.

Obviously, thought Gary, the clerks would never challenge a physician. It was just one more confirmation of the threat Gloria posed. He had to get her a pregnancy test.

"Gloria," he began.

"Oh, Garrison." Her eyes gazed at him adoringly. "We have so much to talk about."

"Please," he said, wincing in spite of himself, "call me Mr. Bernstein."

"Oh, Garrison," she sighed. "I'm going to have your baby and you want me to call you *Mr. Bernstein?* You're so cute!" She leaned forward over the burgeoning mound of her belly. "What am I supposed to say when you meet my mother?" Addressing the chair next to her own, she said, "Hi, Mom. Meet the father of my child, Mr. Bernstein. You know," she went on, "I've been trying to figure out what to do now that I'm showing before we've even announced our engagement. I mean, can you have both an engagement party and a baby shower at the same time? Why not? We'll just skip the bridal shower."

Gary rubbed his temples. "Gloria, I think what we need to do before anything else is have you take a pregnancy test."

"Who needs a pregnancy test?" she exclaimed, standing and reaching for the hem of her skirt. "Just feel my belly, the baby's already started to kick."

"Gloria," he ordered. "Sit down. Right now." His heart was pounding in his chest. At the rate her pregnancy was progressing, she'd go into labor in his office.

"Now listen to me," he said after she sat obediently. "There are two things I want to do. I want you to have a gynecological exam, because I'm really concerned about this pregnancy, and I want you to have a psychiatric evaluation."

"Psychiatric evaluation?" She was on her feet again. "Why do I need a psychiatric evaluation? You cured me. You're wonderful. I no longer have skin dreams. I know I'll be able to work again, when the baby's old enough, of course. We'll get a nanny. Or Mother could baby-sit!"

Gary could feel his stomach sinking. He passed his hands over his eyes, his cheeks, his mouth, trying to get a grip on himself. She was decompensating, unraveling at top speed. He had never seen this before. I've got to get her to the psych ER now, he thought.

"Gloria, we have a lot to do. Let's start right now by getting you— and the baby—the best medical care."

"You're so right, Garrison," she said, swooping down to grab her purse from the floor and placing it on his desk. "Which is why I've been making a list. Let's see," she said, holding up a small notepad. "First there's the wedding gown. And then we have to think about where to get married. I think it should be a synagogue, don't you? But if you don't want to, I'll understand. And then there's the honeymoon. I've always wanted to go to Venice. And then there's the baby layette to think about." She caught his eye and smiled dreamily. "Do you think it will be a boy or a girl?"

Gary felt a sudden pang. This poor, poor woman, he thought. All she wants is a life and all I want is to have her admitted. "Gloria," he said kindly, "listen to me. It's important, I mean, it's really the procedure when a patient, I mean, you know, when anybody gets pregnant, we, just as a matter of course, as a standard procedure"— he was improvising wildly—"recommend that they go in for a psychiatric evaluation. This is a medically oriented clinic and the psychiatrists have the ultimate authority here, and . . . and"—he finished with a flourish—"it would be good for the baby."

Gloria positively beamed at him. *"Our* baby. All right, Garrison, let's go."

"Great. The baby will get the very best of care starting right now."

"You'll go with me?"

"Of course." He stood.

Gloria reached inside her bag and took out a compact. "You know, I have an idea," she said, looking at herself in the small mirror. "Why don't you come to dinner this Friday night? I'm a really good cook and it's time you met my mother." She dabbed at her nose. "She'll really like you."

"Shall we go? It's not far," he said gently, walking to the door.

"Can I leave my purse here?" she asked.

"No, you might need something. Better take it with you."

She reached for the bag and then stopped, transfixed.

Oh God, no, thought Gary, as she picked up the small silver frame. He lunged forward but it was too late.

"What is *this?*" she whispered. Then, with increasing volume, "You're *engaged? Engaged?*" She dropped the Tiffany-framed engagement notice on the floor, breaking the glass. "You didn't tell me you were engaged."

"We were engaged before I even met you," he said automatically.

Her voice quivered with hurt and fear. "You're going to break it off with her, right?"

He reached for her hand. "Don't worry about it, okay? Let's just go . . ."

"No! Answer me. Are you going to marry her?" she pleaded.

Gary tried to think fast. Was the best answer yes or no? He was thinking fast, but not straight.

"How could you do this to me?" she wailed as she ran out of the room while Gary stood frozen to the spot.

My phone rang and I ignored it again. I thought about how ironic it was that, of all the trainees, he was the one who insisted on adhering to the traditional analytic injunction against revealing anything of his private life to his patients. Now, his inadvertent violation of that rule had caused this crisis to escalate. I imagined that Gary was punishing himself for failing to obey his father's teachings.

"So what should I do, Fred?" he repeated.

"Whew," I sighed. "We've got a serious situation here. She's obviously quite psychotic. She needs a psychiatric evaluation and probably hospitalization. The major question is how do we get that done? She probably won't come in voluntarily at this point and I don't know if we've got enough evidence to state that she's dangerous to herself or others. So we might not be able to have the police get her."

We were silent for several moments, thinking. "Even if she's resistant, you've got to try and get her to come in on her own, Gary," I said. "She's a very sick woman. I think you need to do whatever it takes to get her here."

"Like telling her I'm going to break up with Maggie?"

"If you have to."

Tentatively, Gary said, "I guess you're right. I've got to get her in. But . . ."

"But what?" I asked.

"Lying to a patient. It just doesn't seem right."

"I know what you mean. I don't like it either. But in this case, I think it's necessary. Consider the alternatives. You can send the police to bring her in kicking and screaming or leave her out there in her current condition and God knows what will happen."

Gary nodded, looking glum. "Okay, I'll do it, but I won't like it."

"Me either, buddy," I said softly.

Ginger had listened to Gary silently, a look of concern on her face. She reached over and tapped Gary's arm. "I'm really sorry you've got to go through this. It's so bizarre."

"Gary," I said, "I've got to finish up with Ginger now. Would you like to stay?"

"Please stay," said Ginger. "You look so upset."

"No. I've got a patient in ten minutes. Thanks, both of you."

"See you later. And keep me informed about what's going on," I said as Gary left, closing my door behind him.

"So, Ginger, you were telling me about the ER."

"Right," she said. "It's real lively down there. Like, there was this marine I saw today. Menacing-looking Vietnam vet. He had written on his forehead with a ballpoint pen, 'Don't fuck with me.' It was written backward, you know, like he had done it looking in a mirror? And I'm in the room alone with him."

There was a knock at my door. Before I could answer, it opened. "Don't you ever answer your phone, Covan?" said Weenie, looking as harried and agitated as ever.

"What can I do for you, Malcolm?"

"The state is making a site visit in two weeks and they're going to be reviewing the charts. We're having a meeting now to discuss preparation for the survey."

"Now? I've got a full day, Malcolm. I can't go anywhere now."

"But I've been trying to call you. They want you at the meeting. All the department heads are there."

I looked at my calendar. I had an appointment with an inpatient unit chief. "Okay, Malcolm," I said. "Just give me a few minutes to cancel an appointment and I'll be right up."

Weenie said abruptly, "Good," and then disappeared from sight.

"Grrrrrrr," I growled. Ginger chuckled.

"So you're alone in the room with Rambo?"

"He asked me for a cigarette. And when I told him 'I'm sorry, we don't allow smoking here,' he picked up my telephone and for a minute I thought he was going to hit me with it. Instead he smashed it down on the floor."

"Sounds reasonable to me," I said. She smiled.

"How about this one? Yesterday, I was walking a patient from the waiting area to my office and there was a young guy sitting in a wheelchair in a one-point restraint, and he says, real politely, 'Excuse me. Excuse me? Miss? Are you a doctor?' I moved closer to his wheelchair and he starts to whisper something. Now you got to remember that this guy looks real normal. He wasn't agitated or anything. So I lean over him to hear what he's saying. Just then, he grabs my blouse and rips it open. Buttons fly everywhere. I shriek, he's hysterically laughing, and the aides and HPs come running and take him away to the isolation room. I spent the next hour fixing my blouse."

"You could have been hurt," I said.

"It's odd, but I feel safe down there. I know all the HPs and aides. And Parnell's down there to take care of me too. And then there's the cops who have brought people to the ER and are still hanging around. So I feel in control. It's okay, hard on my wardrobe, though. I mean, I could have done without Jack the Ripper."

I laughed with her, but then I said, "Don't kid yourself, Ginger. You've got to be careful down there. A few years ago, one of the attendings in the ER refused to admit some guy who was faking psychosis. He just wanted a warm place to stay for a while. The patient got really pissed off and waited for the doctor in the street and then stabbed him when he got off duty. The attending survived but was pretty messed up for a while." Standing up, I said, "So no heroics. And when the cops bring you someone in handcuffs or restraints, keep him that way. Trust the cops. Okay? They've got more experience with this stuff than you."

I got back from the meeting upstairs and picked up my stack of messages on Lucy's desk. One slip said, "Mr. Bernstein called. Emergency. Call immediately."

While I was dialing his number, Gary appeared at my door, his face pale. "I'm glad you're back, Fred. Gloria's threatening to kill Maggie."

"What? Come in and sit down," I said.

"Gloria left a message on my machine. She said she found a solution to our problem. She says she's going to kill Maggie—right away—for me and the baby."

"Did she say anything else?"

"Yes. She said I shouldn't worry about a thing, she'll make all the arrangements."

"Uh oh," I said. "We've got to call administration and the unit chief of the Mental Hygiene Clinic right away."

When I got Weenie on the phone and told him of the situation, his only advice was that Gary should be sure to "document the episode on the patient's chart in detail." The clinic chief recommended that we send the cops and get Gloria to the psych ER *stat*.

"She's right, Gary," I said. "We've got ample indication that Gloria's dangerous. She's got to be brought in right away."

"I just hate to think of the police scaring her. You know?"

"Well, I've got to call the police. But if you can get her to the ER before they pick her up, that's okay too. I'll call Parnell now and fill him in on the situation so he can alert the ER staff. If the police bring her in, we don't want some resident to release her after deciding that she's just a pregnant physician who got brought in by mistake."

Gary looked distressed by this last thought. "Don't worry," I tried to reassure him. "Once she's in, she won't be able to get out."

Standing, Gary said, "I'm going to try to get Gloria on the phone."

"One other thing," I said. "You'd better call Maggie and warn her."

"Do you think she's really in danger?"

"Might be," I said. "We don't want to take any chances."

At our departmental meeting the next day, attended by the entire psychology staff and trainees, Gary's situation took center stage. Although I had called the cops, when they went to Gloria's apartment, it was empty, her invalid mother gone. They said they'd keep trying to track her down and would return to the apartment tomorrow. But as of this morning, they had still not located her.

Maria asked, "Does she know where you and Maggie live?"

Gary was doing his best to act nonchalant. "She has my home phone number. Fred has us give out our number to patients. But we're not listed, so I don't think she can get our address." A hot discussion of my phone-number policy followed, in which Gary didn't participate. After it cooled down, he said, "The engagement notice listed the name of my father, his institute, Maggie's last name and the name of the company she works for. It's just a matter of time before she shows up at one of those places. Isn't it?"

"They ought to give us combat pay in this place," snarled Rhoda. "Thirteen years ago, I was out on disability for a year after I was attacked by a patient. I was working on an adult inpatient ward and a guy was hiding behind the entrance door. When I came in, he whacked me on the head with a chair. I was almost permanently blinded by the injury."

"Right after that, they put in those Plexiglas windows in all the doors so it wouldn't happen again," said Carl. "We used to call them 'Rhoda Windows.'"

"I never realized this place was so dangerous," said Kitty.

"Too late now," said Nick. "And don't think that two-hour course in basic self-defense they gave us is going to help any. That only teaches you how to escape without hurting the patient. Myself, I started Kung Fu training." He karate-chopped the air.

"And I thought I was the only one who was paranoid. I'm taking a street-fighting course, just in case I come up against something I can't escape from," said Elizabeth. "I'm learning to punch, kick, break fingers, stomp on heads. I'm baaad."

"After my latest adventure in the ER," said Ginger, "Parnell told me that 'like all women' I let my guard down and let patients approach too closely. Don't you think that's a bit sexist?"

"Not at all," I said. "It's true. Parnell and I have done workshops with staff from all over the hospital. In one of the exercises, everyone gets in two lines and one line walks toward the other. As soon as the person being approached feels uncomfortable, he or she holds up a hand and says 'Stop.' Guess who says 'Stop' first?"

"The nurses," said Elizabeth.

"No one," said Mike. "The cops frisk them. The nurses wait for doctor's orders. The social workers refer them to the end of the line. And the psychologists ask, 'What brings you here?' "

"Very funny," I chuckled. "The truth is, the HPs—regardless of gender—say 'Stop' first. Then the rest of the men do it. The women who are not cops are the last to hold up their hands."

"Probably, it's because a woman's orientation is toward intimacy and closeness," said Maria. "But here we have to control that instinct. An attack can come when we least expect it. Most of the time when a staff member is hurt, it's because he or she wasn't paying attention or was ignoring cues."

"But sometimes things happen and there's just nothing you can do about it," said Mike. "Remember the pregnant pathologist who was working in her office on a Saturday afternoon a couple of years ago?"

There was a moment's silence. It was a case we all remembered well. Although none of us actually knew her, Bellevue is our home and it was like a death in the family. Only worse, because we were also afraid for ourselves until the killer was caught.

"She was beaten, raped, and strangled by a man who lived undetected at Bellevue because he was masquerading as a doctor."

"Gloria Nadler is a real doctor," said Gary quietly. "She doesn't even have to wear a costume."

"And don't forget the patient who killed the Bellevue psychiatrist's wife," said Carl.

"I don't think I want to hear this," Gary groaned.

"No, listen. You really should know about it. Just like your case, a patient with a psychotic transference was convinced that eliminating her shrink's wife would get her married to him. Somehow the patient found out where the psychiatrist lived and waited in the lobby of the building."

"What happened?" asked Gary.

"When the wife came into the lobby, the patient shot her while their son watched."

"Oh God," he said, covering his eyes.

"Carl's right," I said, "you can learn from that case. The psychiatrist's big mistake was breaking off contact with the patient. He wouldn't speak with her and that drove her further into the delusion. So don't stop trying to contact Gloria."

"If you'll all excuse me now, I think I'll take that sage advice and go dial her number once again," said Gary, leaving the conference room quickly.

There were many reported sightings of Gloria over the next week. Nick saw someone of her description lurking near the elevators in the lobby. Ginger swore she saw her peering through the glass door of the reception area in the Mental Hygiene Clinic. Kiesha thought she was standing in the doorway of the staff cafeteria. But the apparition always disappeared before anyone could summon the hospital police. She didn't call Gary at work or home when he was there, but he thought she might have on other occasions because there were hang-ups on both answering machines every day. Maggie wondered if the pregnant woman, dressed all in black, wearing sunglasses, who followed her into the subway one rainy morning was Gloria. Gary escorted Maggie to and from work from that day on.

Eight days after the death threat, I met Gary at the departmental mailboxes. "Why haven't the police picked her up yet?" Gary asked.

"I checked with the sergeant this morning. Her house is still empty. The neighbors say she and her mother are away. Maybe a vacation?"

"Do you think she's really gone?" Gary looked hopeful. "Maybe we're all overreacting and just imagining that she's stalking Maggie and me."

murder and mayhem

"I hope so," I said. The strain of the past week was evident on his face. "But still be careful. Okay?"

At the same time Gary thought he was being stalked by Gloria, Weenie was stalking the staff. It was the fourth survey in the last six months and Weenie was in a frenzy, sending back every chart if a treatment plan wasn't fully spelled out, a diagnosis was abbreviated, a signature or initials were missing, an "i" was undotted or a "t" was uncrossed. "If they can't read it, we'll get a citation," he whined.

I understood his concern. As a municipal hospital, we are regulated by agencies from the city, state, and the independent nationwide Joint Commission on Accreditation of Healthcare Organizations, fondly referred to as "the Joint." We are subjected to continuous rounds of surveys, audits, site visits—each agency has a different name for the same process. The general public is rightfully in rebellion against the paternalistic, authoritarian attitude of many physicians. The dramatic increase in health-care costs and the frightening stories of gross malpractice have also fed the uprising. The results can be seen in the proliferation of lawsuits against hospitals and doctors that allege improper treatment. In an effort to protect the public—as well as the hospitals and doctors—the city, state, and the Joint have taken charge. Each has different rules and criteria regarding all matters from the minimum square footage that should exist for each patient to the number of times we write each week in each patient's chart. We must keep our records as if a lawsuit *will* be instituted and we will need to defend our every thought and action in court. It's all cover-your-ass, leave-a-paper-trail work and it consumes fully half of our time. When I run a ninety-minute group for the adolescents in the Bellevue school, it takes another ninety minutes to fill out the charts.

Even worse from the hospital's point of view are the citations Weenie spoke about. Each citation lowers our overall score. Too low a score or one major citation and the reimbursements from Medicare and Medicaid will be cut off. Because we couldn't function without that money, Weenie and his fellow hospital administrators have a right to be terrified. The hospital administrators were

CRAZY ALL THE TIME

originally intended to help us do our jobs, but because their jobs have become primarily to deal with the surveys, our job now is to help them satisfy the regulatory administrators. To make matters even worse for Weenie, but better for the rest of us, the physical plant was also being inspected. This meant that in addition to worrying over charts, he needed to make sure that no graffiti remained on walls, no mouse droppings could be found, the heat functioned properly, the air quality was high, and the patients' rooms weren't overcrowded and had toothbrushes.

Meanwhile, Gary's predicament seemed to have aroused in both the students and staff a preoccupation with violence and homicide. During my weekly seminar for the trainees on psychological testing, David asked me if I had ever done a psychological workup on a killer.

"Sure," I said. "Everyone from Mafia hit men to celebrity murderers like Mark David Chapman. And, of course, I've also tested violent psychotic killers whose acts were completely bizarre."

"What do the tests tell you?" David asked. "Can you pick up violent tendencies?"

"In the case of the hit men, not really," I said. "In the few I have examined there were no indications of acute psychiatric illness. If I hadn't known what they did for a living, I never would have guessed. They could have been merchants or stockbrokers. Which is not surprising, because they were completely professional. One of them even told me, 'It's strictly business. These guys know the rules. They break the rules, they get killed. That's the rule.' "

"So it's like these killers are normal?" asked Kiesha.

"Well, yes," I said. "If you consider it normal to kill people, cut them up into little pieces, and dispose of the bits in various parts of the country. I just said that in the cases of these particular men, there was nothing on their tests or in the clinical interviews I conducted to indicate their occupation."

"But were they abnormal?" persisted Kiesha.

"This brings us back to that old question, What is abnormal? These guys certainly were aggressive, but no more so than a randomly sampled collection of successful businessmen or professionals. What was different was what these guys did with their aggression."

"What about Mark David Chapman?" asked David eagerly. "What was he like?"

"Everyone always asks that question. I wanted to know, too, which is why I, like many others, wanted to interview him. When he was brought to the hospital, it was a media event. He arrived in an armored car with a caravan of police cars. And when he got out wearing a bulletproof vest, surrounded by flak-jacketed, shotgun-toting correction officers, everyone went wild—flashbulbs flashing, reporters yelling, TV cameras going. He was a celebrity and he had become one just by killing a celebrity. Sad, isn't it?"

"So what was it like interviewing the guy who killed Lennon?" Nick asked. "Weren't you ready to kill him yourself?"

"Kind of," I said. "I walked in angry and disgusted. Then I asked him, as a preliminary question, 'What's it like being here?' And he said, 'What do you think?' laughed uncomfortably, and for the next several minutes apologized profusely for laughing. He seemed to me to be one of the most pathetic, pitiful, and self-denigrating human beings I had ever met. And I just couldn't hate him or be angry with him anymore."

"Was he obviously crazy?" Gary asked.

"Well, he wasn't a violent, vicious maniac. He was diagnosed a simple or residual schizophrenic, someone without any prominent psychotic symptoms. It was like he was a shell of a person; even his body seemed to have a doughy quality."

"So what made him do it?" asked Kiesha frowning intently. "Lennon was a big shot, so he figured that by killing a big shot, he'd be one?"

"Yes, he did it to gain attention, but in a more primal sense. Primitive tribes cannibalize their victims as a way of incorporating the spirit, power, and courage of their enemies. Lennon had passion, energy, creativity, all the things that Chapman didn't have and wanted."

"What about the violent psychotic killers?" asked Wayne. "You certainly were able to see something on their psychological tests."

"Yes. Definitely. They have some of the most chilling Rorschach responses you'll ever hear."

"Like what? What did they see?"

"Well, one guy who comes to mind saw bloody parts and described in detail how the bodies had been mangled. He saw that on all the cards. On card four, for example, which doesn't even have red in the picture, he saw a man hanging with hooks through his arms, pieces of rotting flesh were falling from his body; in addition, his penis was swollen and oozing and was being eaten by flies."

"Yuuck," said Nick. "What had that sicko done?"

"Well, I'll tell you, if you insist, although it is probably the most stomach-turning case I ever worked on. He was a twenty-one-year-old schizophrenic who was having a psychotic episode after having ingested a combination of rum, marijuana, hash, and unidentified street drugs. He became convinced that his mother was possessed by the devil and decided to put his theory to the test. He would masturbate in front of her and if he was able to, quote, 'come in her eyes,' this would be proof that she was not possessed."

I looked at the students, whose faces ran the gamut from shock to disgust, and continued. "So he confronted her in the bedroom, which, by the way, is where most matricides take place, and when he began to masturbate, she tried to stop him, as most mothers would. It was a bit of a setup. Now he had his proof that she was possessed. He grabbed her steam iron, bashed in her brains and gouged out her eyes in order to 'release the devil,' and then used her scissors to do surgery on her, cutting up her breasts and her vagina and eating parts of them."

"Peo-ple," sang Nick, drawing out the syllables Streisand style, "eat-ing peo-ple."

"Well, our time is up," I said. "But if you want further installments on this topic, don't forget to come to the next departmental colloquium."

Lucy came running up as we were leaving the seminar room. "Dr. Nadler's on my phone. Wants to speak to you, Gary. She says its urgent."

Gary pushed passed me and ran to Lucy's desk. When I approached a few moments later, he gave me the thumbs-up sign. Hanging up the phone, he filled me in. Gloria had agreed to meet him in the psych ER that evening at nine. She was calling Gary from Connecticut, where she had been for the past few days signing her mother into a nursing home.

Because Gary was extremely nervous about the rendezvous with Gloria and about leaving Maggie alone that night, I invited Maggie to stay with my family while Gary and I went to the hospital.

Opening the door marked PSYCHIATRIC EMERGENCY SERVICE, Gary said, "This always feels like I'm entering Limbo, the outer circle of Hell, the land of the forgotten." I almost accused him of melodrama, until I looked around. Three Port Authority cops were standing next to a small woman in filthy clothes who was screaming something I couldn't make out. A stench of body odor permeated the air. Three HPs, two men and a woman, sat along the wall, laughing and talking. The walk-through metal detector and two red lines on the floor marked the next layer of ER security. Inside the lines, I saw a woman strapped into a wheelchair, clutching pieces of ragged paper. A thin, gray-haired man prowled the perimeter—but never touched the red line—like a caged lion. Catching my eye, he mimed putting a cigarette to his mouth. I shook my head and the man glared at me.

Gary approached the three HPs. "Hi, I'm Garrison Bernstein, one of the psychology interns. This is Dr. Covan, chief psychologist. We're meeting a patient here who's coming in voluntarily, but we expect that we'll be involuntarily committing her."

"No problem," the female officer said. "I'm Perez, this is Matteos and this is Barley. Just let us know if you need us."

"I'm just going to check out the office," said Gary. I stayed put, watching the outside doors as Gary crossed the red line. I turned to see which office Gary would use and saw two men stretched out in chairs, their faces devoid of expression, staring at a wall TV. The woman tied to the wheelchair thrust her sheaf of torn bits of papers at Gary. "Doctor, doctor," she said thickly. "Help me." One of the papers drifted to his feet. He stooped down and handed it back, wordlessly. "Doctor, doctor," she repeated. Gary veered sharply to avoid the pacing man who had asked me for a cigarette.

At ten o'clock Gary nudged me. "Here she is," he said under his breath, nodding toward the doorway of the psych ER.

Gloria was dressed in an ankle-length black coat which she clutched across the mound of her stomach. She wore sunglasses and a black beret that covered her forehead and ears. "Hi, Garrison," she smiled warmly, wiggling her gloved hand at his face. "Long time no see."

"I thought we would talk in my office, Gloria," he said, taking her by the arm while she hesitated.

"I'd rather not," she said. "Why here? Why not in your office upstairs? Or at the coffee shop?"

"I already explained," he said patiently. "I'm on ER duty and I need to stay here until the end of my shift."

"But I don't feel comfortable in there where those patients are. Let's just sit out here and talk."

"But it's private in my office," he said, gently taking her arm. "We have private things to discuss. About the baby."

"About us?"

"Yes, Gloria," he said. "About us."

I followed at a distance and sat in a chair outside the office he had selected. He left the door slightly ajar. From inside the office, I heard her say, "Garrison, I just want you to know I forgive you everything. I understand that you were engaged before we fell in love and know that you've just needed time to let Margaret off easy. I wouldn't expect you to break her heart like that, so cruelly."

"Gloria, you need to listen to me now . . ."

"Really, I understand," she replied. "I do. I'm not trying to rush you, it's just that, since Mother's in a nursing home now, I'm all alone. I just get lonely without you there."

The deep breath Gary took at that point was audible. "Gloria, in my opinion, you are delusional. You've threatened Maggie's life. I think you are dangerous. You're under severe stress. You're out of control. It's my belief that you need to be hospitalized."

"Garrison, of course, I'll go to the hospital. I wouldn't think of having a baby at home. Do you really think I'd even consider having our baby at home?"

"Gloria, I'm not the father of your baby. We never had sex. It's probable that you're not pregnant."

I heard a chair move suddenly across the floor. "What are you talking about!" Then Gloria's scream. "Ahhhhhhh. I hate you!"

I got to the doorway just in time to see Gary pulling her hand from his throat while she went for his eyes with the long red nails of her other hand. "Help!" I yelled to the HPs, still sitting along the wall. "Now!" They were at my side, cloth restraints in hand, before I'd figured out how or where to grab Gloria. Quickly, expertly, the three HPs bound her hands, removed her from the office, and bundled her onto a gurney.

"Come on," I said to Gary, who had smears of blood all over his face. "Let's go get someone to look at your cuts."

"I'm okay," he said, as we watched Gloria struggling against her restraints as they wheeled her to the isolation room.

After Gary had his cuts attended to, we returned to the psych ER and gave the attending psychiatrist the information he needed for Gloria's involuntary admission paperwork. By the time we reached my home again, Gary was completely spent and could only nod or shake his head in response to Maggie's questions. I could only feel relief that the matter was under control, at least for the time being.

The preoccupation with violence among the staff and students continued. At the special departmental meeting I called the next day to discuss the impending state survey, I had trouble getting them on that topic.

"She was so lonely, so trapped with that intrusive, arthritic mother," said Jenny.

"What makes a woman like that crack up?" asked Elizabeth. "And why does she suddenly turn violent?"

"Anybody can be violent," Mike said. "Look at Milgram's famous experiment where ordinary people gave what they believed to be near-lethal electric shocks solely because they were ordered to. The vast majority became willing torturers rather than disobey authority."

"I always thought it interesting," mused Maria, "that none of the subjects were women."

"He was measuring obedience, not compassion," said Carl.

"Then you admit women are more sensitive and compassionate?" challenged Rhoda.

"No, I merely mean that the results would have been the same or worse. Women make even better doormats," Carl grinned.

"We think that murderers are different from us. But Eichmann, who killed millions, was certified normal by half a dozen psychiatrists," said Wayne.

Kiesha gave Wayne a friendly poke. "Don't forget Cain, the first kid on the planet. He killed because he had a bad case of sibling rivalry. It's in our genes. It's part of our heritage."

"But what about the studies that show that people with violent or murderous tendencies were abused or neglected in childhood?" asked Ginger. "That would seem to indicate that nurture is more important than nature."

"I vote with Kiesha," said Carl. "It's genetic. People are born twisted just like their DNA. Look at all those twin studies, where identical twins reared apart since birth marry women with the same name, get the same grades in school, even choose cherry vanilla as their favorite ice cream."

"Cherry vanilla may be built into the DNA but not violence," declared Rhoda, who liked nothing more than a good argument. "All those genetic theories of violence like extra Y chromosomes turned out to be so much hogwash."

"Then what do you think it is, Rhoda? Child beating? Poverty? Unemployment? Homelessness?" said Carl. "Myself, I'm getting real reactionary in my old age. I'm nearly convinced that all those things are just part of the fallout from bad genes, the same way violent tendencies occur."

"Now, Carl, you can't dismiss the role of social conditions," said Rhoda. "Look at the Harry Harlow monkey studies. The babies raised with cloth surrogate mothers grew up to be normal while the babies with wire mothers were violent."

"My guess is it's a combination—nature and nurture," I said. "But we won't figure it out now. So could we talk about the jobs that have to be done before the survey? Anyway, we'll have lots of time to continue this discussion of violence at next week's colloquium. If you recall, Dr. Solomon, the expert on parent killing, is making a presentation. She says she's writing a book on a new theory of the origin of violence that will revolutionize the way we think about it."

Dr. Sydney Anne Solomon had made it obvious from our phone conversations that she was a Major Thinker in the field and should be accorded all the ruffles and flourishes due a visiting dignitary. Mike had gone to meet her at the airport and was standing in front of the room with Dr. Solomon as I entered. I walked over to meet her.

"I came prepared to give an unusual speech," she told me. "It's the first public statement anywhere of the contents of my as yet unpublished work, *Oedipus and Electra: The Natural History of the Parricidal Impulse.*"

She gripped us immediately with her opening statement. "The wish to murder one's parents is universal. So the question we should ask ourselves is not why there are so many parricides but why so few." She then went on to describe how "this wish, this need, this overwhelming urge" develops. "It begins at birth." There was an audible groan at the mention of the birth trauma, but Solomon gave it a new twist. "Think about it," she said, in a dramatic whisper, "the first experience a baby has is rejection from the womb."

"That's *e*jection," someone called out.

"From the womb's point of view," Solomon answered back tartly. "For the baby it's the first in a long series of rejections. So its first emotion in the world outside the womb is rage, pure blinding rage. And it expresses it in a long howling cry of pain, which we euphemistically call 'taking the first breath.' "

She paused and looked at her audience. She then took us through the oral, anal, and genital stages showing how the parental need to socialize the child inevitably leads to frustration. At this point, everyone settled back for what seemed to have become standard Freudian fare.

"As the mother draws out the interval between breast or bottle feedings, as the infant is forced to violate its own need to urinate and defecate when and where it pleases, as the boy child is made to give up his mother as a sex object and the girl her father, the small, hard knot of rage, frustration, and pain that began at birth swells and grows until by the age of five or six the child, and I do not exaggerate here, becomes a seething mass of homicidal rage."

Carl was on his feet, waving his hand high above his head. "Dr. Solomon, do you have one shred of evidence, one piece of data, one statistic to support that statement?"

"Your defensiveness at hearing a buried truth spoken aloud for the first time is a natural one. The answer is that the evidence is in your psyche. Just listen to the tone of your own voice right now."

Carl sat down and Solomon continued. "It is not until puberty, when the child has the cognitive ability to plan and see cause and effect, that the impulse to kill one's parents becomes fully conscious. Suddenly the earlier thoughts, the fleeting wishes, take on a new reality. The child has taken on secondary sex characteristics. He or she has grown taller, stronger, more competent. This is when children who have been spanked or beaten often hit back. It is when the child who has been frustrated is capable of taking action."

This was too much for me. "You're saying that a kid who's made to do normal kid things—like we were all made to do and we now make our kids do—is an incipient killer?" I asked.

Solomon stepped forward and stretched out her hand. "Be honest. We're all professionals here. You have all, I hope, been in therapy. Can you honestly say you have never had a murderous feeling toward one or both of your parents? Can you honestly say you don't see this among your patients?"

There was the sound of muffled conversations in the audience. Jenny Noh raised her hand, then stood and said loudly, "What about the child of parents who are nurturing and giving?"

"All parents will frustrate their children," Solomon intoned. "It is in the very nature of things. Although my parents were nurturing on the surface, with the help of analysis, I came to recognize their abusiveness, their unavailability, their narcissism. I remember only too vividly how my mother would take me on shopping expeditions when I was little and buy clothes she knew I hated. How I had to practice piano for an hour every day. And clean my room before I could play with my friends. And come to dinner on time and eat with my family. And after dinner my sister and I had to do the dishes and clean up the kitchen every night."

After a pause, she continued. "All my patients have reported similar experiences. Let me make myself perfectly clear. The wish to kill one's parents is a totally normal and universal phenomenon."

There was a moment's silence and then Rhoda's voice rang out caustically. "Then why doesn't everybody go out and commit parricide?"

"Right! Right!" trumpeted Dr. Solomon, shaking her fists. "That's the question. Why don't we all do it? The answer is, and my research is irrefutable, that society forces us to repress these impulses, to drive them into the subconscious, because they are so disruptive to the social fabric. And the increase in matricides and patricides is proof of the fact that the impulse exists universally."

"What increase?" yelled Carl. "Cite your sources."

"Read my book. It's all there. It's also based on my experience with my patients. In fact, I came to this conclusion only after virtually every patient expressed the wish to kill his or her parents. Don't be fooled. Your patients may not express it openly, but if you listen, it is there, in their dreams, in their associations, in their references. It may be disguised, it may be symbolic, but it is there."

At this point, it was obvious that Solomon was losing her audience. I stood. "Thank you very much, Dr. Solomon. We're very grateful that you took the time to share these fascinating . . ."

"If we could only take a few moments more," Dr. Solomon interrupted. "I could lead you all through some experiential exercises that would allow you to get in touch with your own murderous rage."

I looked around at the faces of the audience. Most were eyeing each other or grimacing. "I'm sorry, Dr. Solomon, we just didn't allot enough time for your entire presentation But we greatly appreciate everything we've been able to hear." I began clapping and the rest of the audience stood and clapped also as they moved toward the door.

"I don't know about you, but I'm going to be watching my back when I go home to my teenagers tonight," Maria said to me as we walked toward our offices, leaving Dr. Solomon in Mike's care.

"I know what you mean," I said, thinking about how all four of my sons have been obsessed with guns, swords, and martial arts from at least the time each of them learned to walk.

As we passed Lucy's desk she told me that Ginger had called, wondering if she could see me first thing in the morning; things had gotten a bit "bloody" in the ER and she needed to talk to me. I checked my book and told Lucy to tell Ginger that I'd see her at 8:30 but only for a half hour. What was she talking about? I wondered. And why had Ginger missed the colloquium?

The next day all anyone in the hospital seemed to talk about was the suicide in the ER. The hospital rumor mill had gone into overdrive, providing varying accounts of the episode. "The guy was carrying a gun when he came in." "He wrestled it from a cop." "The cops killed him and said it was a suicide." "He was killed in a crossfire." And so on.

I was getting worried because Ginger had been in the ER and had left that message with Lucy about things getting bloody. When she missed our 8:30 appointment, I became really concerned. And later that morning, when Lucy said that Ginger had called in sick, I called her at home. She said only that she had been in the ER, had seen the suicide, that she was okay, just a little tired and felt like she had the flu.

"Ginger, are you sure you're okay?" I asked.

"Oh yeah, sure," she assured me. "I'm fine. It's just a bug. I'll be over it tomorrow."

We rescheduled our appointment for the next morning.

Ginger missed the next day as well. Two days later, she was standing at my door, somewhat the worse for wear. Her auburn hair looked unwashed, her suit rumpled.

I welcomed her in. "Ginger, how are you?"

"I'm fine," she said in a monotone, not moving from the door. She looked tired, maybe even depressed. There was a bland, emotionless quality to her voice known as "flat affect."

"You don't look so good."

She waved her hands dismissively. "I'm really okay. Ready to get back to work."

"Sit down. Let's talk a minute before you go."

She pointed to the slim gold watch she always wore. "I'm running late at the ER, Fred." She forced a smile. "See you."

"Ginger," I called after her. "Why did you come by?"

"I just wanted to let you know I was okay. I'll see you later."

A half hour later she was back. "Fred, I'm losing it," she said. She had gone into the ER, thinking how good it was to be back after two days of chicken soup and soap opera. One of the hospital police had come over to ask about the "incident" as she put it. "Ginger," he had said teasingly, "I heard you were there when Ortiz messed up the floor." A female cop called her a heroine. While she tried to talk to them, a patient in an army jacket kept barking orders to invisible troops.

"It sounded like I was in a wind tunnel, Fred," she said. "Every time the guy gave a command, it reverberated. All I could think about were the cops' guns. Did they all have their guns? Were the guns in their holsters? Then all of a sudden I looked down at the floor and it had red streaks across it, like . . ."

She breathed out. "When I blinked, the floor was clean. At that point, I just walked out and came up here to see you."

"Ginger," I said, "tell me about what happened when that guy shot himself. I never heard the whole story."

Pushing back her hair from her shoulder, she said hesitantly, "Well . . . you know . . . it was like everybody's been saying. This guy, Ortiz, was brought into the ER by the cops who had picked him up at Penn Station because he had been yelling and threatening the commuters. His hands were cuffed behind his back, but then when he got to the ER, he asked one of the cops if he could go to the bathroom. He had calmed down and seemed pretty reasonable, so the cop undid one of the cuffs and he grabbed the cop's gun. That's all there is to it."

"That's all? Then how did he wind up dead?"

"Oh that?" she said with a shrug as though I'd asked her where she put my pen. "He was waving the gun around, yelling, and I tried to get him to give me the gun. And for a moment there I thought he might, when all of a sudden he just . . . shot himself."

"He put the gun to his head?"

"To his temple. Yeah."

"Are you aware that you're exhibiting symptoms of posttraumatic stress disorder? You're familiar with those symptoms, right? Exaggerated startle response, intrusive reliving of the experience, flashbacks, hypervigilance, impaired concentration and attention, flat affect. I think you've got PTSD. It's appropriate, given what you went through."

Human beings have the most remarkable ability to survive some of the worst horrors imaginable. But at a price—the separation of thought from feelings. It may seem a bargain when you're purchasing survival, but the actual cost afterward can be a lot higher. Try as we may to forget, ignore, suppress, or cast out these "bad" feelings, they come back in the form of the classic PTSD symptoms. It would be nice if they could be excised like a tumor or erased with a forgetting pill, but the only way we have to exorcise them is to drag them back, as painful as that can be, into the light of day.

"What should I do about it?" Ginger asked.

"Well, there's a technique called crisis intervention debriefing. It's used with emergency workers—like police or firefighters— who've experienced a traumatic event. That's what I think we should do now."

"What do we do?"

"You'll recall the entire event, alternating between what happened and what you thought and felt about it. You'll concentrate and bring up the event in great detail, as well as all your thoughts and feelings during it all. Eventually the PTSD symptoms disappear."

"I'll give it a shot," she said.

Then she told me about the event. She was just getting ready to leave her office in the psych ER, when she heard the sound of footsteps running. Then, she told me, it was like it was happening in slow motion. She recalled the city and hospital police moving past her like underwater swimmers. Then, almost as an afterimage, the guns. Larger than she imagined when they were holstered, with big black barrels. Then a pulse throbbing painfully in her throat.

She ran, walked? She didn't remember. She was moving but they weren't. A frozen semicircle of police with their guns drawn. And then Ortiz, *standing,* no longer chained to the gurney, his eyes wild and desperate and terrified. And in his hand, the handcuff still dangling from his wrist, a gun identical to the others, the black barrel pointing to his temple.

Someone grabbed her arm as she tried to walk past him. A cop. "Stand back, lady," he warned.

"I'm a psychologist," she said. "Let me talk to him."

He let go of her arm. "Don't walk any closer," he said.

Behind Ortiz, she could see the other patients, a tableau of horror and fear, their eyes riveted on the shabbily dressed armed figure. A fat, unkempt woman tied to a wheelchair, was caught in mid-act, her hands still clawing the air, her mouth forming an unspoken word.

Ginger felt eerily calm, in control. It was up to her.

"Mr. Ortiz, I'd like to talk to you a minute. Please put down the gun."

She took a step toward him.

"Any closer and I'll shoot," he said. His eyes darted wildly.

For a moment her mind spun absurdly. Oddly, she thought of the movie *Blazing Saddles,* its black star holding a gun to his own head, saying, "Don't move or I'll shoot the nigger." But this was real. This was happening.

She stayed where she was. She was quiet, calm, in control.

"Put down the gun," she coaxed. "We'll work things out together. You're not alone in this."

"You don't know *anything,*" he screamed.

"I'll help you," she said. "I'll help you through this."

Ortiz looked at her and began to tremble, his gun arm shaking.

Tentatively, walking a tightrope, she moved the toe of her left foot a half step in front. The silence was overwhelming, the very air alive. She could feel everyone breathe with her, take the step with her.

He was hesitating. "Please," she soothed. She took another step. Calm, in control.

"Stop!" The sound of his voice boomed like thunder. Her right foot hung just above the floor.

CRAZY ALL THE TIME

"It's all right." She let the ball of her right foot touch down.

He moved the gun away from his head.

Now, she thought. She could feel the cops stirring in back of her.

Then a blur of motion, the film speeding up. Ortiz jerking his arm toward the patients, screaming, his arm swinging back. She suspended in midstep, unable to move. He raising his arm. The sound ripping through her body. Blood. Ortiz lying on the floor. Blood and brains on the floor. Herself throwing up.

"What have you been thinking about since the episode?" I asked when she was finished.

"I was thinking about . . . how I should have been . . . able to save him." Her tone was dispassionate, but her hands were clenched.

"So you were thinking you should have been able to save him," I repeated. "Could you explain that to me some more? How was it that you think you should have been able to save him?"

She bit her upper lip, and for the first time since we had been talking looked away from me, her voice coming from a far distance. "If I were a really good psychologist, if I understood really how people think . . ."

"Yes?" I prompted.

"I would have been able to connect with him better; I would have known what to say. If I had been able to *distract* him, so the cops could grab him. I just know I should have been able to stop him." She closed her eyes for a minute and rubbed them, leaving traces of mascara on her cheeks. "See, I don't know how, and that just shows that I'm not a good psychologist. I should have been able to do it."

I leaned forward and tapped her gently on her tightly laced fingers. "Really?"

She took a deep breath and sighed. For a moment some of her old spunkiness returned. "Look, Fred, come on. Let's say somebody walks out on a ledge and is going to jump, who're you going to call? You call the psychologist. Right? The police call in people who are mental health experts to do this. You and I should be able to do it too."

"Ginger, those people get special training to do that kind of work.

I haven't been trained to do it. To my knowledge, you haven't had that special training. Have you?"

"Not really."

"I think that maybe you're being a little bit hard on yourself right now."

Regarding me dubiously, she bit the knuckle of her index finger.

"I know that being hard on yourself has always done good things for you," I continued. "It's gotten you to be where you are. You've been your own taskmaster and that's good and healthy. However—"

She flinched, almost physically warding off my words. "Ortiz was a troubled man under great stress," she said huskily. "He wasn't a raving psychotic. So I should have been able to somehow convey to him that I was there for him. That I could help him. I should have been able to do that. And I *didn't*." She was rocking back and forth on her chair.

"You wanted to save him and you didn't. But to say that you should have saved him and didn't is a bit grandiose." I waited while she took this in, then added, "What do you think, you're God or something?"

She started to respond, then stopped and laughed softly. "Grandiose, huh?"

I smiled and she continued: "You know, during it all, I kept thinking about how it was so much like a movie. I was even comparing it to movies. Maybe I got a little too caught up in all that. Started thinking I was John Wayne, or something."

"Yup," I said. "I think you should let this all sink in for a while. Get a good night's sleep. I'll be in by eight thirty if you want to check with me tomorrow."

"Great, I'll see you then."

Protect Me from Love

Chapter 8

Ginger Baron had almost not made it to Bellevue. During the interview selection process, Carl had argued against her, pointing out that she came from a dysfunctional family, had dropped out of high school at sixteen, and left home. She had a pattern of running away when things got tough and "hair-trigger" emotions, he said, that made her a risk at a place like Bellevue. But I and others on the staff fought to get her accepted because we were impressed with what she had gone on to do after leaving home—from waiting tables to supplying homemade desserts to neighborhood restaurants to running her own $200,000-a-year catering business, Ginger Snacks. Then she went into therapy and decided to become a psychologist. As far as I was concerned, she had everything I look for in a therapist.

After my session with Ginger following the Ortiz incident, she appeared to recover rapidly. Although she continued to show an exaggerated startle response every time there was a loud sound, like someone slamming down a book, in all other respects she was back to normal. I checked with Parnell in the ER, who told me she was doing fine, her sense of humor and vivacity still intact. I was also supervising her work with an adolescent outpatient.

Angelica Thompson was a twelve-year-old black child who had

been placed into foster care by her alcoholic parents at the age of two; she had been sexually abused by both the father and the grandfather in the foster family from the age of six. Six months before she had come into therapy, Angelica's biological parents, having gone to AA and been sober for more than a year and now working at full-time jobs, applied for and received permission to take their daughter back. They had also become deeply religious. Unfortunately, Angelica had discovered that the one surefire way to gain attention and affection was to freely offer oral sex to the boys and men in the neighborhood. The Thompsons were ready to raise the little girl they had abandoned and were doing a halfway decent job with the three-year-old girl they had had in the interim, but their older daughter's sexual practices had come smack up against their fervently held religious scruples.The more they tried to control her, the more she rebelled. They appealed to her teachers, to their minister, and finally to the court. Angelica became a PINS child (person in need of supervision) and the judge remanded her to Bellevue for evaluation. After three weeks she was released back to her family with a recommendation that she and her parents continue in therapy as outpatients. That was two months ago and Ginger had been seeing Angelica ever since.

"I think I'm starting to get through to her now," Ginger told me.

"What did you do?"

"I got her to promise to lay off 'the boys,' as she calls them, although some of them are in their thirties. And she's to concentrate on her schoolwork."

"How did you do that?" I marveled.

"I told her she ought to charge money for what she's doing."

"Say *what*?"

"That's exactly how Angelica reacted. She goes, 'No way. I'm no hooker.' So I go, 'Only fools give it away for free.' Then she puts her hands on her hips and says in this sassy way, 'What you be talking about? Everybody do it for free. I bet you be doing it too.'" Ginger laughed affectionately.

"So I told her, 'Yeah, I do that with my husband and before that only with a guy I really cared about. I mean, it's my body and I was very choosy about whom I touched and whom I allowed to touch

protect me from love

me.' Then she blows a big bubble from the gum she's chewing, pops it, and says, 'Yeah, but the guys like me when I do it.' 'They like what you *do,*' I say, 'not who you *are.*' And then I said, 'I like you for who you are. And so do your parents, believe it or not. They love you and they fought to get you back. But do you know who the most important person is in your life?' And now I've really got her attention. She goes, 'Who?' I poked her in her chest and said, 'You. When you care about yourself and really like yourself, you won't be giving away blowjobs or charging for them. You'll wait until you're older and meet a guy who feels about you the way you feel about yourself and loves you for who you are and not for what you can do for him.' "

"Sounds like it's going well," I agreed. We talked some more about how adolescents mask their depression. "It's interesting that adolescents who are depressed often act out as a way of covering their depression," I said. "For instance, I've worked with very depressed boys from the Bellevue school who steal and sell drugs because the excitement is a distraction from how shitty they feel. Angelica's way is to act out sexually. But her acting out is so extreme and she has such poor judgment with no awareness into the dangerousness of it, it is a kind of passive suicidal behavior. You'll have to work on getting her to recognize her feelings and her needs," I said. "And then find more appropriate ways to express them. I don't think this will be an easy case."

Two weeks later, Ginger was in my office telling me that Angelica's passive suicidal behavior had turned into a real attempt. "I didn't get home until six in the morning, Fred." Ginger's entire body sagged, her eyelids were half drawn.

She had gotten the call from the Thompsons at two in the morning at home and had gone to the pediatric ER to meet them.

"Ginger," Angelica cried happily when she saw her. They were in one of the treatment cubicles in the pediatric ER. Angelica held up her arms. A dishtowel had been wrapped around one wrist and a washcloth tied around the other. For a moment Ginger had felt queasy thinking about the blood.

"You want to see what this girl did to herself?" Mrs. Thompson asked Ginger. And then she looked at Angelica accusingly.

"They locked me in the closet," Angelica bleated, "for *six* hours. I could have suffocated." Her eyes looked puffy and her cheeks bore scratch marks.

Ginger wondered how she had gotten them.

Angelica couldn't have suffocated, Mr. Thompson informed us, because he had drilled air holes in the door. The parents told Ginger how Angelica had lied to them, broken her promises and sneaked out "to see the boys." They had slapped her across the face, then locked her in a closet for six hours, with only a sandwich and a soft drink that she had to eat in the dark.

"They don't let me *live,*" Angelica cried. "You've got to help me, Ginger." Ginger had briefed the child psychiatrist on the case, who decided that Angelica should be admitted as an inpatient to the adolescent ward.

"I'm going to the ward after this to see her," said Ginger. "They still have a suicide watch on her."

"We're going to have to work out a plan for her discharge that makes sense and won't just be a revolving door for her. You notified Special Services for Children about the abuse?"

"Oh, Fred," she said in a weary voice, "why do parents do such things?"

"They love her. That's why."

She shook her head. "I don't understand."

"We only abuse the people we love," I said. Parents abuse their children, children abuse their parents, husbands and wives abuse each other. And what does each of these people say? *'I love you.'* If you say those three magic words then you have the license to commit the most inhuman behavior in the world."

"If that is what love means," said Ginger somberly, "then protect me from love."

I was just digging my way through the congealed, gooey fruit topping on my yogurt, starving after my session with Ginger, when Nick sat down next to me at the staff cafeteria. I cupped my hand protectively around the dish.

"Okay if I join you?" Nick asked, setting down a can of Coke.

protect me from love

"Sure," I said. Lucky for me, I thought, there was nothing for him to get his hands on. "What's up?"

"I don't know. Maybe nothing." Noisily popping the top, he took a long swig of Coke. "You remember Inez's daughter, Luz, the kid I fought so hard to get in here when Inez was trying to starve herself on the ward?"

"Sure. You were just telling me how well she and the kids were doing. Is Inez back in the hospital?"

His black eyes darted toward my yogurt and then away again. "She called me a few days ago. Luz had a vaginal infection and I arranged for her to see an ob-gyn resident I know at the hospital. The doctor just called me to tell me she ran a routine HIV test on her because her mom has it and her dad died of it and vaginal infection is a common first sign of AIDS in women."

I put down my spoon. "Nick, you don't really think Luz could have AIDS, do you? I mean, she's eleven years old."

His brooding eyes belied his offhand tone. "Yeah, too old to have been born with it, and too young to be involved in sex or drugs. Besides, the doctor says she's a virgin."

"Then you probably have nothing to worry about," I assured him.

Before Ginger's rotation on the ER began, she had been on the adolescent ward, which—until she had witnessed Ortiz's suicide—she had thought was a far more dangerous place. For one thing, she pointed out, the ER was protected by hospital police with nightsticks and city cops with guns. For another, it did not have unpredictable, acting-out adolescents. She still shuddered when she thought about the time one of the girls had thrown her bed against the wall after being told she had to stay another three weeks. It took three aides to subdue her.

Ginger told me how apprehensive she was when she visited Angelica on the ward. She had found Angelica propped up on a pillow, earphones on, listening to a cheap cassette radio as she watched TV. While her face was no longer puffy from crying and the scratches were almost gone, the bandages on her wrist remained as a grim reminder of the ordeal she had gone through when the surgeon had stitched her up.

CRAZY ALL THE TIME

"Hi, Ginger," Angelica greeted her cheerily, taking off her earphones.

"Where'd you get that?" Ginger asked, pointing to the radio.

"My mom sent it up. They wouldn't let her see me."

"Did you want to see her?"

Angelica turned her head away. Ginger wondered again about the scratches on the girl's face.

"No way, not after what they done to me."

Sitting down on the bed, Ginger delicately traced a scratch on Angelica's face. "Who did that to you?"

"I did it to me," she said. "I was alone in that damn dark closet for six hours. I wanted to kill someone."

"So you hurt yourself? You wanted to kill yourself?"

"I wanted to hurt *them*. Show them what they were doing to *me*."

"Then you didn't want to die?" Ginger asked.

"Yes, I did. If I could hurt them by dying, I'd do it," she said in a petulant tone.

"I understand how angry you felt, Angelica. But the one you really hurt when you scratched your face and you cut your wrists was yourself. Next time you might die, and I don't want that to happen."

Angelica sat up in bed, her eyes flashing. "Then tell them not to lock me in a closet and be keeping after me all the time. They be after me if I'm five minutes late. They unplug the TV in the middle of my shows. They be dressing me like a three-year-old, like my baby sister, Chandra. That's the worst thing."

Ginger took her small hand in hers and patted it. "We've been all through that, Angelica," she said. "And just last week you told me that you would stop seeing the boys and you'd do your homework. Now your parents told me that you broke your word and you sneaked out. Is that true?"

Pulling back her hand, she tucked it under her chin and gave Ginger a sulky look. "Could you get me a tootsie pop? I'd like a tootsie pop."

"You didn't answer my question, Angelica."

"Get me a tootsie pop and then I'll answer your question."

protect me from love

Ginger laughed. "You can't *bribe* me. The truth, now. Did you sneak out of the house?"

"She wouldn't answer my question," Ginger told me. "She just put on her earphones and turned up the volume high enough for me to hear the rap music and tuned me out. Finally she says, 'What if I did? If I can't have my boyfriends, then I don't want to live.' And then when I took off her earphones, she says, 'Just don't make me go back there, okay?'"

Ginger looked at me now. "What are we going to do?"

"About what?" I asked.

"About her going back to her parents."

"We have to work it both ways," I said. "You'll work with Angelica to get her to control her behavior. She has to see that not only is it destructive to herself but the way she acts makes it impossible for her to live with her parents. At the same time, Kiesha is working with the Thompsons on getting them to be less rigid and see that Angelica is a disturbed child who is entering adolescence."

Ginger sat back. "I don't know," she said. "The situation looks to me like it can't be resolved. Angelica and her parents look like they're on a collision course. And we can't put her in yet another foster home, considering what she's gone through."

"Hey, Ginger," I said. "Whoa. You're jumping too far too fast. Give the therapeutic process a chance. We got some things going for us. The Thompsons are no longer drinking and they're trying to work with us. And underneath Angelica's bravado, there is a scared little girl, who is desperately in need of love."

"That she needs to be protected from?" asked Ginger, the irony evident in her tone. "I'm really worried," she said. "All this is going on and all Angelica will really talk about is her so-called boyfriends."

Things came to a head with Angelica after she had been on the adolescent ward for about three weeks. Although she had made one or two unsuccessful attempts to get to the boys' side of the ward, she was no longer considered a suicide risk and was generally well enough behaved to be given off-ward privileges and al-

CRAZY ALL THE TIME

lowed to attend the public school in the hospital, P.S. 106.

All the students at the school have been diagnosed as severely emotionally disturbed, often with a history of criminal behavior, such as teenage prostitution and drug dealing. Some were inpatients like Angelica who continued after they were discharged, some live in residences and group homes in the community, others are referred by their guidance counselors, and still others come to P.S. 106 because they have heard about it from friends. As one of them explained to me: "I was thirteen years old. I had a hundred-dollar-a-day job, a nice car, a nine-millimeter, seventeen-shot automatic, and all the girls coming around me. But then I stopped selling drugs and I didn't have the girls anymore. So what was I doing to do? Bag groceries for the rest of my life?" The kids come because they know that the school is a safe haven with caring, nurturing adults—perhaps the only ones they have ever known in their lives—and it represents their last chance at having a reasonably good life rather than ending up in a state prison or in Bellevue's morgue.

Ginger entered the school warily, feeling the way she did when she entered the psych ER or the adolescent ward. There were just so many places around the hospital where violence could erupt at any moment. Not ten feet away from her two adolescents were pummeling each other on the floor.

"He stole my headset, man," bawled the lanky youth who had been on top.

"Bull*shit!*" said the young teenager, a head shorter but more powerfully built. "I'll show you the receipt."

"You never got nuttin' in your life with a receipt on it," sneered the first one.

Ginger walked away quickly. A bespectacled, mild-looking man came up to Ginger and glanced at her ID. "Hi, Ms. Baron. Can I help you?"

"I'm looking for Angelica Thompson. She didn't show up for her appointment with me."

The teacher gave a quick look around. "Angelica? I could have sworn I saw her this morning."

A teenage girl with clanky gold earrings, wearing an oversize man's shirt that coincided with the hem of her tight black skirt, stopped to listen to them. "Oh, Angelica booked with those guys."

The teacher walked over to her. "What guys, Melissa?"

"You know," she said counting on her fingers, "Jesus, Michael R., Richie, Jimmy Red, and Fats."

"She ran away with five boys?" asked Ginger, incredulous.

"These boys are day students. She could have gone with them for a cigarette," the teacher said.

"Don't you check to see if they come back?"

"I didn't know they left. They're not in my class."

He looked at his watch. "I'm sure somebody would have soon noticed, if they already haven't, that the kids are gone." He turned back to the girl. "How did you know about this?"

"I heard them whispering about it this morning during English."

"And you didn't tell anyone?" he asked accusingly.

Melissa blinked at him with heavily mascaraed eyelashes as if to say, Are you kidding? and loudly popped her gum.

Taking Ginger by the arm, the teacher said, "I'm Tony. Let's go to my office where we can talk."

About thirty-six hours later, Ginger walked into my office. I was talking to a prospective trainee on the phone and asked Ginger to sit down.

"Angelica's back," she said when I had finished.

"What's up?" I asked. "You don't look all that happy about it."

Angelica had danced into Ginger's office at noon the next day, wearing a tank top about two sizes too big. Her jeans, which bagged around her legs, appeared to have also come from one of her "boys." They had all gone to the movies and then to the apartment of a cousin of one of the boys.

"Then she puts her hands on her hips and says to me, 'He's like thirty and he's cool. Has his own place and everything.' So I asked her if she gave him a blowjob too."

"Sounds reasonable," I said.

"She stands up, knocks over her chair and yells, 'Fuck. What's your problem?' and I just took her by the hand and said, 'Angelica, we're going back to the ward.' "

CRAZY ALL THE TIME

Ginger gave me a look somewhere between anger, worry, and disgust. "How can she do such a thing, Fred?"

"What thing?"

"You know, give blowjobs to every Tom, Dick, and Harry."

"Well," I said, "what do you think about it?"

"I'm like of two, maybe three, minds about it. There's the therapeutic side of me that tries to help her understand it, realize why it is dangerous. Then there's the side that is worried and concerned that what she is doing is really dangerous, so I wind up lecturing her. Then there's the third part of me which is thinking, 'What are you doing, you little slut?' And oh," she laughed, "there's also this part of me that wants to lock her in the closet and never let her out."

"Now you're connecting with the parents' feelings."

Ginger snorted. "Great. I'm in league with the torturers."

I smiled. "Now you can understand how frustrated her parents get," I said, "and why they do some of the things they do. They don't have any of the distance that you can get on this and they don't see any alternatives."

"Yeah, but what they do is real child abuse."

"Oh yes," I agreed.

"I mean, I might have this fantasy of locking her up because I want to protect her, not because I'm following some kind of biblical injunctions to drive out the devil from my sexually acting-out child."

"It's true that their behavior is maladaptive, abusive, and just doesn't work—"

"And is causing her to be even more rebellious and acting out," Ginger broke in. "Their punishments keep making her do exactly the things they don't want her to do."

"Exactly. But, Ginger," I said, "you can understand their sense of desperation and the very real fear for Angelica's safety that you share with them. That will enable you to connect with them rather than just judge them."

She seemed lost in a trance.

"What are you thinking about?" I asked.

She looked up, startled. "Oh nothing. It's just, to tell you the truth, sometimes she's like . . . like a real brat. Her behavior seems so willful."

"I know it looks that way, but it's usually no will and all impulse. It's like a runaway car without a driver. You're familiar with the term *acting out* but now you've had a chance to experience it. It can make you crazy. But you're the therapist. Getting angry at them for having the very symptoms that brought them to us in the first place may be a normal reaction but it's not very helpful."

"I know she's in pain," said Ginger. "But she won't let me in."

"That's right," I said. "Because she doesn't want to let *herself* in and feel it. Also she doesn't have the verbal skills to tell you what's going on. You have to look beyond that brattiness to what's behind it—her very real depression and fear and low self-esteem."

She sat there for a moment, saying nothing. Then she took a long breath and blew the air out. "You know what frightens me the most, Fred?"

"What?"

"That Angelica is so hurt by her parents' rejection and abuse and angered by their control that she'll continue this negative attention-getting behavior. It's behavior learned from all the sexual abuse she suffered from her foster parents, but she knows it has the power to make her parents go ballistic."

"You're right," I said. "It gives her a feeling of power. She can cause them pain in retaliation for the pain that they have caused her. So there is nothing pushing her to stop, even though the consequences come back at her in the form of abuse. It's even more complicated because her behavior gets her attention from them and from the boys. She is no longer ignored. She has no motivation to change."

"That's just it," she said. "This kid has had a lifetime of abuse. First being abandoned, then being sexually abused by her foster parents, then back to these crazy Bible-thumping, self-righteous, ex-alcoholics. I'm really scared for her. She is going to end up in the streets. She is going to end up being beaten up and running away again. She'll be one of these kids that New York swallows and spits out."

"Or pregnant," I added, "or with AIDS, or both, or even murdered."

"Thanks." She looked down at her hands in her lap.

"What are you thinking about?" I asked.

For a moment she said nothing. Then she looked up and sighed, "I don't know. I just wish there was something more we could do."

I gave her the standard warning, like the message on the side of cigarette packs. "This is tough work. And if you're not careful, it may be hazardous to your health. You have to dance the line between being a mother and a therapist, between giving Angelica the help she needs and rescuing her. You can be moved to tears, but if you're overidentified, you lose your objectivity and you'll quickly burn out."

"I know," she murmured.

"Just remember that you have a lot going against you on this case and you might not succeed."

"Right," she said, grimacing.

"There's a limit to what we can do. We can't undo all the horribleness, all the pain. But sometimes we can be successful; sometimes we can change people's lives."

She gave me a weary smile. "You know, I could always bake cookies for a living."

I touched her hand. "This is better," I said.

Several weeks later, Ginger appeared to have completely recovered from her posttraumatic stress syndrome. Her old energy level was back, she was enjoying her work, and even bringing in exotic concoctions in the morning in her search for the perfect cookie. Her latest effort was a buttery, praline affair with splatters of dark chocolate that looked like a drip painting. "I call it chocolate meltdown," she said. I called it indescribably delicious.

She often took some cookies to Angelica, visiting with her for a few minutes before reporting to work in the ER. I asked Ginger if she didn't think she was getting overly involved with her young patient. But Ginger said that there was nothing to worry about, she was in touch with her feelings, and if she felt at any point that she was becoming overly identified, that there was some problem of countertransference, she would talk to me about it. Her main concern, she said, was to bond with Angelica, to let her see that adults could be helpful, nonexploitive, and worthy of her trust. Ginger hoped that the child could then learn to transfer some of those good feelings to her parents.

Apparently some of Ginger's approach was working. Angelica stopped pushing her away at every turn. She began talking about going home, seeing her friends, even her baby sister. At the same time, the Thompsons kept asking when they could bring their daughter home. I decided that maybe the time was ripe for a family session. Kiesha, who had been meeting with the parents, would conduct the session. Ginger argued that she should be there as well. But I said that it would be best to have Kiesha do it alone. The parents trusted her, she knew the case, and Angelica would not try to manipulate her against her parents, which she would do with Ginger. I expected that Angelica and her parents would have difficulty communicating their real feelings to one another, so I told Kiesha to try a technique that I thought might work.

The day after the session, I was sitting with Ginger in my office, when Kiesha came in with a big smile.

"How'd it go?" asked Ginger.

"Great," said Kiesha. "Really great."

A cloud seemed to pass across Ginger's face, but then it lifted as she listened to Kiesha's account.

"It really didn't start off well," said Kiesha. "At first all they did was yell at each other. Mary Thompson called her a 'devil child' and complained that whenever they left Angelica with her three-year-old sister, she would beat up the child. In response to which, Angelica accused her parents of favoring her baby sister over her. They all adopted their usual antagonistic positions and held their ground. We weren't getting anywhere.

"That's when I decided to try the technique you suggested, Fred. When I squatted next to Angelica's chair, she says, 'Kiesha, what are you doing?'

"I told her to just sit there, quietly. I said, 'I'm going to talk for you.' And suddenly, Gabe and Mary Thompson get very quiet. And then I say in a small voice, 'I do these things, because I'm not really sure about you.' And Mr. Thompson goes, 'What?' But Mrs. Thompson just touches him with her hand and says, 'Shussh, Gabe.

Listen to her.' And then I say, 'You sent me away when I was only two years old and then all these terrible things happened to me.' And it was just like you said it would be, Fred. Mr. Thompson starts talking to me as though I were Angelica, saying things like 'It wasn't our fault. We were kids ourselves. We were alcoholics.' And then Mrs. Thompson joins in. 'We couldn't help it. We had no money. We couldn't take care of you.' And Angelica is looking from one to the other, biting her lips. And I say, 'Just listen to me. Listen to my feelings. I'm telling you, I don't trust you, Mommy and Daddy. You don't really love me. And the only people who do, who really care for me, really want me, are those boys. They give me attention. All you ever do is punish me and make me feel bad.'

"And Mr. Thompson clenches and unclenches his fists and says, 'Yes, it's true that we punish you, but . . .' And he stops. And I just go on: 'I'm telling how I feel. I need you to be there for me. I need to feel safe. I need to feel that no matter what I do, you'll always love me. You'll never send me away again. No matter what. And I don't think I can feel that.'

"And then there was this long silence. Mrs. Thompson started to speak and then she closed her mouth and Mr. Thompson just sat there. I could hear his breathing. And then Angelica started to cry. And Mrs. Thompson ran over to her and hugged her and cried, 'My baby, my baby, my baby, what have we done to my baby?' And then they started to talk about her coming home. Angelica didn't say much, but she certainly listened."

"That was great, Kiesha," I said.

"Thanks. I came away feeling pretty good. I think the parents are really trying."

"I think you're right," I said. "Hopefully, Angelica can now start to see that in spite of her parents' punitive behavior, they do love her and want her back. Not that there aren't still many problems to be resolved. But if the family continues to work with us once she leaves, at least we may be able to contain some of Angelica's acting out and her parents' overreaction."

Ginger looked dubious.

"What do you think?" I asked her.

"I don't know whether Angelica was crying because of her love for her parents or because she was remembering the pain they inflicted on her all these years."

"Ginger," Kiesha said, "she was crying out in love. They all were. Even me. We used up a lot of tissues."

"I don't know," said Ginger slowly. "I'm just not sure."

"Ginger, believe me," said Kiesha. "I know. I was there."

"I know, Kiesha, and I appreciate that. It's just that I know Angelica so well. She has so much anger against these people who abandoned her and are so strict with her now and lock her in the closet. I just can't see her doing a complete about-face."

"Yeah, but she must also have some good feelings about them," said Kiesha. "Maybe from when she was little. They're still her parents. And when her mother hugged her, it was like she was giving the kid what she needed so badly. What do you think, Fred?"

"I don't know. This is a tough call. You're both right about Angelica's feelings, and her parents sound like they're on the right track. But Angelica's so insecure and so impulsive she has a lot of growing up to do. Ideally, that's what therapy is all about. I think that the confrontation helped the Thompsons to see what they've been missing all along, the terrified, needy child under all her bravado and sexual acting out. And it also let Angelica see that her parents really care for her."

Kiesha nodded, but Ginger still looked doubtful.

"I just don't know," I said, "if Angelica can control herself enough so that her parents can get past her provocative behavior."

"I'm worried about that too," said Ginger. "Sure, they can talk about their little girl, their little baby now. But what happens the next time she goes off with some boy? Or sneaks out of the house? She may learn to modify her behavior, but I can't see her turning into Miss Goody Two Shoes, either."

"You're right," I said, "but you're going to continue working with her and Kiesha will continue to see the parents."

"Can I say something, Ginger?" Kiesha asked.

"Sure."

"I think you're being a little too hard on the parents. They've worked really hard to get where they are now. I mean, they had Angelica when they were both sixteen and were always drunk. Now they've been through rehab and are working. Do you have any idea how hard that is? And they've stayed together all these years."

"That's true," said Ginger. "And they got religion so they could righteously beat the shit out of Angelica."

We both looked at her. "I'm sorry," she said. "I wish I could put as much faith in the parents as you guys, but I think these are very limited people."

"And they're doing their best with the limited resources they have," I said. "But it's interesting. Let's look at what both of you are saying. Ginger is saying that Angelica has really suffered at the hands of her parents. And Kiesha is saying that you have to look at where the Thompsons came from. Look at their modeling— they're all from abusive families."

"Now you put your finger on what's bothering me, Fred," said Ginger. "You have one abused generation abusing another generation which then abuses the next generation. We have to find a way to cut into this."

"I agree," I said. "We have to stop this cycle of abuse."

"But maybe the only way we are going to stop the cycle is to get Angelica out of this family. I'm worried that these people are not going to be able to handle their daughter because they are too scarred themselves."

"And I say we should give them a chance," said Kiesha.

"You're both right again," I said. "Ginger's right to be concerned about the parents continuing to do to their children what they have had done to them. But Kiesha's also right that we have to work with the parents because the best way to stop the cycle is to teach them how to be better parents. If abusive behavior can be passed from one generation to another, so can the behavior of caring and loving and nurturing."

Hurrying to a meeting late that afternoon, I nearly bumped into Nick, who was walking, face down, mumbling.

I took his arm. "Nick. You okay?"

He seemed to be emerging from the depths as he slowly focused on me.

"I just got the AIDS results from the doctor," he said.

protect me from love

I literally got cold feet. "Are you . . . ?" I couldn't even get the words out of my mouth.

He looked at me, uncomprehending. "Am I . . . what?"

I gulped. "Aren't you talking about your AIDS test?"

He stared at me blankly, then brightened. *"Me?* No. I got the results a month ago. I'm fine."

"Nice of you to share it with me," I teased, remembering how anxious he had been. Then I realized who he was talking about. "You mean the results for Luz, Inez's daughter."

He nodded, his features so tightly drawn it seemed the air had been sucked out of them. "The doctor just called me. She was freaking out. Luz has AIDS."

The word hung in the air with an awful finality. "What?" I gasped. "How?"

"That's what I'm going to find out," he said. "Inez and Luz are coming in to see me tomorrow. My God, Fred, first her husband, then herself, now her daughter. How much does this poor family have to suffer?"

The next morning Ginger showed up with her latest creation, pecan-almond sandies. "These are all for Angelica," she said. "Her going-away present." An hour later she was back in my office to tell me what happened.

When she walked into the adolescent ward, she told me, Angelica was nowhere to be seen. Her roommate—she was now sharing a double room—lay on the bed reading a magazine. In contrast to the wall on Angelica's side, which was filled with snapshots of her "boyfriends," the heavyset teenager sharing the room had hung magazine photos of Mel Gibson, Tom Cruise, Cindy Crawford, and Michael Jackson.

Ginger continued to look for Angelica, peering through the window inserts of each room. Finally she peeked into the activity room, where a handful of girls were scattered among the chairs and sofas writing letters or watching TV. But no Angelica. If she had somehow managed to elope the day before she was due to be discharged, then she had blown everything, Ginger thought.

She walked into the room and sat down on the nearest sofa, wondering what to do next, when she spotted Angelica in the corner, hunkered down alongside a magazine rack. She crouched down next to her and patted the top of her head.

"Here you are," she said. "I've been looking everywhere for you." Angelica buried her head between her knees.

"I came to say good-bye. I got a whole bunch of cookies for you. You can share them with your folks and Chandra."

"The only reason they want me home is to baby-sit Chandra," said Angelica, not looking up.

"That's not true," said Ginger. "Kiesha told me about what happened in that session. How your mother cried and held you. You saw how they really love you."

Angelica raised her face far enough so that Ginger could see just her eyes above the round knobs of her knees. "Then why did they give me up?"

Ginger put her arm around Angelica. "They wanted to keep you. It was the booze. And as soon as they could, they took you back. And you heard what they said about wanting to take care of you."

But Angelica shook her head. "They've said a lot of things before. And then they locked me in the closet."

"People change. Believe me. I know."

"How do you know?"

"I know from my own life. They love you. They're willing to change for you because they love you. They're still together because there is something there between them. They made it work. And now they'll make it work for you."

"Don't make me go back, Ginger."

"Sweetheart, you have to. They're your parents."

"I don't want to go. Let me stay here."

"In the hospital?"

She nodded.

"The hospital is not a place to live. You need a home. A family."

"Then take me home with you."

She threw her arms around Ginger, who could feel the child's heart beating.

"*Please, please,* I wanna go home with you. I wanna go home with you. Don't make me go back. They'll hurt me again. Take me home with you. I'll be good," she entreated. "I promise. No more boys. Nothing. Don't make me go back. Please."

Late that afternoon, Nick burst into my office, his face black with murderous rage.

"That fucking bastard," he spat out, shaking his fists. "Oh God, oh God. If only I could bring him back to life and string him up and torture him and watch him die slowly."

"What guy? Who? What are you talking about?"

"Ramón. Inez's husband."

"I don't understand."

He raised his right fist and for one moment I thought he was going to slam a hole in my door. But then he sat down, his hands dropping helplessly into his lap. "I just met with Inez and Luz," he said tonelessly. "You know how Luz got AIDS?"

I shook my head.

"She got it from her father."

"How? Did he give her drugs?"

"He gave it to her the same way he gave it to Inez."

"Jesus. You mean . . ." And then I stopped. "I thought the doctor said she was a virgin."

Nick shut his eyes and massaged his temples. "He sodomized her, Fred. Luz said he told her that way she was still a virgin."

"That's so sick."

When he opened his eyes again, I could see the pain in them.

"I thought I had seen everything as an AIDS volunteer. Young men dying the most god-awful death. But this is like . . . I can't stand it. I can't stand this."

I wanted to help him, reach out to him in some way, but it was all I could do to meet his eyes. "There's nothing I can say, Nick."

And there wasn't.

About an hour later, as I was picking up my scooter helmet and locking up for the night, Ginger came to my door.

"Fred, could you just give me a few minutes?"

"Ginger, can it wait until morning?" I asked. "I've had one hell of a day."

"Well, it's just I was wondering, you remember I told you what Angelica said to me this morning?"

"Yes, what about it?"

Ginger looked at me intently. "Do you think she's right?"

"About what?"

"About not wanting to go home?"

"Ginger, we've been all through this. It's the best solution all around."

"Well, I was just wondering . . ." She fiddled with the strap of her bag as she talked. "I mean . . . is there a possibility . . . ?"

"Yes?"

"I know this sounds ridiculous, Fred, but . . ."

"What sounds ridiculous, Ginger?"

"Well, maybe Angelica could live with me? Maybe at least until things can be worked out better with her parents. I don't think Kyle will mind. We've been talking about having kids. And this doesn't have to be permanent."

"Ginger," I said, setting down my helmet and inviting her to sit. "Our job is to treat patients, not rescue them."

"I know," she said. "It's just that I feel that something has to be done."

"Something *is* being done. You and Kiesha have done wonders. The Thompsons have gained some insight into their behavior and they understand that they can't keep coming down on their daughter that way. They've agreed to stay in therapy. You're right that Angelica is still scared and distrustful, but she is beginning to understand that they *do* love her. And she'll continue to stay in therapy with you."

"I know," she said. "But people lie. They make promises they never keep. They say anything to get what they want. We both know that."

"Listen, Ginger, there's no way we can predict how things will go. The whole vicious cycle of abuse that we talked about can start up again. We can't be there every minute. But we have Special Services for children involved and the family is in treatment. Beyond that, we can't protect her. But what we can do, what you can do, is nurture the strengths that she has. Make her psychologically hardy so that she can survive this abuse and whatever other abuse life may have in store for her."

Ginger nodded. "And that's it? That's all we can do?"

"Yes. You can give Angelica your love and strength. And you can also give her a teddy bear that she can hold when she feels scared and lonely. It will remind her of you and it will let her take your voice home with her."

"Okay, Fred," she said. "But I have to tell you, this is hard. I remember what you told me about this being a tough business. And you're right. I'm not so sure I'm cut out to do this."

"Yes, you are, Ginger. You're a real nurturer. And you have everything going for you—intelligence, insight, candor, humor, relatedness, enthusiasm, courage, resourcefulness, dedication. Do you want me to go on?"

"Please, no," she laughed. "But you're wrong about one of them. I don't have courage."

"How can you say that? Look how you tried to get the gun away from Ortiz? That took guts, even if it was a little bit crazy."

"That didn't take courage. I wasn't even thinking about myself at the moment. Working with Angelica and not being able to stop her from doing things that are bad for her and watching her getting hurt—*that* takes courage. And I'm not sure I have that."

I started to argue that with her, but she cut me off.

"Listen to me please, Fred. I've been thinking a lot about this. I have a wonderful husband. He has a good job and can support the two of us. I made big bucks in the dessert catering business. And now I'm working on these cookies. Maybe I'm not cut out to be a psychologist. Maybe I'm meant to be an entrepreneur. You say I'm a nurturer. Well, I can nurture people with cookies."

"It's not that I don't think you're a great pastry chef, Ginger. Believe me, I love your cookies. It's just that I think you have more to contribute to the world as a therapist."

She shook her head. "I don't know, Fred."

"Look," I said, "this isn't anything you have to decide now. You've put in five years of your life toward getting a Ph.D. You're almost there. You've got to finish and then make up your mind."

"What's the point if I'm not going to practice? The thing with

Ortiz was bad enough. But that was a fluke, really. I mean, how often in your career is someone going to kill himself in front of you? But Angelica is a different story. This kind of thing is going to come up again and again. And if I have difficulty separating myself from the patient, then I'm going to burn out. You said the same thing yourself."

"That's true," I said. "But you're just starting out. You can learn to deal with the feelings that come up with patients in your own therapy. But the point is that you do feel deeply about other people and you do care. And that is something I can't teach. So what I want you to do, Ginger, is hang in there, just as you are going to tell Angelica to do. And think about what we've talked about. We've only got a month to go until the internship year is over. Get your Ph.D. and then decide. Think about why you went into this field in the first place. And then think about what you'll be giving up."

"Okay, Fred. And maybe you ought to give me a teddy bear too, so I can hear your voice while I'm thinking," she smiled.

A
Question of
Commitment

Chapter 9

Alone among the interns, Kiesha Wright came from poverty and a tough neighborhood. Her father left the family when she was eleven, overnight turning Kiesha into a "parentified child," caring for five younger siblings and her mother, who cleaned apartments for a living. It was Kiesha who made sure that everyone's homework got done. And when her younger brother was arrested at age twelve as a lookout for drug dealers, it was Kiesha who went to court, persuaded the judge to release him on probation, and then got him into an after-school treatment program. I thought that her Harlem-bred street smarts would be useful in her new rotation on the forensic ward. This was a forty-bed, all-male psychiatric prison hospital run jointly by Bellevue and the NYC Department of Corrections. "Patient-prisoners" are brought in for competency evaluations and for treatment of severe psychiatric problems.

At our supervisory session, Kiesha described in vivid detail what her first day had been like. It was both scary and exciting, she said, to hear the solid "thwump" of the heavy steel-barred door shutting behind her as she entered the reception area. In front of her a corrections officer unloaded his gun over a steel-walled, waist-high sandbox, barrel down in case of accidental discharge, before

CRAZY ALL THE TIME

handing it over and walking through the second steel-barred door onto the ward. She greeted the CO guarding the room, whose belt sported a long chain of handcuffs like a piece of kinky jewelry. Looping her thumb under the collar of her dress, Kiesha jiggled her ID at the CO, who gave her a thumbs up and buzzed her in.

On her way to the unit's dining room, where she had been told her patient was eating lunch, Kiesha passed by the patient rooms, not wanting to look through the Plexiglas walls that revealed everything—bed, sink, toilet, the most private human functions. At the back of the rooms, she could see the bars on the windows.

She found Sid Waters sitting at a table with benches that were bolted to the floor. He had just finished eating.

"Good afternoon, Mr. Waters," she said crisply. "I'm Kiesha Wright. I'll be working on your evaluation."

Picking his teeth with a plastic fork, Waters peered at her through half-lidded eyes. He looks like something the cat dragged in, she thought. He was twig thin, and the bones of his young face stood out like knobs against his sallow, pitted skin and scruffy beard. His hair was as nondescript and colorless as plank wood. Only his eyes, yellow-flecked and canny as a cat's, seemed to have any real life in them.

"You a shrink?" he asked scornfully, jerking a thumb in her direction.

"I'm a psychology trainee," she said. "Mr. Waters—" she began.

"Sid. Just call me Sid."

"Just Sid?" she asked, looking at his chart. "That's short for Sidney?"

"It's short for Siddhartha," he said.

"Sid Arthur," she repeated.

"It's one word," he said glumly.

"I'll stick with Sid. Tell me, Sid, they feed you enough here?"

Curling his lower lip, he regarded her dubiously under pale sparse eyebrows that almost matched his skin. "Yeah. Why?"

"And what about when you were in Rikers Island?"

"It was okay." He narrowed his cat's eyes. "What are you getting at?"

"I was just wondering if you needed to supplement your diet." She held up the chart. "It says here that while you were at Rikers you swallowed the following items: two razor blades, one pencil stub, two odd-shaped bits of metal, and an assortment of nuts and bolts. Why did you do that, Sid?"

"Don' know," he shrugged. "Just did."

"Just did," she repeated. "It seems to have gotten you a lot of attention, Sid, especially the razor blades. How do you do that anyway? Do you swallow them whole or chew them up like peanuts?"

"Whole, of course," he said proudly. "Get me a razor blade and I'll do one for you. They took all mine away. I can swallow anything—metal, wood, plastic, glass, you name it. I've been doing it all my life."

"All your life, huh?" said Kiesha, tapping his chart with her pencil. "And how long have you been picking pockets?"

"As long as I've been eating things. I can pick any pocket, swallow any object."

"You're a regular Houdini, Sidarthur. How'd you get that name anyway? Your parents make it up? Name you after two people, Sid and Arthur?"

"My folks were hippies," he said, as though that explained it. "I was born in sixty-six in the East Village, just off Saint Mark's Place. They were flower children and I was their flower."

Kiesha folded her arms and looked at me challengingly. "I think he's faking."

"Faking what?"

"Being crazy, what else? It's so manipulative. My kid brother did the same thing."

"Your kid brother was a swallower?"

"No, he held his breath just like some brat in the movies. I knew he was just conning me, but the first few times he did it I got sucked in. Stood there shaking him, yelling 'breathe, breathe,' while he was practically turning blue in the face. Then I figured he was trying to manipulate me and the best thing I could do was ignore him. So the next time he pulled that stunt, I said, 'No problem, William. You just keep holding your breath and then you'll pass out. And then you'll start breathing again whether you want to or not.' That was the last time he pulled that bull on me."

"Isn't William the brother who had a drug problem?" I asked.

"Yeah. So?"

"Was that manipulative behavior?"

Her eyes narrowed. "What do you mean?"

"Do you think William used drugs to get your attention?"

She gave me a steely glance. "I think William did drugs for the same reason anyone does drugs in Harlem. It's there. It's inevitable. It's considered remarkable if you *don't* do drugs."

"Yeah," I said. "But he got strung out. And you got him into a rehab program. So is it possible that he got strung out to be manipulative and get attention from you?"

She opened her hands. "I can't answer that. I really don't know. What are you getting at?"

"That from what you've told me, I don't know if Sid is swallowing stuff to be manipulative. When you manipulate, you have a goal. What would his goal be?"

"Not to go to prison, obviously."

"How? Incompetent to stand trial? Or an insanity defense? If he succeeds with either one, he might do a longer stretch in a hospital for the criminally insane than if he goes to prison on these charges."

"But he's a repeat offender, and according to the guidelines he could go to prison for a long, long time." She crossed her legs. "Fred, the guy is smart enough to figure out that if he just carries off this swallowing gig, ingesting everything he can get his pickpocketing hands on, he can stay in the state hospital rather than do time in the state prison."

"But the hospitals for the criminally insane are no cake walk. He's been around the system long enough to know that."

"I don't know. I've known scammers, and my gut tells me he's scamming," she said.

"Even if your gut is right and he is malingering, the judge is going to want your opinion to be based on hard facts and test data. So you have to find out more about Sid and why he does what he does. He says he's been swallowing things and picking pockets most of his life. Ask him what happened the first time he swallowed some nonfood substance and how his parents reacted. Do a good history. He says he was the kid of two hippies. What did that have to do with anything besides the fact that that's how he probably got his name."

"What is that name, Sidarthur?"

"Siddhartha," I corrected. "It's the title of a book by Herman Hesse that was very popular in the sixties. Siddhartha is the name of the Buddha."

"Hmmm," said Kiesha, looking thoughtful. "I wonder where his folks were at when they gave him that name."

I smiled at her encouragingly. "That's another good question to ask. If he is just malingering, I'd like to know how he came up with this way of getting what he wants. Think about it, Kiesha. We all manipulate in one way or another. I'm manipulating you right now to get you to ask him all these questions and try this way of working. It's called supervision."

Kiesha rolled her eyes and sighed. "Okay, Chief. Whatever you say. But I'll tell you right now, Fred, this guy Sid, Sidarthur, whatever, can tell me anything he damn pleases. He's the product of two white, spoiled, middle-class hippies who cared more about being acid heads than taking care of him. You're right. He's been in and out of the system. He knows how it works. He's faking, and you and I both know it. He even boasts about his being transferred to Bellevue."

"But, Kiesha, even if *he* thinks he's manipulating the system, the irony is that he might be more crazy than criminal anyway. It's not exactly considered normal behavior to risk your life eating razor blades just to get an indeterminate sentence in the state hospital as your reward."

Standing up, Kiesha slung her book bag over her shoulder and said with a smile, "You know what you are, don't you, Fred? You're a typical white, bleeding-heart liberal."

I smiled back. "Yeah, well, not everything is all black and white."

"Touché," she said.

• • •

Kiesha left and Kitty came in. "I'm worried about Brenda," she said, bringing me up to date on her schizophrenic patient. "I think her paranoia is moving in a direction that could cost her her job."

What's going on?" I asked.

"Yesterday Brenda told me that the women in her office were sending secret messages to one another about her just the way the CIA and the FBI do. She said that one of the women went to the window and opened it wide." She looked at me significantly. "You know what that means, don't you?"

I shrugged. "They don't have sealed windows in her office?"

"Come on, Fred," said Kitty. "Everyone knows a window represents the vagina, and by opening it wide the coworker was telling the whole office that Brenda's vagina was wide open. And then she found the sleeve of her sweater that she had hung on the back of her chair turned inside out. The sleeve is also a vagina. So by turning it inside out, they were showing everyone her vagina, which was another way of telegraphing that she was promiscuous."

"Has she actually shared these insights with her coworkers?" I asked.

"Not directly," said Kitty, brushing an unruly lock back into her pageboy. "But when she walked in after lunch they were laughing and she threatened to punch one of them."

"That's bad," I admitted.

"I told her that she wasn't to do that. That no one was going to hurt her and she was not to hurt anyone."

"Right."

"But listen to this," urged Kitty. "Last night she called me at home about midnight." She flinched involuntarily. "Unfortunately she woke up Tom again, who was still angry about the last time. But I knew Brenda wouldn't call unless it was important. She told me she was going to go in there and punch the living daylights out of that woman and then give notice."

"Uh oh," I said.

"I managed to calm her down, but, Fred, I really think we have to do something. I'm afraid that her paranoia is getting out of hand

and she'll lose her job and end up homeless. Her employer told me that the only reason he lets her stay on is because he feels sorry for her and up to now she hasn't been any trouble. But, he says, if she starts giving him trouble, she'll be out of there in a heartbeat. And I can't see her ever getting another job."

It was interesting to see just how far Kitty had moved from her original position of hospitalizing Brenda and giving her antipsychotic drugs. Then she had wanted to "cure" Brenda's schizophrenia. Now her goal was to keep her out of the hospital.

"Is she taking her medication?" I asked.

"Oh, it's the usual thing of one pill every few days. She just refuses to take the medication as it's prescribed. I've discussed it with her psychiatrist, who prescribed the medication, and he's stumped too. He told me that the amount she's taking is useless."

"Kitty," I said, "as much as both you and I want to keep Brenda out of the hospital, we may have to consider it if she's serious about hurting anyone. Remember, she got violent once already at the animal-rights demonstration."

"I don't think we're at the hospitalization stage yet," she said. "I was able to calm her down and I think I can keep her that way. She has agreed to call me if she feels threatened or scared by any of her coworkers or she thinks about harming them. But I'm still worried that she might lose her job just because she's acting crazier than she did before."

"Why don't you prepare for that possibility by applying for SSD?"

"SSD?"

"It's Social Security disability for people who have worked and paid into the system for a certain number of quarters and are now disabled. I think Brenda would qualify. She's been working on and off for her whole adult life. Why don't you speak to Pam Wyatt, the social worker in the Mental Hygiene Clinic, about applying for it?"

"You mean Wayne's, uh, friend? Okay. I'll do that."

I had just come from a Therapeutic Environment Committee meeting where the main topics were discharge planning and educating patients about their illness and how to cope with it. I was making

CRAZY ALL THE TIME

a note to discuss some of the points brought up with Kitty in re-gard to Brenda when Kiesha and Gary arrived for their joint su-pervisory session.

Kiesha told us that she had seen X rays of Sid's stomach and then confronted her patient with what she had been told.

"The X-ray technician identified four shirt buttons," she told Sid, "but what was the big round object?"

"It was an AIDS button. I really liked it," he said. "It said, 'DO IT' in big letters and underneath in little letters it said, 'with condoms.'"

"The kind of button you pin on? What about the pin?"

"No problem. I just—"

"No problem?" she jumped in, annoyed. "How's it going to come out? I assume the shirt buttons will come out fine the usual way, but the pin? What if they have to cut you up to get it out? Or they don't and it gets hooked on your intestines? Is that what you want?"

"You angry with me, Kiesha?" he asked.

"Why do you keep doing this stuff, Sid?" she asked. "It says in your chart you've had fourteen operations to remove foreign ob-jects. Is that true?"

"Man," he snickered, "I've been cut up so many times, I look like a map of the New York subway system. I've probably had more stitches than a patchwork quilt."

Kiesha laughed.

Sid grinned. "I made you smile."

Kiesha told Gary and me that she then asked Sid what it was like being the child of two hippies. "He told me about his happy child-hood with his teenage druggie parents. Mom was a garbage head, crystal meth, phenobarb, Valium, ludes, heroin snorting. Dad was a major dealer whose drug of choice was coke. They both did enough acid to blow out their synapses, or as Sid says about his mom, 'She has trouble connecting the dots.' So he was left alone a lot while they 'did their thing' and when he was five his dad split never to be heard from again. After that, he remembers a whole succession of men who came to the house, some of them moving in for a few months and calling themselves 'dad,' and others telling him to get lost."

She drummed her pencil on the cover of her notebook. "About the only bright note in this story was his mother got a dose of clap, which left her sterile, so Sid's an only child."

"Built-in damage control," I said. "Did he tell you how he got started with picking pockets and swallowing?"

"It just started with taking things from the men who slept over. He was a real sly kid. He'd creep into their room at night when they were sleeping off the drugs and booze and he'd lift their wallets, steal only a few bucks, so they wouldn't notice. Sometimes his mother would catch him, but she was so ineffectual. She told him to stop doing it, but would then sometimes ask for a few bucks. He felt he was entitled to the money because he never had anything of his own. He got secondhand clothes and secondhand toys, when she remembered to get him anything."

I looked at Kiesha. "Doesn't sound too much like spoiled, middle-class white folks to me."

"Okay, okay," she said, raising her hands. "I got it. But I was right about one thing, the reason he swallows stuff. The first time he re-members doing it was when he was three or four and swallowed a bunch of his mother's Valium. She rushed him to the hospital and they gave him medicine which made him throw up. And then she spent the next few days really watching him. He remembers her buying him a game, Candyland, and they sat on the floor and played it together. So you see, Fred, he very quickly got the atten-tion and the feedback he wanted. And he soon learned to manip-ulate it. I think he even got off on the surgery. All those doctors and nurses fawning all over him."

"That's interesting," I said. "The swallowing and pickpocketing go together. They're both about taking and possessing. What do you think, Gary?"

"I was wondering if this kind of pathological swallowing might not be an infantile expression of very primitive oral needs," Gary said. "From what you've been saying, Kiesha, being raised by these drugged-out, neglecting parents, Sid was always hungry. Hungry for food, hungry for clothes and toys, hungry for attention, hungry for love."

"Always hungry," Kiesha repeated. "So his swallowing razors

and buttons and nuts and bolts is a way of feeding himself, giving himself what he never got from his parents? Do you agree, Fred?"

"It's one possible interpretation," I said. "One that you should definitely consider."

Leaning on her notebook, Kiesha said, "But I still think he's using the swallowing to get out of going to prison. And that's the bottom line."

"Well," I said, "the behavior could be manipulative and he may be taking advantage of his well-honed talent to get out of Rikers and avoid prison. But what doesn't fit into that neat package is the fact that he originally devised this behavior when he was a child who just needed attention and love."

"You're saying that I have to figure out whether he's crazy, desperate, or both."

"Or possibly retarded."

"No. The intelligence test I gave him ruled that out." She shifted uneasily and twirled her pencil like a baton. "You know, Fred, I got curious about his name, Siddhartha. I wondered why his parents gave him that name, whether Sid himself ever read the book and whether it would help me to understand him better. So I read the book."

"What did you get out of it?"

"That I never would have been a flower child in a million years. You see, it's about this Indian guy who loves to eat and drink and screw around, and then he gives it all up and becomes the Buddha. So I wondered where his parents were coming from. Maybe they already had had it all, were rich kids like Gary here."

"Hey," he said, shaking his head in denial while Kiesha continued.

"So they didn't have to work very hard at not wanting anything anymore. And that sure isn't me."

"It isn't me, either," Gary said.

"I'm a string of wants," Kiesha went on. "I wanted to get out of my house, get out of being poor, get out of my neighborhood. I've never even considered not wanting or needing more, much less giving up what I've got and being satisfied with nothing."

"That's true of me, too," said Gary. "Believe it or not, I don't have it all. My parents do. I'm still trying to get mine."

"Maybe Sid is too," I said. "It sounds like he had lousy parents. Maybe they believed in universal love just like the Buddha but they sure weren't cutting little Sid in on any of that."

Looking at my watch, I realized I had told the Penne's gang I'd be at the restaurant five minutes ago. I invited Kiesha and Gary to join us.

When we found the table, Jenny was just pouring iced tea for everyone from a big pitcher. "Please sit down," she said, offering Kiesha a glass. "I'm in training to be a wife, for when I find the right man, that is."

"Who is this ravishing creature?"

Sitting down, Kiesha favored Parnell with a smile.

"Haven't you met Kiesha Wright? You spend too much time in the ER, Parnell. She's been one of our trainees for about ten months now," I said. "Kiesha, this is the eminent Dr. Parnell Walsh, psychiatrist, philosopher—"

"Bullshit artist," Jenny added.

Parnell waved Jenny away with a flick of his hand. "And to what part of the wildlife conservation park have they rotated you, my dear?"

"Conserva . . ." Kiesha started as she picked up a breadstick. "Oh, you mean the zoo?"

"Precisely," said Parnell, delighted.

"I'm in forensics."

"Forensics," he exclaimed. "That unholy alliance between the church of psychiatry and the state of law."

Kiesha pointed her breadstick at him. "I like this guy."

The conversation at the other end of the table was about declaring someone incompetent to stand trial. Sitting next to me, Mike yelled down to the others, "It's easy. You ask the alleged offender what the lawyer's job is. 'He's there to help me.' What does the jury do? 'They decide what happens.' What is the prosecutor's job? 'He's out to get me.' What does the judge do? 'He sits up there and says things.'" Mike gaveled the table with the edge of his butter knife. "Competent!"

"Right," I said. "And incompetent is when he says, 'I don't need

CRAZY ALL THE TIME

any help, God is my lawyer, and the jury will find me innocent or be struck by lightning on the spot.'"

Having dispensed with the issue of competency in criminal cases by the time the appetizers came, we went on to civil commitment, where the object is to prevent violence against oneself or others.

"Of course there's no real way to predict future violence," I said, munching on a piece of celery. "When I was in training, I worked with a group of severely disturbed kids. One of them was an angelic-looking, blond, six-year-old boy. He was so sweet, so adorable, so normal looking, I wondered why he was there. I noticed that all the other kids kept their distance from him and then found out why. The angel had poked out the eyes of his pet rabbit with his finger. I always wondered what happened to him."

"Eeeuw," said Maria. "So we'd all expect him to do something horribly violent against someone. When? When he's a teenager? An old man? Should we keep him confined forever, just in case?"

"Maybe just keep him away from rabbits," Mike said.

"That reminds me," said Parnell, pausing to rake an artichoke leaf with his teeth. "I recently testified regarding an application for the involuntary transfer of a patient to a state hospital. The patient comes in to the court dressed in a conservative suit with a meek expression on his face. He looks like the kind of guy you'd trust with your taxes. He sits there docilely, nodding at everything I say, while I describe his borderline personality, his dangerous paranoid tendencies, his difficulties with impulse control. But the guy has yet to really harm someone. His lawyer is making notes; they're whispering to each other. The judge is looking bored. He says, 'Dr. Walsh, can you give me any example of these tendencies?' So I told him about how the patient, who is a sports fanatic, was watching a baseball game and disagreed with the umpire's call. He smashes the TV screen with his chair, takes an ax and a shovel from the basement and drives across the George Washington Bridge to the Palisades where he finds a secluded place, digs a grave, and waits for two hours for a victim to show up. Finally, when no one comes, he gives up and goes home."

"Doesn't the guy believe in making appointments?" asked Mike.

"Sounds like some of my dates," chuckled Jenny. "Not the ax murderer, the no-show victim."

"Anyway," Parnell continued, "when the judge asked me if I thought he was a danger to the community, I said, 'Only when he watches ball games, Your Honor. Inasmuch as that's all the time, I think you better hold him.' The judge agreed."

"You're right about danger to self being more of a judgment call," said Mike between mouthfuls of minestrone. "I was at a conference recently where several psychiatric residents were discussing a difficult treatment case. The patient was the wife of an eminent surgeon. So it was a high-profile case, which made their lack of success even more embarrassing. The woman kept attempting suicide. First she cut her wrists. Then she overdosed on pills a few times. They concluded that she was manipulative and her behavior represented suicidal gestures, which were a way to get attention from her workaholic husband."

He took another mouthful of minestrone and continued talking. "Finally, one day she jumped in front of a subway train, severing her leg at the hip. And while lying on the tracks being treated by the paramedics, she was struggling to grab the third rail and get electrocuted."

"Shocking story," murmured Parnell.

"And even this they called a suicidal gesture," said Mike. "So in the discussion afterward, I pointed out that she had to keep upping the ante in order to prove how desperate she really was. And if after her leg was cut off and she almost succeeded in electrocuting herself, they continued to use the label 'suicidal gesture,' what the hell does a woman have to do to demonstrate that she's serious? For some reason they didn't want to acknowledge that she was psychotically depressed and suicidal and not simply out to get her husband's attention."

"Maybe it was too close to home," I said, "the idea that one of their colleagues or their own spouse could do that."

"Or maybe it was because she was a hysterical woman," said Rhoda tartly. "I wonder what their treatment would have been if the spouse were a man?"

CRAZY ALL THE TIME

"Come on, Rhoda," Mike scoffed. "A man wouldn't have been such a failure. You know the rule in suicides: women try, men succeed."

"Or they get someone else to do the job for them," said Jenny ruefully. "One of my first patients was a very depressed, acting-out black kid who began burglarizing the homes of friends and acquaintances who lived right around him. Soon the whole neighborhood was gunning for him. One night he showed up at a local concert wearing a floor-length white mink coat, when he knew that many of the people who were after him would be there. When he stood up at intermission, he couldn't have been more conspicuous if he had worn a bull's-eye."

"What happened?" asked Kiesha.

"They pumped him full of holes," said Jenny. "Right through his beautiful coat."

"You must have felt terrible," said Kiesha.

"Yes, such a nice coat," said Parnell.

"Shut up, " said Jenny. "Yes, Kiesha, I felt terrible. I still do. I thought he was making progress. Speaking of progress, Gary," she said, quickly changing the subject, "how's your girlfriend?"

"Maggie? She's—"

"No, I mean the patient who thinks she's engaged to you and is the mother of your child, whom you had admitted a few weeks ago?"

Gary put his hand over his eyes and moaned, "Oh God, will I ever live this down?"

"C'mon, Gary," I said. "After what everyone went through with Nadler's stalking you and Maggie, you've got to tell them the rest of it."

"Actually it gets better and better," said Gary. "First, they gave her a pregnancy test and it came out negative. So they started her on Thorazine."

"So?" asked Jenny eagerly.

"Then a nurse noticed that Gloria was lactating . . ."

Maria's eyebrows went up. "Lactating?"

"Lactating," said Gary, nodding. "The nurse asked the attending to order another pregnancy test."

"And?"

"And it came out positive."

"Oh my God," said Maria. "She really is pregnant?"

"You old devil," said Parnell, "you didn't really . . . ?"

"Wait, wait," said Gary, holding up his hands for silence. "Meanwhile, I'm going nuts. This woman says she's having my baby, I have her committed for it, and the tests say she's pregnant. I thought I had just kissed my career good-bye."

"So, tell us already," begged Jenny.

"You then suggested an abortion?" snickered Mike.

"Don't think it didn't cross through my mind. But luckily the attending knew that Thorazine can cause lactation and it can also produce false positives in pregnancy tests. So they did a sonogram and some other tests and confirmed it was a false positive."

"Incredible," said Parnell. "A full-blown case of pseudocyesis, hysterical pregnancy, complete with laboratory evidence and milk production."

"So everything's okay now?" asked Rhoda.

"Not quite. Unfortunately, Gloria noticed the milk coming out of her breasts and it reinforced her delusion that she was pregnant."

"Oh no. The poor woman," said Maria.

"The marvels of modern medicine—antipsychotic drugs that reinforce delusions," Parnell mused. "There's probably never been anything like this case in the annals of psychiatry."

"Let's hope," said Gary. "Anyway, they changed her meds and are waiting for the effect to kick in."

"What a story," said Jenny. "I hope they can help her. Have you seen her?"

"No. Her attending thinks that it's best that I don't. And, to tell the truth, I was relieved."

"Meanwhile, she's knitting booties in her activities therapy sessions," I quipped.

After returning to Bellevue, I felt my shoulder being tapped just as I reached the psych department secretarial area. Turning around, I saw the imperious figure of Gordon Bishop, one of the staff psychiatrists.

"Frehhhd," he said, drawing out my name in his BBC accent. He peered at me through his oversize glasses. Smiling broadly, he said, "This is your lucky day."

"That's always good to hear, Gordon," I said. "What's up?"

"I'd like you to do some testing for me."

"I don't think I can squeeze it in just now, Gordon," I said, reaching for the doorknob.

His french-cuffed hand shot out, stopping me. "Frehhhd, why are you acting like this?" he asked in hurt tones.

I stepped back. "Well, since you asked, Gordon, I'll tell you. Any time you've asked any of us to do psychological testing for you, it's been a disaster. First of all, you don't respect the psych tests, and second, if you disagree with the findings you just dismiss them. You're condescending and discourteous and you act as though psychologists are inferior to psychiatrists."

Placing his hand over his heart, he said, "If I've unintentionally offended you, Frehd, please accept my apologies. Shall we go into your office and talk?"

"Just for a minute," I said, thinking I'd regret it. "I'm expecting Rhoda any second."

He sat down in *my* chair and said, "Well, it's a fascinating case. A Lady Godiva picked up roller-blading nude on Fifth Avenue. Seems she caused a near riot."

"Why do you need my help?"

"Her stay here is almost up and I want her transferred to a state hospital. I need you to testify at the involuntary commitment hearing."

"What for? It sounds cut and dried."

"She is very intelligent and can sound quite rational and the new judge is grossly incompetent. If he should happen to be on the bench next Tuesday, I'm afraid that her lawyer might get her off, regardless of my testimony. But you know how judges are. They like tests, numbers, things that are quantifiable, never mind the impossibility of pinning down the human mind as if it were a butterfly specimen."

"So that's where I come in?"

"I've heard that you've been successful as an expert witness in cases outside of the hospital. If you could do your mumbo-jumbo with the inkblots and present it in the courtroom, I'm sure we could clinch this case."

"Do my mumbo-jumbo," I repeated in his Oxford drawl. "What if my testing turns up something that disagrees with your diagnosis and then the report is in the chart? You'd really be—"

"Not a chance," he said dismissively. "You'll agree with me because I'm never wrong about my diagnosis. This woman is a dangerous paranoid schizophrenic."

Clapping me on the shoulder, he gazed sincerely at me with his granite eyes. "I think this might be a really good career move for you, Frehd. And I'd really like to help you."

I did a slow burn inside. Good career move? Help me? You pompous ass, I wanted to say. But instead I said sarcastically, "Thank you, Gordon. I never knew you were so magnanimous and concerned about my career. I'm really touched."

"Of course, I'm concerned about you, old man," he said, patting me on my shoulder again. "I've always felt that way. Wait till you see the patient. She's a knockout." He extended his hand. "I'm really glad we're going to be working together on this."

You may not be, I thought.

Rhoda came into my office and exchanged pleasantries with Gordon. As soon as he left, I asked her, "So what's going on with him? Why is this case he wants me to do so important to him?" As a friend of many of the psychiatrists, my operative in the BIA (Bellevue Intelligence Agency), and a yenta, Rhoda was someone I could count on to fill in the blanks.

"Gordon's been shot down on his last two cases," she said authoritatively. "And he can't afford to strike out. There's been talk about his lousy track record. The hospital is supposed to keep in dangerous psychotics, not let them roam the streets."

"So he really needs my help," I mused.

Rhoda chuckled with satisfaction. "It must have killed Lord Bishop to ask. And then to put it that he was helping you. Did you kiss his ring?"

Later that day, Kitty came in asking if I could spare a minute. Things had not gone too well at her meeting with social worker

CRAZY ALL THE TIME

Pam Wyatt about Brenda's case. It started off great with Pam taking her arm and welcoming her.

"Kitty, hi. What brings you here?"

"Pam, I need the services of a social worker."

Removing some papers from a chair so that Kitty could sit down, she said, "Just name it and I'll see what I can do."

Kitty explained the situation with Brenda, showing her the relevant portions of her chart, and ended with "so Dr. Covan and I thought it would be good to apply for Social Security disability for her. Can you help?"

"Sure, Kitty," said Pam, standing up and rummaging through some papers on her wall shelf. When she sat back down with the SSD application form, Kitty told her how wearing contacts had done wonders for her and she complimented her on her new jacket.

"Well, you should arrange for her to be admitted."

Kitty was surprised. She could feel her cheeks flushing. "Admitted?"

"Yes. Then she'll be under the protective umbrella of the hospital system."

She closed her eyes, registering this information. "Why?"

"Because if she is stabilized on medication, she could be referred to a day hospital program and from there eventually to a sheltered workshop and finally to a supervised group home."

Taking a deep breath, Kitty forced herself to remain calm. "Pam, I don't think you understand our goals for Brenda. She's a patient whom we've managed to keep out of an institution going on thirteen years now. She may be delusional, but she is still able to function as an outpatient. She lives in her own apartment, cares for herself, has a job, goes out with friends. There's no problem with any of that. Our only concern is that she might lose her job. That's why we want the SSD in place. That's all."

Pam said coldly, "Excuse me, Kitty? But didn't you say that the woman was diagnosed as a paranoid schizophrenic?"

"Yes, but—"

"And didn't you say that she's delusional and won't take her medications properly?"

a question of commitment

"Yes, but—"

"So how can you really think she can function without a protective environment?"

"She already *is,*" snapped Kitty, exasperated.

"You call talking about beating the daylights out of a coworker *functioning*?" Pam asked sarcastically.

Kitty felt her cheeks redden again. "I already told you I discussed that with Brenda and I think I can keep her under control."

"You *think,*" said Pam. "All that the trainees have been doing all these years is laboring under their own delusions that she is a functioning person. But from what you told me this woman is put together with spit and glue. And she's one step from sleeping on the streets."

Kitty was furious by now. "Jesus, Pam, what's the matter with you? Brenda is a person, not a name on an application. Whatever self-respect she has comes from being self-supporting and living on her own. If you met her you'd see that she's not really dangerous."

Pam stood up, looking distinctly unfriendly. "I've dealt with a lot of this, Kitty. It's my job. I may not ever meet the patients, but from the facts I'm given, I can usually tell which ones have to be hospitalized to be safe from society and society safe from them. In my judgment, your patient is definitely one of them."

"No," said Kitty, struggling to remain calm. "I just want to apply for SSD. She's entitled to it and she needs it. She does not need to be hospitalized."

"It's not that simple," said Pam frostily. "I think she needs hospitalization and I'm going to talk to my supervisor about your stubbornness. Because it's my job to see that Brenda gets all the benefits she is entitled to. This is the way I see it. This is my recommendation. And this is what I am going to do."

"You can't do that," said Kitty. Leaning over Pam's desk, she covered the application with her hand.

"Oh yes I can," she said, snatching the application from under her. "I'm a staff member and you're only a trainee."

After she told me the story of what happened, Kitty said, "She's a real bitch, you know that, Fred?"

"Bitch?" I teased her. "I've never heard that word come out of your mouth." It was the first time I had ever seen her really angry, and I wanted to cheer.

"She's an effing bitch. I'm sorry. Make that fucking bitch."

"It's ironic, Kitty. She sounds like you did a few months ago. But you are absolutely right. SSD is our backup to be used only if we can't get Brenda through this latest crisis and she loses her job. Pam thinks Brenda needs institutionalization for her own good. And we think that Brenda's own good is keeping her outside the hospital and functioning at the highest level she's capable of."

"So what should I do?"

"Get her SSD. Pam may be a staff member and you a trainee, but you're the primary therapist on this case."

"But what about Pam's supervisor?"

"Don't worry about her supervisor."

"I'm sorry, but—"

"Kitty, you're a talented therapist and I enjoy working with you, but please stop apologizing for everything."

She giggled. "You sound just like my husband. He says, 'Say "I'm sorry" one more time and I'll really give you something to be sorry about.'"

"What?"

Embarrassed, Kitty covered her face. "He's only kidding."

"By the way, did you give him any of the books I recommended?"

"Yes," she said, looking even more embarrassed.

"What did he say? Is he going to read them?"

"He says he doesn't have to read them. He could write them."

"So what happened?" I asked Kitty when I saw her later.

"I fired Pam," she said happily.

"You what?"

"I went to her office and I said, quote, 'You may be a staff member and I may be a trainee, but I am the primary therapist on this case and I will find someone who can tell me how to apply for SSD and I'll do it myself. So consider yourself off the case.'"

"What did she say?"

a question of commitment

"She just shrugged and said, 'Have it your way.' Not a word about her supervisor. I feel great. I can't wait to tell Tom."

Gordon was right, I thought, when I met Mercedes Williams to administer the psychological tests. This woman is beautiful. In addition, the Wechsler Adult Intelligence Scale showed her to be in the superior range. Beautiful and brilliant.

I detected no evidence of organic brain damage on the Wechsler or on the Bender Gestalt test. At that point, I was becoming excited by the prospect of disputing Gordon's diagnosis.

An hour into the testing she said, "This is fun. I was very good at school."

"Where did you go to school, Ms. Williams?"

"Here or on the Pleiades?"

The hair on the back of my neck stood up—my most reliable indicator of schizophrenia. "Pleiades?" I asked. "Like the star?"

She nodded. "Actually the stars. There are seven of them, but only six are visible to the naked eye from Earth. I'm from Electra. I came here through a wormhole," she added as casually as someone might say "I flew here from L.A. on a jet."

Batting her thick lashes, she said in a voice soft as silk, "I hope you can get me out of here, Dr. Covan. We Pleiadians get our nourishment from the sun and I haven't been able to eat since I've been on the ward."

Gordon, I thought. You were right!

Minutes before I was about to leave for the courtroom the following Tuesday, Kiesha came to my office extremely upset. "It's Sid," she began, her voice trembling as she struggled for composure. She had gone to see her patient on the ward but he was nowhere to be found. Then she spotted Sid's attending psychiatrist as he was leaving and ran over to him. He told her that Sid was on the operating table.

"Fred, he swiped a nurse's bifocals, stomped on them, and swallowed the pieces of glass. He started bleeding internally and they had to rush him to surgery. I asked the psychiatrist if he'd be all right and . . . and he said he didn't know, that it didn't look good because Sid had all this scar tissue from his previous operations."

She looked at me, worried. "They can fix him up, right? I mean, we've got great surgeons here."

"I'm sure they'll do their best," I said.

She bit her lip, then said almost in a whisper, "Fred, I'm so scared. He could die."

"We don't know that, Kiesha," I said. "Look, I've got to go to court, but I'll be back in about an hour. We'll talk then. Hang on."

"I've got to admit," I said, slipping into the tubular fabric-covered chair next to Gordon's, "you were right about her."

"Good boy," he said. "Judge Nitwit is presiding," he murmured, inclining his head toward a bald, middle-aged, black-robed man wearily watching the proceedings from his high-back leather chair. We were sitting in court, the small hearing room in Bellevue where every Tuesday commitment hearings are held.

People who are just a little eccentric or quirky aren't then summarily locked away in Bellevue like in the movies. Involuntary confinement, also known as commitment, is a complex process in which a patient must be clearly found to be a danger to self or others according to the criteria of Sections 9.39 and 9.40 of the New York Mental Hygiene Law. The laws require certification of the patient by two psychiatrists if he or she is to be held for more than forty-eight hours. After a specified time period of either seventy-two hours or fifteen days, depending on which law governs the admission, a hearing must be held if the psychiatrist believes further hospitalization is necessary and the patient wants to be released. The court proceedings, which generally last less than forty-five minutes, are often extraordinary human dramas in which a psychiatrist and the hospital's attorney, who want to keep the patient confined, battle against the patient and the lawyer from the Mental Health Information Service, who want the patient released. The hospital has the burden of proving that commitment is warranted ; it is not a case of the patient's needing to prove that release is appropriate.

Gordon testified first and immediately I could see why he ran into difficulty. Being an expert witness is a performance art in which everything—your voice, presentation, body language, responses to cross-examination—needs to radiate genuine sincerity as well as authority. Arrogant, smug, self-satisfied, Gordon made no effort to establish rapport. He crossed his legs, slouched back into the witness chair, gazed at the ceiling, and spoke to the light fixture. "Ms. Williams is a dangerous paranoid schizophrenic who is under the delusion that she is an alien, specifically from the star cluster known as the Pleiades," he said.

"Objection," sang out the patient's lawyer, a very young-looking woman with short frizzy blond hair, suited up in powder-blue pinstripes. "Dr. Bishop improperly characterized my client as 'dangerous.'" She let her eyes rest for a moment on Mercedes Williams, who, with her hair neatly tied with a black velvet ribbon and wearing a smartly tailored, long-sleeved black dress zippered up to its high collar, looked anything but.

The hospital attorney, an older man with a dignified, businesslike manner, said crisply, "Your Honor, Dr. Bishop is an expert and thus he can state his opinions, including the opinion that she is dangerous."

"Overruled," said the judge in his bored voice. "Continue."

"Her delusional system includes the belief that her blood is green and that she photosynthesizes her energy from the sun. And the only way she can feed herself is by, um, exposing herself to the sun or fluorescent light. Consequently she has refused all food since she has been on the ward, constituting a clear danger to herself. She has also tried a number of times to, um, undress herself in full view of the male patients—"

"Objection," cried the patient's attorney. "Hearsay. The witness has not seen any of this failure to eat or undressing behavior himself. Both may have been nothing more than rumors on the ward, for all we know."

"It is part of the history and medical record, Your Honor," argued the hospital attorney.

"I'll allow it," said the judge reluctantly, glancing at his watch. It was getting toward lunchtime. "Please continue."

"As I was, ah, saying, she believes she can extract energy from people looking at her, and the more intensely they stare, the greater the energy. This, combined with her undressing propensity, has made her a management problem on the ward."

"In your opinion," asked the hospital attorney, "does the patient constitute a danger to herself?"

"Certainly," mumbled Bishop without any clarification.

"Is she a danger to the community?"

"Due to the usual natural male reaction to female nudity, I would say yes," Bishop said, fingering his eyeglass temple piece.

"What does that mean?" I heard Mercedes whisper to her attorney.

"Does the patient have any judgment or insight into her condition?" asked the hospital's attorney.

"I caan't say that she does," he drawled.

"Your witness," said the attorney, sitting down.

Buttoning her jacket, the patient's attorney stood up. "Dr. Bishop, was it a warm day when the patient was picked up?"

Bishop leafed through his notes. "Um, I believe it was."

"One of the first beautiful days we've had this spring?"

"Riiight," he said warily.

"The kind of day where a brash young man might take off his shirt? Or a young woman might wear shorts?"

"Yes. But this young lady was totally nude."

"But you agree that a young man might strip down to his shorts without having the police pick him up and restrain him in a strait-jacket?"

"I would think that a young woman—"

"Please, just answer the question, Dr. Bishop."

He stroked his beard into a vee. "Uh, yes."

"So if on a beautiful balmy day, the first after a week of unrelenting rain and chill, an athletic young woman on rollerblades should skate exuberantly down the street, and in a kind of spring fever, start removing her clothes because she is intoxicated by the feel of the wind on her skin—"

"Could counsel please get to the question?" asked the judge, resting on his elbow.

"I'm just getting to the patient's state of mind, Your Honor," said

the attorney. "Should this behavior, which could be fairly characterized as nonconformist or bohemian, be considered reason
enough to restrain someone in a straitjacket, confine her against
her will in a psychiatric hospital, and then, adding insult to injury,
seek to extend her confinement for an indefinite period until the
institution which shut her up in the first place should decide her
behavior no longer constitutes a *danger,* not a nuisance but a *danger,* to herself or to the community?"

"Your Honor," said Bishop, taking off his glasses and shaking his
head haughtily like a dowager refusing a drink, "the woman is a
paranoid schizophrenic."

"Your Honor," said the attorney, "my client is a poet and an artist,
and as such has a gifted imagination. I do not believe this constitutes mental illness."

The judge rolled his eyes as if to say, Where do they get these
people? "Counsel, the issue is not whether she's mentally ill, just
whether she's a danger."

The psychiatrist in the next case on the calendar leaned over
and whispered to me, "What is this? Now they have trainee
lawyers?"

"Yes, Your Honor. I'm getting there, Your Honor. My next question goes to the central issue of whether my client constitutes a
danger to herself or others."

"Good," he said.

She turned back to Gordon. "Hasn't Ms. Williams been a model
patient on the ward, friendly both to staff and other patients?"

"She has refused medication and as I said in my earlier testimony tried to disrobe in front of the other patients."

"I don't think Ms. Williams's disrobing could be considered unfriendly, Your Honor," observed the attorney dryly, making the judge
laugh out loud and even Bishop titter behind his hand. "And as to
refusing medication," she said, her voice growing stronger, "since
it is my client's contention that she does not suffer from a mental
illness and since the medication as stated in your own testimony
carries the risk of serious, even irreversible side effects, isn't it reasonable that from her point of view she should refuse it?"

"Madam," said Bishop in his most imperious tone, "have you

ever known a severely psychotic person who did not insist that he or she was perfectly sane?"

"Counsel," sighed the judge. "Danger? Remember?"

"Yes, Your Honor," she said, flustered. "Dr. Bishop, what violent or danger-inducing incident or incidents has Ms. Williams caused?"

"I don't have any information about them now, but I'm sure there have been many."

"Based on what?"

"Based on my beliefs and knowledge about human nature."

In spite of his arrogance and seeming indifference, I thought Gordon had done fairly well.

"If counsel has concluded with Dr. Bishop, I'll call our next witness," said the hospital's attorney.

On the witness stand, I gave a brief description of the tests I had given Ms. Williams. The Thematic Apperception Test, I explained, consisted of a series of cards showing people involved in various activities. The patient is asked to tell a story about what the people in each card are doing and thinking. Looking the judge straight in the eye, I described several of Mercedes's stories and how she spoke of people who weren't in the pictures, ignoring those who were. When she did talk about the people in the pictures, she said that they were Earthlings being controlled by Pleiadians or Pleiadians disguised as Earthlings. In the Rorschach tests, I pointed out, the images Mercedes described were entirely arbitrary, bearing no relationship to the inkblot pictured, and even after a long explanation from her, I couldn't connect the two.

In conclusion I said, "Although Mercedes Williams presents superficially as an organized and intelligent woman, if you look slightly below the surface you see a complex matrix of a paranoid delusional system involving aliens and their influence on humans. Her grasp of reality is totally distorted. She shows very little ability to acknowledge reality or have judgments and perceptions that are consistent with reality. Her actions, such as roller-blading nude down Fifth Avenue and not eating food on the ward, are based solely on her delusional system. I, therefore, would agree with Dr. Bishop that the patient is a danger to herself and, considering the near riots she caused, maybe even a danger to the community."

"Thank you, Dr. Covan," said the hospital's attorney. "Your witness."

"Isn't it true that many paranoid schizophrenics survive nicely outside a hospital setting? Are you telling us that just because you believe she is a paranoid schizophrenic she must be committed?"

"No, of course not. I fully agree that many paranoid schizophrenics survive outside the hospital setting if their delusional system is such that it is consistent with the basic requirements for survival. For example, a paranoid schizophrenic may believe that the CIA has implanted a transmitter in his ear, but still recognize the need for adequate food, shelter, and safety. That person can probably do fine outside a hospital. But Ms. Williams believes that she is not human and that she has no need for the basic requirements of human life. Thus, she is a danger to herself."

"Dr. Covan," said the patient's attorney acidly, "isn't it true that these psychological tests are not objective in the way that, say, a test for the AIDS virus or a CAT scan for a brain tumor might be?"

"It may not be to the same level of concreteness," I said, "but—"

"That in fact they are quite subjective and will vary from practitioner to practitioner?"

I leaned forward and said, "That's not true."

"Aren't they really just a matter of opinion?"

"That's just not correct," I declared. "These tests are objective, based on many years of research and training, and there is often more agreement between various psychologists in interpreting the results of these tests than one finds between radiologists interpreting the same X ray."

I could see her backing down just from the force of my delivery. As I said, it's a performance art.

"So someone else," she continued in a more subdued voice, "looking at a patient's responses to a particular Rorschach inkblot or TAT card would come up with exactly the same results you would?"

"They may not use the same words, but their conclusions would essentially be the same," I said.

"Thank you, Doctor," she said, sitting down. "I have nothing further."

I stepped down feeling fairly confident. The extent of your effectiveness as a witness usually can be gauged by the brevity of the cross-examination. And this was brief.

There was one more witness, a social worker, who testified about a phone interview with the patient's mother who indicated her willingness to take care of her daughter but who was unable to come to court this day.

"If there is no other testimony," said the judge, "I will now make my decision."

"Looking good, old man," said Bishop, thumping my knee.

"I agree," I said.

"Excuse me," said Ms. Williams, raising her hand timidly. "May I speak?"

Putting on the glasses that were hanging on a leather string around his neck, the judge gave her a long look. "Of course. Bailiff, swear in Ms. Williams."

"Would you prefer that I testify from the witness stand, Your Honor?" she asked after being sworn in.

"No, that's all right. You can speak from there."

She smiled angelically at Gordon and me, and turned back to the judge. "Your Honor," she said in a silken voice, "I just want you to know how much I appreciate all the time you have taken with my case. And I know that you will make a fair decision. Now it's true that for several months I believed that I came from Pleiades and that my blood was green and that I drew sustenance from the sun. In fact, I thought I would starve to death if I were locked up in the ward. But now, thanks to the care I've had in the hospital and my amazingly effective therapy with Dr. Bishop, I no longer believe any of these crazy things."

The judge took off his glasses and stared at her. "Is this true, Ms. Williams? You no longer believe these things?"

"That's right," she said, with a dimpled smile. "So you see, there is no reason to hold me any longer."

Gordon jumped to his feet, displaying uncharacteristic passion. "She's lying, Your Honor. Paranoids can do that."

The judge banged his gavel. "You're out of order, Dr. Bishop. Sit down."

a question of commitment

Gordon whispered to me behind his hand. "Judge Nitwit is about to do it again."

"Tell me, my dear," he said kindly, "were you really not eating on the ward?"

"I was eating, Judge. Just not when anyone was looking."

"And if I release you, will you promise to return as ordered for outpatient treatment?"

"Of course," she said in dulcet tones. "I don't want to be sick again. And I'll do whatever Dr. Bishop thinks best."

"And you now understand that you get your nourishment from food? Human food?"

"Naturally," she laughed. "Where else would I get it from?"

The judge laughed with her. "And you'll keep your clothes on?"

She looked shocked. "Of course, Your Honor."

"I'm going to make my decision," he said.

Gordon's face was a sickly white. "Here it comes," he groaned.

"I find that the hospital has failed to meet its burden of proof in this matter. It has failed to show that Ms. Williams is at substantial risk of physically harming herself or physically harming other persons. Her convincing testimony shows that she has both insight and judgment into her condition, and that she is now able to care for herself and has agreed to continue with medication and therapy. She is to be released immediately into her own custody."

"Oh God," moaned Bishop.

"What does that mean?" Ms. Williams asked her lawyer excitedly.

"It means you're free to go, dear," said the lawyer happily, hugging her client.

Mercedes Williams turned around and, facing Gordon and me, winked.

"Did you see that?" demanded Gordon. "Did she really do that?"

Later that afternoon, Kiesha came to my door.

"I spoke with the attending who spoke with the surgeon," she said. "They've finished operating. Sid's in the recovery room. He's going to be all right."

"That's great," I said.

"Oh, Fred," she said, collapsing into a chair. "He could have died and it would have been all my fault."

"Kiesha, he's been doing things like this all his life. He's had fourteen operations."

She shook her head. "You remember that story Mike told us about how the doctors kept calling the physician's wife's attempts to kill herself 'suicidal gestures'? And Mike said that she had to try more and more dangerous things to prove how desperate she was? Don't you see?" she implored. "That's what I was doing to Sid by telling him his swallowing was a ploy to get out of going to jail. I forced him to do crazier and crazier things in order to convince me."

I touched her gently on the shoulder. "Kiesha, you don't know that. Besides, he's eaten glass before. And razors and pins. He didn't up the ante. It's just more of the same behavior."

"All Sid ever wanted was to be noticed, to be paid attention to, to be loved," she said. "I was paying no attention to the psychological factors involved."

"You're a good psychologist," I said. "The work you're doing with the Thompsons is helping them deal with Angelica in ways that are helpful rather than harmful. Sid Waters is a difficult judgment call and we may never learn his underlying motivation. Maybe you were a little too hasty in saying that he was scamming, but the fact is he is a career criminal, and they're not the most trustworthy of people. So don't be too hard on yourself, Kiesha. This is a learning experience. Especially because," I teased, "he got you to read *Siddhartha,* so maybe you'll become unattached to wanting to make a good salary and having good clothes and living in a nice apartment."

"Fat chance," she said, looking a lot better. "Now, if you'll excuse me, there's a guy I have to see in the recovery room."

Bombay Juliet

Chapter 10

Elizabeth Driver was one of five high-achieving children of two
Stanford University academicians who placed their faith in science, humanism, and rationality. They celebrated no holidays,
passed on no traditions, had minimal contact with their families
back east, and, although they venerated "culture" in the form of
books, music, dance, art, film, and cuisine, they held that no culture was inherently better than any other. Elizabeth was incredibly intelligent, a model student, whose treatment charts were used
as demonstrations for psychiatry residents. But in her last assignment on the adolescent psych ward, when she came up against an
age-old religious and ethnic rivalry, she found that passionate beliefs in feminism and reason could take her just so far.

Elizabeth had been assigned a sixteen-year-old Hindu girl who
was admitted to the adolescent psych ward after a joint suicide attempt with her seventeen-year-old boyfriend.By the third session
with the patient, Maya Patel, she had managed to piece together
the story of what had happened and was now telling David and me
about it in joint supervision.

"She came here with her family when she was ten years old,"
Elizabeth told us. "Her father's brother owns an Indian restaurant
in the neighborhood, which her father manages, and Maya and her

brother, who's two years older, help out after school. She goes to Stuyvesant High School."

"Stuyvesant," said David. "She must be really smart."

"She's up there. She's on the math team and she's doing research at an NYU lab after school on a Westinghouse science project. She's pretty, but she's shy. Before she met Rashid, she had almost no experience with boys, not even as friends."

"How did they get together?" I asked.

"In her chemistry class. He was her lab partner. She started talking to him because he was from Bombay, like her, although he is a Muslim. They discovered they had a lot of things in common: poetry, music, science. He wants to be a doctor, she a molecular biologist. They started eating their lunches together at the river near the school and taking walks after school."

"Wasn't she worried about his being a Muslim?" asked David.

"Well, she knew that her parents, who are conservative Hindus, would freak out. They don't even like her to be alone with a boy. She's supposed to go out only in groups. And a Muslim is out of the question. But she didn't really think about the consequences of what she was doing."

"She was in love," I said.

"Right," said Elizabeth. "And she also told herself her parents would understand. Her father was always going on about how the Muslims were a minority in India and were trying to take over and should be thrown out. And he could recite every battle between the Muslims and the Hindus from year one. But he is a gentle man and believes in nonviolence, Maya says. And anyway this was America. He'd just have to realize that she was growing up in a different world."

"So what happened?" asked David.

"They fell in love. And they just decided one day that they would have sex."

"Yeah, but, the way she was brought up. I mean, wasn't losing her virginity a big deal to her?"

"Not really. This was the U.S., the nineties. All their friends were doing it. And they saw virginity the way most of us do, as an antiquated concept, something that had meaning only in the context

of arranged marriages, which they rejected. And anyway, they were
in love and that's what you do. So they start making love every afternoon in the apartment of one of Maya's friends, whose single
mother works during the day. This goes on for three months and
one day the woman comes home early because she's feeling sick
and she finds Maya and Rashid in bed together in her daughter's
room. She hits the ceiling and takes it upon herself to call Maya's
mother, whom she knows from the PTA, to tell her that her kid is
sleeping with a boy."

"Uh oh," said David. "Small world."

"Maya goes home that night and her parents are furious. They
ask her how she can do such a thing. They call her a whore, tell
her that she's wrecked her chances for a good marriage. Then her
mother says, maybe it's not all that bad. You're sixteen. You can
wait a few years and then get married. No one has to know. Who
is this boy? Does he come from a nice family? Maya tells them
about Rashid and at that point the shit hits the fan. Her father tells
her to go to her room and not come out while he and her mother
decide what they are going to do. She does what he says, but after
about an hour she can't take it any longer and for the first time in
her life she disobeys him and comes out. She tells him that he's
treating her like a child and she's not a child. She tells him she
doesn't see things about Hindus and Muslims the way he does, that
she and Rashid have talked about these things. It is not just any
Muslim she loves, it's Rashid, who writes poetry, plays the violin,
is probably going to win a Westinghouse scholarship and become
a doctor."

"She's a gutsy kid," I said.

"Her father is in a state of shock, and that's when he tells her
that he and her mother have decided what is to be done. Her
brother, Raj, is to accompany her back and forth to school every
day. She will be permitted only to work in the restaurant and return home. Meanwhile he will make arrangements with his family in Bombay for her to return to India and live with them. She
tells him it's an impossible solution, he's ruining her life. But he's
adamant. This time he won't listen to anything she says."

"So when do the kids decide to kill themselves?" David asked.

"Shortly afterward. Her brother can take her back and forth to school but he can't stop her from talking to Rashid once she is there. And she tells him about her parents' decision. They talk about how terrible it is that her father won't listen and that she has to go back to India. It becomes real to her that if that happens, she'll never see Rashid again. If she can't be with him, she doesn't want to live. And he says he doesn't want to live without her. And that's what happened. The cops picked them up unconscious on a bench by the river the next morning and brought them here. They had over-dosed on pills."

"Is she still talking about killing herself?" I asked.

"No. All she wants to do is see Rashid."

When I mentioned the case to Maria, she told me that she was su-pervising Nick, who was assigned to an adult psych ward and had Rashid for a patient. We decided that it might be a good idea for me to see both Elizabeth and Nick in joint supervision to coordi-nate the planning and the treatment of both cases.

"What's he like?" Elizabeth asked Nick when he had sat down.

"He's shy, studious. Very bright."

"What does his family think about the situation?" she asked.

"They're fit to be tied. It seems the whole family has put their hopes on this kid. He's the golden boy, the one who taught himself to read, set up a lab in his bedroom, owns a thousand books. The father and his two older sons have been squirreling away their money so that this kid can go to Harvard, become a doctor. And they're furious and heartbroken that the light of their lives is throw-ing his life away."

"Yeah," said Elizabeth sympathetically. "I can see that."

"The father in particular can't understand what's going on," said Nick. "He said to me, 'I don't care if he sleeps with a girl. But why try to kill himself over her?' "

"You mean, he doesn't care if she's Hindu?"

"Well, he doesn't think it's a bright idea. And he certainly doesn't want him to marry her. His feeling is Rashid'll get over it. He's sev-enteen. He'll meet other women."

Elizabeth frowned. "There's still such a double standard," she complained. "Maya's family calls her a whore and is ready to put her under house arrest in India. It shouldn't be that way."

"Right," I said. "And Muslims and Hindus shouldn't kill one another."

"Yeah," she sighed, "I know. Well, what should we do about this particular Muslim and Hindu so that no one gets killed? Maya told me her brother is telling everyone he's going to avenge her honor."

"The same thing is going on in Rashid's family. His older brothers want somebody to pay for the fact this girl talked their kid brother into almost killing himself."

"But that's not what happened," protested Elizabeth.

"Well, that's how his family sees it," said Nick, turning to me. "So, Fred, what do we do to stop this?"

"To tell you the truth," I said, "I really don't know. This is one of those cases that teach humility."

"But, Fred," said Nick, "there's a real potential for violence here. We have to do something."

"Well right now, they're both in the hospital," I said, "so the situation is somewhat under control. But if the brothers decide to kill one another, there's not much you can do. You can talk to the families, let them vent their feelings, try to alert them to the danger, and let them know there are other ways of working it out."

"Do you think it will help?" asked Elizabeth.

"God knows," I said.

"Or Allah," said Nick.

"Or Shiva," said Elizabeth, throwing up her hands.

When I saw Elizabeth in the hall the next day, I asked her how it had gone with Maya.

"Well, it could have gone better."

"What do you mean?"

Elizabeth told me she had gone into Maya's room and found her reading, while her radio was playing classical music. She asked her what she was reading and Maya told her it was a basic text on cellular biology that she needed for her Westinghouse project.

Elizabeth was glad to see her taking an interest again in the things she cared about and told her so. Then Maya asked her if she had spoken to her parents.

"I did," Elizabeth told her, "and they've agreed to put off the decision to send you to India until they're certain you're okay. They really love you, Maya. And they don't want anything bad to happen to you."

At that point, Maya got very upset, saying she understood that her parents wanted the best for her, but why couldn't they understand how she felt about Rashid? "I can't give him up," she said, "and I can't go back to India. I can't give up my friends, my school, everything I have here. It will be a thousand times worse with my relatives." Then she started to cry. "Oh God," she said, "why didn't they just let Rashid and me die!"

Elizabeth waited until the girl stopped crying. Then she said, "If you want to stay in this country, Maya, you ought to cool it when you get out of the hospital and not see Rashid, at least until I can get through to your parents."

"No," she said emphatically. "I can't do that."

"You don't want to go back to India but you insist on doing the one thing that will make your parents send you back. You're not being rational."

Maya gave her a scornful look. "Go away, Elizabeth. Leave me alone."

Elizabeth looked at me. "You were right, Fred. We're really up against it. Not only is she rebelling against her parents, which is age appropriate, but she is fighting a thousand-year-old cultural tradition as well as religious strictures. And her parents won't listen to reason. They want to pull her out of school and send her back to a wholly different life. At the same time, it's hard to get her to listen to reason because she's in love and her hormones are raging."

"Which is also age appropriate," I said.

"God," Elizabeth laughed. "I've almost forgotten just how intense sixteen can be."

While Elizabeth and Nick were struggling with their Hindu and Muslim clients, I was having cross-cultural problems of my own.

Late one afternoon, Lucy marched into my office. Her hair, somewhere between lemon and orange in color, was pulled back into a severe bun, signaling muddy waters ahead.

"Fred," she said in a threatening tone, "I want to talk to you about that woman."

"Which woman is that?" I asked.

"You know who I mean," she said, folding her arms and glaring at me like a third-grade student's nightmare of a teacher. "That woman who doesn't even speak right who thinks she can give me orders."

"Lucy," I said calmly, "are you talking about one of the staff members?"

"Just because she's Hispanic, she thinks she can throw her weight around here."

"You mean Dr. Santiago?"

"Maria Santiago," shouted Lucy, jabbing her finger into the air. "That's the one. She tells me that I didn't type up a report correctly and that I have to do it again. And then she gives me a letter to type. Just who does she think she is?"

"Lucy," I said, getting up from my desk and walking over to her, "you work for Dr. Santiago the same as you do for me. That's your job. If she tells you to do something over, then that's what you do."

Lucy glared at me and then patted her bun. "Well, it's not right."

"What isn't?"

"That I should have to take orders from that woman who doesn't speak English as good as I do. What does she know if a report has been typed correctly? She talks with an accent."

"Does she write with an accent?"

She pulled out a hairpin from her bun and with a quick, deft flick of her wrist reinserted it. "What are you talking about, Fred?"

"Did she write the report with an accent?"

"No, of course not."

"Then you shouldn't have any trouble," I said, showing her the door.

Later, on my way out, I stuck my head in Maria's door. "I hear Lucy's been giving you problems," I said, telling her what she said.

"Me?" she laughed, her brown eyes dancing. "I thought she was after you."

"Say what?"

Maria walked over to where I was standing. "She was just in here, wailing. 'I can't work for Fred,'" she said, imitating Lucy's whine. "'I never understand what it is he wants me to do. He keeps changing his mind. He's driving me crazy!' Oh, she also said she knows you don't like her."

"Don't like her?" I scoffed. "She's the best-paid nonpatient secretary we have."

Maria nodded sagely. "She's the only one."

"The reason she's pissed at me," I said, "is because when she complained to me about having to retype a report for you, I told her that working for you was part of her job, even if you do have an accent."

She clapped her hand to her chest. "*I* have an accent?"

"Well, yes."

"Me?" she said, smiling and stabbing her chest with her finger. "I've been here since the age of twelve."

"It's really nice. I like it. It's musical."

She walked back to her desk and sat down, her chin in her hands. "I have an accent?" she said wonderingly to herself. "I never knew I had an accent. Do I really have an accent? I can't believe I have an accent."

I left Maria, quietly raving to herself.

"He's been released."

"Released? Why? Maya's still here."

"I don't make the rules, Elizabeth," said Nick. "I imagine it's because the psychiatrist decided Rashid was no longer a danger to himself."

"And Maya *is?*"

It was now only two days after my joint session with Elizabeth and Nick, and the boy had been discharged.

"I don't understand," Elizabeth said.

"Well," said Nick, folding his arms and crossing his legs out in front of him, "to begin with he was an honor student who—"

"So is she," Elizabeth snapped.

"And he had no history of psychiatric illness or prior depressive episodes."

"Same here."

"And the father convinced the psychiatrist that he could take care of the boy and that he was in no danger of trying suicide again."

"Excuse me," said Elizabeth, taking off her glasses. "I just don't see any difference between Rashid's situation and Maya's, except she's a girl and he's a boy. Why is Rashid sent home while Maya has to stay in the hospital?"

"Maybe it's just as well she's in the hospital," I said. "It's either that or being shipped off to India."

She shook her head. "No. I've talked to her parents. They're willing to at least listen. Anyway, it's the principle of the thing. Why is Rashid diagnosed as less disturbed and as less of a risk?"

Nick sat up. "Okay. You want to know the real truth? The psychiatrist told me, 'Look, it was two kids screwing. It's his first time and he's following his dick. But the girl's full of romantic bullshit and she talked him into a suicide pact.'"

Elizabeth stared at Nick. "That is the biggest piece of male chauvinist crap I've ever heard."

Nick elbowed me in the ribs. "I knew that would get her."

She turned to me. "I mean, what do you think, Fred?"

"I agree with you. It's like saying boys will be boys."

"Yeah," laughed Nick. "That's just what the psychiatrist said. He also said that boys were more rational than girls."

"More rational?" she scoffed. "He doesn't try to stop her? He volunteers to kill himself along with her and the psychiatrist calls that *rational* behavior? Oh you mean that he went about it in a more rational way, like, maybe taking the pills one by one instead of swallowing them in bulk?"

"Well, in his defense," said Nick, "I've got to say that it does look like the girl put him up to it. I mean, it was her idea. She brought the pills."

"Oh I see," Elizabeth smiled. "She was tempting him, sort of like Eve tempting Adam with the apple? Is that what you're saying?"

"Well, now that you mention it, Elizabeth, that's not a bad analogy."

"Elizabeth," I said, "I'm sure that as soon as Maya calms down she'll be released."

"Calms down," she repeated.

"Yeah," said Nick. "The psychiatrist also called her histrionic."

"You mean, she expresses her feelings?"

"Yeah," said Nick. "Like you."

Picking up a box of paper tissues from my desk, she hurled it at Nick, who caught it deftly.

"Light objects only," I said.

Elizabeth laughed. "So you guys think I'm overreacting? Well, I agree that Maya is pretty intense, but then so is Rashid. First love is kind of like that, I guess."

"I'll never forget my first one," I said. "We were twelve years old."

Nick sat up. "Really? What did you do?"

"We made out in the back of her father's car in the driveway."

"God, Fred, you were so precocious," Elizabeth said, rewarding me with a raised eyebrow. "I didn't do anything until I was thirteen."

"I was eight," Nick announced.

"Seriously," said Elizabeth, "have you ever loved someone so passionately you could kill yourself for them?"

Nick thought for a moment and then said, "Nah, and I'm Latin."

"What about you, Fred?" she asked.

"I'm Jewish. I'm passionate, but I'm not stupid."

As I predicted, Maya was released the next week, and her parents promised to let her continue in therapy as an outpatient while they deliberated her future. Elizabeth hoped that at the very least they would let her finish the school term, which ended in a month. And she still clung to the belief that since reason and logic were on her side, it was only a matter of time before she could overcome their objection to Rashid.

"Look," she said to me while we were riding down in a crowded elevator on our way to the cafeteria, "I did group therapy with men in San Francisco who abused and beat their wives. These guys had attitudes out of the Stone Age and yet we got some of them to change their beliefs and their behavior."

"Elizabeth," I said, trying to wedge myself deeper into the rear, without offending the woman behind me, as half a dozen people got off the elevator and about fifteen more got on. "I'm the first person to defend the concept that changing beliefs can lead to changed behavior, but in this case we're dealing with centuries-old ingrained cultural patterns and traditions. You also are making the assumption that your beliefs are superior to theirs."

"She's sixteen years old, Fred," said Elizabeth, who raised her voice, leaning across the young Chinese resident who was standing between us. "She knows her own mind. I think she has a right to keep seeing this boy."

"Well, here's what I think," I said. "You're from this culture and this society. Her family is not and thinks differently and what you want could be dangerous. You have to consider the whole ecology of the system. You can't just have her go against her whole family and culture."

"It's like the Prime Directive," interjected the Chinese resident. "The first rule of The Federation is not to interfere with a planet's development and learning curve. Just try to imagine what Spock or Captain Kirk would do in such a situation."

"Uhmm," said Elizabeth. "They'd probably go to the computer to get more information on the culture."

"We have every nationality in the world represented right here in the hospital," I said. "Let's go find us a cultural consultant."

" 'Star Trek,' " said the Chinese resident getting off the elevator. "It works every time."

By God, I thought, there *is* a common culture in this society.

Finding a cultural consultant proved to be an easy task at Bellevue. No institution could be a better example of New York City's "gorgeous mosaic," where the staff and patients come from just about every country and ethnic grouping in the world.

The cultural consultant I found for Elizabeth was Dr. Shiela Singh Gupta, a young pediatric resident. We sat with her in her office, balancing the cups of tea she had made for us. After pointing out that India was an ethnically and religiously diverse society of more than 700 million people and that she herself was a Sikh married to a Hindu with her parents' blessing, she predicted that a marriage between a Hindu and a Muslim would be a catastrophe that ranked only slightly lower than a monsoon flood.

"The grandmothers would just freak out," she said. "The gossips would have a field day. The family would fall from grace. It would take years to overcome."

"But why is there such intense hatred between Hindus and Muslims?" Elizabeth asked.

"It's buried so deep in history and religion. The Muslims invaded India and some of the earlier rulers had mass conversions, where Hindus and Sikhs had to choose between Islam and death. There are obvious religious differences. The Muslims, who are monotheistic, consider the Hindus, who have a pantheon of gods, to be stone worshipers and tried to destroy every statue in Hindu temples. Six hundred years ago they razed the temple at Ayodhya, which is said to be the birthplace of Ram, one of the main gods of Hindu mythology, and built a mosque in its place. Then recently, fundamentalist Hindus destroyed the mosque, leading to the bloodshed now going on. Unfortunately, some unscrupulous politicians play off these religious differences and age-old enmities to gain votes and power. It's really barbaric when this kind of thing happens. You get families killing families because their families were killed. And it never ends because it is blood retribution."

Shiela leaned back in her chair and smiled. "And yet having said that, you must understand that most Hindus and Muslims get along. They can be the best of friends, visit each other's homes. But when it comes to intermarriage, it is a big no-no. Indians talk about equality and not being prejudiced but it's like the blacks and whites here. Everything's fine as long as it's not too close to home."

Besides going out with a Muslim, Maya had broken a taboo by going out at all. If an Indian girl is seen with a boy, Shiela told us, people talk and she gets a "reputation." Most important, it ruins her chance for a good match.

"You're talking about an *arranged* marriage?" said Elizabeth. "I would have thought that was no longer the case among middle-class, educated people."

"It's still the norm among Indian families," said Shiela. "But it's not as off the wall as you think. The idea is that if the couple come from similar backgrounds with the same fundamental beliefs and values, the marriage will endure far better than if they are swept away by passion. Indians believe that love will follow. And then there is the matter of economics. Parents always try to marry their daughter to someone who is preferably higher on the economic ladder, because even though a girl from the middle class is educated today and usually works, the husband is still the primary breadwinner and the wife's income is considered incidental."

But Maya's biggest sin was that she had had sexual relations with Rashid, she said. "For the boy, it will simply be considered a mistake, something that happened in his past, but for the girl it is an indelible smear on her character. It is almost like being handicapped. She is damaged goods."

"That's just the phrase her parents used," said Elizabeth. "It sounds like something out of a Victorian novel."

"Of course, things are changing in India as they are everywhere. But men still want perfection in their wives. Just look at the advertisements in Indian magazines. They want someone who is slim, fair—meaning light-skinned—good-looking, educated. In the Hindu religion, your husband is your god. You fast for him in certain festivals the way you do for a god. A wife is expected to please her husband in every way, fetch him water, bring him tea, make his meals, feed him first before she eats. Indian men do nothing around the house. Even my father and my father-in-law, who are very modern, broad-minded men, don't know how to boil an egg or use the toaster."

"But," she added, noting the look of horror on Elizabeth's face, "as with everything else in India, there is always another side. Indian women are very strong and have a lot of say in what goes on in the family, often running things behind the scene."

●   ●   ●

"Worship your husband like a god?" Elizabeth said to me as we were walking down the hall after leaving Shiela's office. "Did you ever hear of such brainwashing in your life?"

"I don't know," I said. "Sounds good to me. Who says all these superachieving women are happy?"

"Fred!" she yelled and then laughed. "You're just yanking my chain. I know you're married to a lawyer."

"But you're so much fun to tease, Elizabeth."

Raising her glasses, she scrutinized me. "You know, underneath that bantering exterior, I never know whether a male-chauvinist heart is beating."

A very anxious-looking, foot-tapping Weenie was waiting at my door when I got back to my office.

"Covan," he said, waving a sheet of paper in my face. "What the hell is this?"

"A moving piece of paper," I said.

"It's a letter from one of our employees, Ms. Rosselli, informing me that she is resigning because of a Jewish–Puerto Rican conspiracy against her."

"Lucy? My secretary?"

"What does that mean, Jewish–Puerto Rican conspiracy?" he asked, puzzled. "Is it a conspiracy of the Jews against the Puerto Ricans? Or the Puerto Ricans against the Jews? Or the Jews and Puerto Ricans against some other minority group? Fred, if there is something going on here, you better tell me because we can't be too careful when it comes to cross-cultural sensitivity."

"You're right," I agreed. "Let's see, you're Jewish. Maybe she thinks you're plotting against her?"

"Me?" he asked, clapping his hand to his chest. "She's your secretary. You're Jewish too. Maybe she's talking about you?"

"Maybe," I admitted. "But you're a member of the bureaucracy. You're in a position of authority."

He looked at me suspiciously, uncertain as to whether I was putting him on. "That's true," he said slowly. "But who's the—? Wait a minute," he said, catching himself. "She specifically mentions you and Dr. Santiago as being difficult to work with. And Dr.

Santiago is Puerto Rican," he said triumphantly. "So you two must be whom she's talking about."

"We weren't conspiring against Lucy," I said, "unless you can call one person asking her to type a report and the other saying she has to do it a conspiracy. People who think that other people are conspiring against them when they're not are paranoid, which gives me an idea." I put my arm around Weenie. "Maybe we could get her admitted as a patient and then she could work for us free under the volunteer rehabilitation program?"

"Very funny," he said, quickly moving away from me. "If you and Dr. Santiago did not conspire against her then I want you to document that there was no Jewish–Puerto Rican conspiracy."

"Oh," I said. "Let me get this straight. You want me to document a conspiracy that didn't take place. How do you expect me to do that, Mal?"

"That's for you to figure out, Covan. Because the next thing you know, we'll have all the Italians after us. You know how sensitive they are because of the Mafia thing. And," he said, smiling, "I want it first thing tomorrow."

"Would you mind it in longhand?" I asked.

"What are you talking about?"

"You want me to write a memo about why my secretary didn't leave because of a Puerto Rican–Jewish conspiracy that didn't take place and have the secretary I don't have type it?"

"You got it, Fred," he said turning on his heel.

About a week later, Elizabeth came to my office, visibly agitated, accompanied by a bewildered Nick.

"I asked Nick to come along because I wanted him to hear this. You remember the other day when we were talking about how men were more rational and less emotional than women?" she asked in a chilly tone. "I just got a call from Maya. Her rational brother and his rational friends have just beaten Rashid so badly that he is now in the ER of this hospital."

"Jesus, no," Nick breathed.

"A really fine example of rational male behavior," Elizabeth went on.

CRAZY ALL THE TIME

"How did it happen?" I asked.

Elizabeth took a deep breath. "Since her discharge two weeks ago, she's been under house arrest. The only activity she was allowed other than going to school was her work at an NYU lab three afternoons a week. And then she was to immediately report to the family restaurant. But in reality she was using the lab hours to see Rashid. Yesterday her father turns on the phone machine at home and hears a message from school asking Maya if she had given up her Westinghouse project because the lab said she was taking off until the fall."

Nick grimaced. "So he sent out a posse."

"Actually, it was her brother Raj's idea," said Elizabeth. "Her father supposedly knew nothing about it, although no doubt his attitudes set the stage for what happened. Raj called his friends, told him how this Muslim kid had taken advantage of his sister. It was diabolical. They actually followed Maya and Rashid and then tailed Rashid after he and Maya had split. They jumped him in a parking lot under the FDR drive."

"Shit," Nick said.

"What is it about men that makes them so violent?" Elizabeth demanded, looking first at Nick and then at me. "Men rape women, beat their wives, kill their girlfriends, beat and kill other men in the name of honor. And it's not just Hindus and Muslims. It's Latinos and Jews and WASPs and Catholics. It's in every culture."

"It's true," I said. "And men also create armies and go to war. It's called man's inhumanity to man."

"And women," she said bitterly.

"But," I added, "women's hands have not been bloodless either. I think that in general human beings have the potential to be aggressive and dangerous animals."

Nick's face was pale. "I really hate violence, Elizabeth. I hate it as much as you do. Where is this all going to end? Rashid's brothers are not going to take this lying down."

"I know," she said quietly. "That's what makes me so scared, that cycle of retribution that Shiela talked about."

"What you really need is to meet with the whole family, Raj included. Find out what's going on with them, what they want, what they believe, what they think and play it from there. But if Maya wants to see Rashid after all that's happened, there's not much you can do. If she's willing to defy her parents, her religion, and her cultural traditions, how can we expect that she'll listen to you?"

"Rashid's no longer my patient," said Nick. "And the family won't come in for therapy. But we got along. Maybe I can try to get him to head off his brothers. I'll talk to him as soon as he's well enough."

"Good," I said. "We'll try working it from both ends."

When Elizabeth asked Maya's parents to come in with Raj for a family meeting at which they would discuss, among other things, whether Maya would be sent back to India, her father invited her to hold the session in his house. This was highly unusual, but not unheard of at Bellevue. Occasionally therapists go to the patient's house, such as when Kitty went to Brenda's apartment to help clean it and get rid of the roaches. Therapists may also make home visits if the patient is physically incapacitated or there is some other reason why they can't come to the hospital.

The next day Elizabeth told me what had happened. She arrived at seven P.M. to find seven family members present—Mr. and Mrs. Patel, Maya, Raj, Mr. Patel's older brother and his wife, and his uncle, a man in his late seventies. She was about to sit down in the living room, when Mr. Patel said, "First we eat, then we talk."

"That part was great," said Elizabeth. "We had three different curried dishes, two kinds of breads, and half a dozen condiments." Finally, when they finished, Mr. Patel led the way into the living room. "What is it you would like to know, Miss Driver?" he asked.

"I thought we could start by talking about your plans for Maya," she said.

"It's why we're meeting," said Mr. Patel.

"Good," said Elizabeth, "because I'm sure you'll agree with me that in making any decision, you have to consider the consequences involved." She looked at Maya, who stared into her lap.

"Your daughter," Elizabeth said, "is blessed with unusual intelligence and talent. And I think that those talents could best be realized in this country. This is not to denigrate India, but many Indians come here for advanced studies. Her science adviser tells

CRAZY ALL THE TIME

me that she could win a Westinghouse scholarship, which would probably mean that she could attend a top college and from there go on to her Ph.D."

"We believe in education for women," said Mr. Patel, "although usually it is to the level of the baccalaureate."

"But," Mr. Patel's brother said, "times are changing. My sister-in-law is a gynecologist in Bombay. And her daughter is studying architecture."

"Still, I really don't understand why women need all that much education," said Mr. Patel. "It is so many years of work. When would she have time to marry and have children? If she works and has a family, she'll end up either neglecting her family, in which case her husband and children will suffer, or she will not be able to do the work for which she is trained and will become frustrated. In either case, she will be unhappy. I have seen that with too many American women."

First Elizabeth argued that Maya would feel frustrated if she didn't get a chance to reach her full potential, which would not contribute to the happiness that he wants for her. Then she remembered Shiela's comment about parents wishing to raise their daughter's economic status. "If your daughter is well educated," Elizabeth said, "she can contribute to the family income and have a higher standard of living. She will be able to afford household help as many do in America and I know that the wealthy do in India."

Mr. Patel smiled and said, "You are a very clever woman. Your husband will be a lucky man. I will think about what you say."

Elizabeth felt encouraged that Mr. Patel was willing to listen to reason.

"But," said Mrs. Patel, "if she stays, how do we know she won't see that . . . that—?" She stopped, refusing even to say his name.

Grateful that Mrs. Patel had broached the subject for her, Elizabeth asked the Patels, "What is your understanding of Maya's relationship with Rashid?" Immediately, she could feel the tension in the room.

Mr. Patel clapped his hands together as if he were killing an insect. "It's over. They'll never see each other again. It was a terrible mistake but now that's all in the past."

Over in his chair in the corner, Elizabeth saw Raj give a smug smile.

Elizabeth said, "I understand how you feel. And I know that there is a long history of animosity between the Hindus and Muslims. But let's look at it from another perspective. This is America, New York City, and we all have to learn how to get along."

"Miss Driver," said Mr. Patel, shaking his head, "we have no problems with the Muslims. We lived next door to them in Bombay. They were our friends and neighbors."

"Well, then," said Elizabeth, "if you feel that way, why is it that Hindus and Muslims can't marry each other?"

Mr. Patel smiled at her, indulgently, as if she were a child. "We can live side by side with Muslims, work together, have them as friends, but intermarriage is a recipe for disaster." Then he laughed. "Who is talking about marriage here anyway? Maya is a child. You cannot take her feelings seriously. It will pass. She will forget about all this."

"Maya nearly killed herself," Elizabeth pointed out, "because you refused to let her see Rashid. And now your son and his friends have beaten him up and it's very possible that Rashid's brothers could retaliate. Aren't you concerned about this?"

"Maya acted very hysterically," said Mr. Patel, "which is why she is seeing you. She must learn to get over this hysterical reaction, which I agree with you is very bad. Do you think that just because you don't get what you want in this world you should try to kill yourself?"

"No," said Elizabeth. "But—"

"As for my son, I am very unhappy with what he's done. It was very unfortunate. But it may have the fortunate effect of bringing the young man to his senses so that he will leave my daughter alone."

Once again, Elizabeth tried to reach the more flexible, reasonable side she felt he had shown earlier when they talked about Maya's education. "Don't you think that now that you are living in a different culture, the culture that your children are exposed to everyday, that there is room for change? You yourself said times are changing. I know that attitudes are changing among Hindus in India as well."

"That's true," said Mr. Patel's uncle. "We are doing things differently now. For instance, when we arrange a marriage between two young people, the boy and girl must give their consent. And they can and do say no."

Elizabeth picked up on this. "So you do believe that young people should have a say in whom they marry?"

"Absolutely," said Mr. Patel.

"Then why are you rejecting this young man who is an honor scholar, who will also probably go to one of the top universities in the country, who will probably become a doctor and make a very good living, and for all I know might be willing to bring up his children as Hindus?"

Mr. Patel turned around to his brother and shrugged, as if to say, How can I reach this woman? His brother leaned forward and said, "Miss Driver, this is a very complex issue, involving centuries of history and tradition. If you wish, you can come to my restaurant and you and me and my brother will drink tea and discuss this for hours. I like you. You are a very nice young woman and very pretty, too, I might add."

Elizabeth looked around the room at the women in their saris smiling at her, at the men looking at her in their charming, flirtatious way, at the tea in their flowered china cups, at Maya staring into the distance, and at Raj, sitting grim and straight as a warrior in his chair, and suddenly felt that the scene was unreal. Here were two young people, Maya and Rashid, who had made a serious suicide attempt; Raj, the son of one family beating up Rashid, the son of the other family; Rashid's family vowing to kill Raj; and nobody seemed willing to confront what was going on.

"Look, all of you," she said. "You have to face what went on between Maya and Rashid. They were intimate together. They had sex. They went against everything their families believed in and taught them because they were in love."

The silence was deafening.

Uh oh, thought Elizabeth.

Mr. Patel stood up. "It has been very lovely talking to you," he said, extending his hand. "We're very happy you came, Miss Driver."

Thank you very much. We'll take it from here. We know what to do."

"And then he led me to the door. I really blew it, Fred," said Elizabeth. "I blew it so bad, these people will never talk with me again. I just know it."

This was the first time I had seen Elizabeth completely frazzled. Her brow was creased with worry lines and there were bags under her eyes.

"This is kind of a new experience for you, isn't it?" I asked. "Blowing it."

"Yeah," she admitted. "I'm usually so on top of things. And the funny part is I kind of knew what I was getting into. It was just seeing them sitting there so smugly, so firm in their convictions, I just wanted to shake them up, let some air in."

"Sounds like you did just that."

She winced. "But I didn't mean to drive them away. That's the last thing I wanted to do. God, how could I have blundered like that, just when I was beginning to reach them? It even looked like they might let Maya stay here. Now, who knows?" She put her head in her hands. "I'm such a fuck-up."

"Welcome to the real world," I said. "It's good to fuck up occasionally. Reminds us that we're human. Anyway, don't be so hard on yourself. Sooner or later, you would have come to an impasse with this family. The cultural divide between your attitudes and beliefs and theirs is almost unbridgeable. Maybe you were premature in bringing up the unmentionable, but I don't think it would have been any different if you had first established a ten-year relationship with these people and then brought it up. And sex and loving the wrong guy are just the least of the problems. You were dealing with prejudices and irrational blood hatred that go back more than a thousand years."

"I know," she said, massaging her temple. "I hear you. You're saying there is just so much I can do."

"*Right.*" I said. "If she continues to go out with the boy, God knows what her family will do. Or what his family will do to her brother. But there's really nothing you can do about it, anymore than you can stop the fighting in Bosnia or Northern Ireland or India, for that matter. And it's not your job. You're a psychologist, you're not the United Nations peacekeeping force."

"Yeah, you're right," she said with a sigh of resignation.

Early the next morning Kitty Webster came charging into my office. "I've left my husband," she announced.

"Wait a minute. Just last week, you were trying to work things out in your marriage. Why'd you walk out? What happened?"

Kitty sat down and pushed back stray pieces of hair that were sticking out from her barrette. It was the first time I had ever seen her hair not perfectly arranged. "I got home late from work and then I had to go get some groceries," she said. "So I came in feeling good and Tom starts complaining about dinner not being ready and how I'm letting the house go. All of this, before I even put the grocery bags down. And usually I would just say, 'I'm sorry,' and run around like a maniac cooking and cleaning and in half an hour we'd be sitting down to dinner in an immaculate house. But this time, I didn't. I just looked him straight in the eye and said, 'I work as hard and as long as you do. I did the grocery shopping. Why don't you do the cooking for a change? You never do anything around here.' I mean, I couldn't believe I was saying that. I never ask him to do anything."

"So then you talked about that?"

"Well, no. He said he refused to be a cook. He works hard as a surgical resident and refuses to work at home too. So I said, 'Then I refuse to work at home because I work hard as a psychology intern.'"

"Then what happened?" I asked.

"He walked out. Slammed the door. He stays away for four hours and then he stomps back in and doesn't say a word. And he just keeps stomping around the house and I keep asking, 'What's the matter? What's going on?' And finally he says, 'I don't know what's gotten into you. You didn't used to be this way. You're not like the woman I married.' And I said, 'What do you mean I'm not like the woman you married? We've known each other since high school. How can you say that?' And he says, 'Because you're not. You turned into this New York bitch.' And you know what I said, Fred? You're not going to believe this."

"You said you're sorry."

"I said, 'Tom, you're right. Maybe I'm not the woman you married. But you're not the guy *I* married. You used to be sweet and nice and fun to be with. But you've turned into a nasty, surly guy I don't recognize.' And then he goes on and on about all he has to do and how hard it is being a surgical resident. And I said, 'Yes, but you don't have to take it out on me.' And then he said, 'If you don't like the way I am, you can leave.'"

"And you just walked out like that?"

"Not then. It was the middle of the night. I went to sleep on the couch and the next morning when I woke up, I thought maybe I had overreacted. And I was ready to go in and apologize. And then I realized that's what I've always done. As long as I kept my mouth shut and the house clean and did what he wanted, everything was fine. But the moment I stood up for myself, I was obviously not the woman he married. Well, maybe I'm not. This past year has really changed me and I just can't go back to being the same old compliant Kitty. I decided that nothing was going to change unless he believed I was really serious. So I went back home at lunchtime, packed a bag, and left him a note that I was moving in with Elizabeth for a while."

"What did your note say?"

"Not much. That I was moving out because we both need time and space to figure out what kind of marriage we want."

"That's it?"

"No. I also suggested that he read the relationship books I bought him because . . ."

"Because?"

"Because I love him and want to be his wife, but I'm not the only one who has to change."

As I told David when he asked me about whether we ever followed up on patients, sometimes we find out what happens serendipitously. A week before Elizabeth was to go on vacation she came in to see me.

It had been a beautiful July day and she was walking home instead of taking the bus as she usually did, when she spotted the

278

CRAZY ALL THE TIME

sign BOMBAY DELIGHTS. It was the name of the restaurant on the card Mr. Patel's brother had given her. She peeked in through the door and saw that there was only one person sitting at a table. As she stood there, Maya came out of the kitchen, wearing an apron over her shirt and jeans and with a plate of food in her hand.

"So I walked in and asked her how it was going, and she said, 'I'm not seeing Rashid anymore, if that's what you mean. I had no choice. It was either that or wait for someone to get killed.' She told me that her brother, Raj, had bought a gun because he figured if Rashid's brothers came for him, he wouldn't go to jail if he killed in self-defense."

"You wanted logical thinking, Elizabeth," I said. "That's certainly logical."

"So," Elizabeth continued, "I asked if Rashid's brothers were looking for Raj. And she said, 'No. That was part of the deal. Rashid told them we were no longer seeing each other and if they tried to get back at Raj, he would take his own life. And they knew he meant it.'"

Elizabeth gave me a sad smile. "You know, all the time Maya was talking, she showed no emotion whatsoever. I thought how different she was from American teenagers, from the way I was at her age. She was so stoic. And then it hit me what had happened. I said to her, 'So you both decided to sacrifice yourselves for your families, is that it?'"

"Did she react to that?" I asked.

"No. She was completely impassive. She just said like her father, 'It's over. Now I must think of other things.' Then she brightened and said, 'My parents are going to let me work at the lab during the summer.' I told her that was wonderful. And then she said, 'I have to go back to work now. They'll be here soon.' As she walked me to the door, she told me about the research she was doing. She hugged me and said, 'Elizabeth, you were such a wonderful help. I'll go to college, get my Ph.D., and maybe someday I'll get married to someone my parents and I can agree on.' And then she smiled and walked back inside. And that was that."

"So you really did help after all, Elizabeth," I said.

"Yeah, I guess so. But I keep wondering, Fred."

"About what?"

"What did she feel giving him up? Will the person she marries be someone she loves? Are the Hindus right when they say make the right match and love and passion will follow? Or will Maya marry someone acceptable and be haunted all her life by the love that might have been?"

"You know, Elizabeth," I said, "for a rationalist, you're a big romantic."

"You're so right," she laughed. And she was out the door.

Epilogue

Just as had happened with the trainees before them, the year at Bellevue had changed each of the students in the development of their clinical skills and their acceptance of themselves as professionals. There were other changes as well, less predictable, even wholly unexpected by them or myself at the beginning of the program a year ago.

Kitty, more confident and less perfectly put together than in her "stewardess" days, continued to live with Elizabeth while trying to figure out what to do about her marriage. She was staying on at Bellevue as a staff psychologist. Kiesha, who was dividing her time between an adolescent storefront clinic she helped set up in Harlem and teaching psychology at New York University at night, moved into her own apartment for the first time. Wayne, who had graduated from nerd to mensch, had a fellowship to study sex therapy and was talking marriage with Pam Wyatt. Much to our amusement, Nick, the antiauthoritarian rebel, was now in administration, defending his decision to direct an AIDS program as a means of reaching many more people than he could as a clinician. David broke with his fiancée, whom he called "Barbie Doll, my unintended," and had a brief fling with Elizabeth before leaving for Philadelphia to run a psychotherapy program for the disabled. Elizabeth rejected a staff position at a prestigious New York hospital in order to do a year of postdoctoral study in family therapy. Gary, who had spent his life in the shadow of his famous father, turned down an offer to join his institute and became a member of our staff. He and Kitty have gone on to become two of the people most dedicated to Bellevue.

Some of my students knew what they were going to do before leaving and the others let me know when they settled, except Ginger, who had finished the year without making up her mind whether to stay in the field. I said good-bye to each of them before I left for summer vacation. When I got back to the hospital, there was a package waiting for me.

It was a tin box of cookies labeled Meringue Madness. As I bit into one of the white puffs, I looked at the card that came with it. On the front, Dorothy was skipping down the Yellow Brick Road with the Tin Man, the Scarecrow, and the Cowardly Lion. Inside it read, "I needed courage and heart to make it to Oz. You helped me see I have both. I'll be starting work as a staff psychologist at Mass General in two weeks. Enjoy the cookies, Ginger."

Fred Covan has been a Manhattanite since birth. After graduating from Clark University in Worcester, Massachusetts, he returned to New York for his Ph.D. from Yeshiva University, an internship at Bellevue, and then eight years working with adolescents at Harlem Hospital. During the past thirteen years, he has been committed to Bellevue's Department of Psychiatry as its chief psychologist. He is also clinical assistant professor at the New York University Medical School's Psychiatry Department and has faculty appointments at several universities. He is president of DC 37's Local 1189, the union of psychologists employed by New York City, and has a private practice where he specializes in psychotherapy and forensic psychology. He is married to Diane Tolbert Covan, a lawyer from Miami and Key West, and has four sons, Alexander, Daniel, Zachary, and Benjamin.

Carol Kahn, an award-winning medical and science writer, is the author of *Beyond the Helix: DNA and the Quest for Longevity* and coauthor with Paul Segall, Ph.D., of *Living Longer, Growing Younger: Remarkable Breakthroughs in Life Extension*. She is contributing editor to *Longevity* and her articles have appeared in *Omni, New York, Vogue, McCall's, Glamour*, and other magazines. She has two children and lives with her husband in New York and Woodstock.